KEYBOARD MUSICIANSHIP

PIANO FOR ADULTS

BOOK ONE

ELEVENTH EDITION

SECOND PRINTING

BY

JAMES LYKE

Professor of Music, Emeritus
University of Illinois, Urbana-Champaign, IL

TONY CARAMIA

Eastman School of Music, Rochester, NY

GEOFFREY HAYDON

Georgia State University, Atlanta, GA

RONALD CHIOLDI

Northeastern State University, Tahlequah, OK

Published by

STIPES PUBLISHING L.L.C.
204 West University Avenue
Champaign, Illinois 61820
www.stipes.com

TO KEVIN

DESIGN, LAYOUT AND ARTWORK BY IS PRODUCTIONS, CHICAGO, ILLINOIS

SECOND PRINTING

Copyright © 1969, 1974, 1979, 1983, 1988, 1993, 1998, 2003, 2009, 2014, 2019

STIPES PUBLISHING L.L.C.

WWW.STIPES.COM

ISBN 978-1-60904-745-0

Preface

Keyboard Musicianship, Piano For Adults, Book One provides the first-year adult pianist in college group instruction with necessary music materials for the development of a well-rounded keyboard musician. A well-rounded keyboard musician sight reads well, plays in a variety of keys, is able to harmonize folk and popular melodies, improvises, and composes. In addition, the well-rounded keyboard musician plays repertoire from all the eras of keyboard literature with understanding and taste. The first-year keyboard student also develops necessary technical skills to function well in ensemble and accompanying situations. With these things in mind, this book is organized sequentially, with technical work and practice in accompanying in each chapter.

The eleventh edition follows a similar plan in each chapter. As new musical elements are introduced, they are reinforced through a variety of keyboard activities. These are included in sight reading, transposing, harmonizing melodies, and improvising and composing. Piano solos, duets, and accompanying selections are all interrelated with new elements introduced in each chapter. Evaluation of progress and understanding appears at the end of each chapter under the heading Suggested Playing Exam Topics.

The text's eight chapters and appendices A–C reflect a typical first-year college piano curriculum for non-piano music major students. Normally, the first semester student would work through chapters one through four. The second semester student would complete chapters five through eight. Within each chapter references are made to various appendices (A–C) for definitions and additional work with scales, arpeggios, and holiday music.

The eleventh edition of Keyboard Musicianship, Book One, contains a special feature in each chapter. The student is introduced to song arrangements by great American songwriters such as Jerome Kern, Irving Berlin, George Gershwin, Richard Rodgers, and others. These arrangements complement the many folk song arrangements from around the world.

ACKNOWLEDGEMENTS
Senior author, James Lyke, would like to acknowledge the contributions of composers Tony Caramia and Dr. Geoffrey Haydon for their fine original compositions. Dr. Haydon and Dr. Lyke have also arranged solo works, ensemble works, and accompaniments. Dr. Ronald Chioldi served as an excellent proof reader. Christophe Preissing, of IS Productions, contributed engraving and design skills that added to the book's handsome look.

NOTE TO THE INSTRUCTOR
Keyboard Musicianship, Book One, is **not** intended as a page-by-page text. Rather, the teacher should plan and assign a variety of materials in each chapter, keeping in mind the ability of the student. For instance, one class session might focus on reading, harmonization, chord patterns, rhythmic patterns, etc. It is suggested that students select an accompaniment, a solo, and a duet early on to allow time to perfect their choices. Technical patterns should be assigned early to allow time to overcome any challenges. Good planning is essential for effective instruction, thus enabling students to reach their full potential at the keyboard.

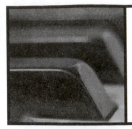

Table of Contents

CHAPTER THREE

CHAPTER FOUR

1
chapter

Keyboard Basics, Counting, Melody Playing, Pattern Recognition, Reading Studies, Repertoire, Musicianship Activities, and Technical Studies

NOTE TO MUSIC MAJORS: The first several pages of Chapter 1 serve as a quick review of keyboard music essentials. Feel free to move rapidly through these pages.

Exploring the Piano Keyboard

On the piano keyboard, high sounds or low sounds may be produced. These sounds, or *pitches*, become higher as you play keys to the right.

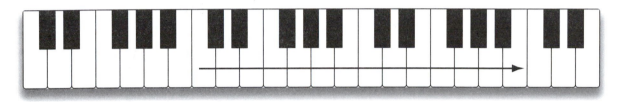

Pitches become lower as you play keys to the left.

Find two black keys in the middle of the keyboard. Using your right hand (RH) pointer finger and middle finger, push down these two black keys, then move to the right and push down the next set; finally, move right again to push down one last set of black keys.

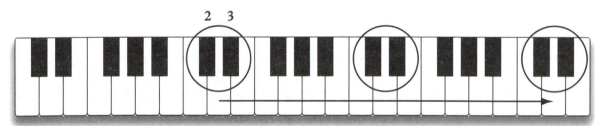

Using your left hand (LH) middle finger and pointer finger, find two black keys in the middle of the keyboard. Push these two black keys down; move left and repeat with the next set; and move left again to push down one last set of black keys.

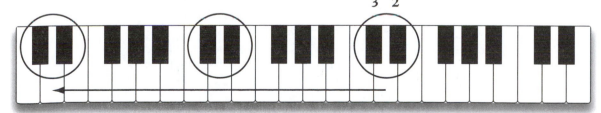

Finger Numbers

The fingers of each hand are indicated by numbers.

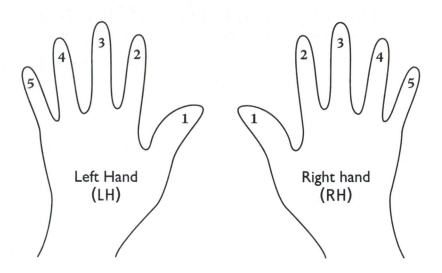

Left Hand
(LH)

Right hand
(RH)

Hand Position

Build a "bridge" with the knuckles of each hand. Allow the fingers to taper to the keys. Bring the thumb up to the tip of the second finger. Let the fingers that are not playing rest on the adjacent key tops.

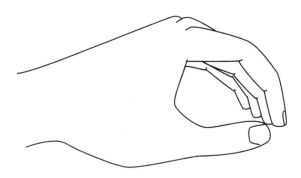

Sitting Position

Sit forward on the piano bench and lean slightly toward the keyboard. Arms should hang loosely from the shoulders. Hands should be placed level with the keyboard. Elbows need to be flexible to accommodate various movements. Feet should be placed squarely on the floor with the left foot slightly behind the right.

Black Keys

Find three black keys just to the right of the middle of the keyboard. Using RH fingers 2-3-4, push down all three black keys; then move to the right and push down the next set; finally, move right again to push down one last set of black keys.

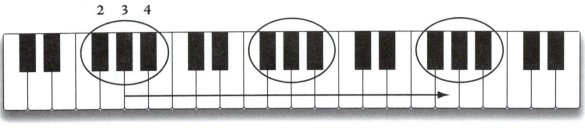

(middle)

Using LH fingers 4-3-2, push down the set of three black keys to the left of the middle of the keyboard; move left and repeat with the next set; and move left again to push down one last set of black keys.

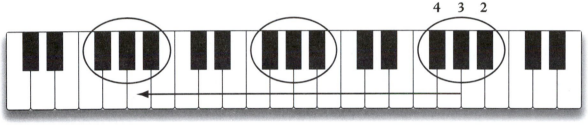

(middle)

White Keys

White keys are easily named by their relationship to the group of two black keys and the group of three black keys.

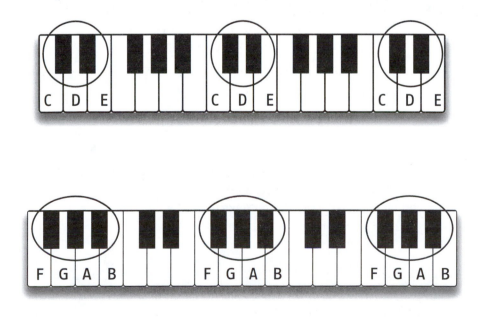

4

Staffs

Piano music is writen on two five-line *staffs* which are joined together. The upper staff is called the *treble staff*; the lower staff is called the *bass staff*. In most of our beginning tunes and pieces, the right hand will play in the treble staff while the left hand plays in the bass staff.

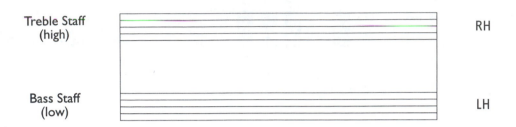

Grand Staff

When the treble and bass clef staffs are joined, the *Grand Staff* is formed. The treble clef, or *G clef* (𝄞), is placed on the upper staff, and names the treble staff G line (above middle C). The bass clef, or *F clef* (𝄢), is placed on the lower staff, and names the bass staff F line (below middle C).

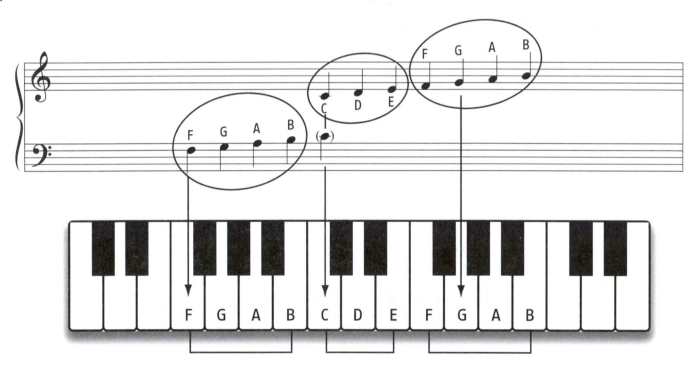

Line Notes and Space Notes

Music is written (notated) on *lines* and in *spaces*. With line notes, the line goes through the middle of the notehead. With space notes, the note head is in a space (between two lines). Notes can repeat, notes can step and notes can skip. Note stems may extend up or down from the note head (♩ or ♩).

line note   space note   repeated notes   stepping notes   skipping notes

Note Values

A *quarter note* (♩) lasts for one count. A *half note* (♩) lasts for two counts. A *dotted half note* (♩.) lasts for three counts. A *whole note* (o) lasts for four counts. Chant and tap the following rhythm pattern with both hands.

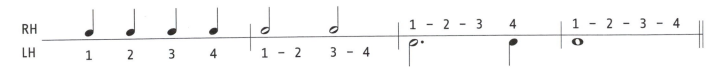

Measure Bars and Time Signatures

Music is much easier to read when divided into *measures*. Measures are marked off with single *bar lines*. The last measure of every piece has a double bar line. *Meter* in music is shown at the beginning of every piece with a *time signature*. The top number indicates the number of pulses in each measure. The bottom number shows which kind of note receives one pulse, or count. Tap the rhythm pattern once again with each hand; observe the time signature and measure bars.

Rests

Rests are symbols for silence. Every note value has a corresponding rest. Study the chart below.

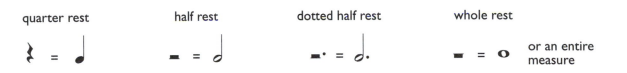

Tap the following rhythm patterns observing all rests.

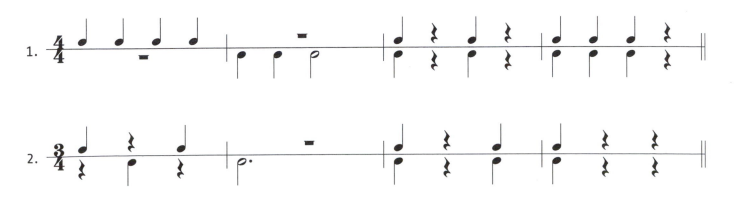

Playing Treble CDE Groups

Play the three CDE groups shown below. Start on Middle C. Count and say the names of the notes as you play. *8va* means to play one octave (eight notes) higher than written. *Loco* means to return to the actual written notes.

Playing Bass CDE Groups and Using Leger Lines

Occasionally, added lines (*leger lines*) appear above and below each staff. Leger lines facilitate reading. Play the following melody which utilizes leger lines above the 𝄢 staff. An *8va* sign below the staff means to play those notes one octave lower than written. (NOTE: Sometimes an octave lower sign is written as *8vb*.)

Playing CDE Groups Using Both Hands

Play the melodies below which use CDE groups in each hand. Observe the *8va* signs. The *repeat sign* (:‖) means the tune is to be played a second time with no interruption in the rhythm.

Sharps, Flats, and Naturals

A *sharp* (♯) placed before a note indicates that note be played one half-step *higher*. It lasts through the remainder of the measure *unless cancelled by a natural* (♮).

A *flat* (♭) placed before a note indicates that note be played one half-step *lower*. It lasts through the remainder of the measure *unless cancelled by a natural* (♮).

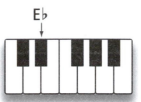

A *natural* (♮) shows a cancellation of a sharp or flat and a return to the natural (white key).

Study and play the various sharps and flats shown below. A knowledge of sharps and flats becomes necessary when building various major pentachords, or 5-finger patterns.

 Sharp: one key up from the closest white key. This may be a black key or a white key.

 Flat: one key down from the closest white key. This may be a black key or a white key.

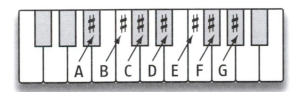
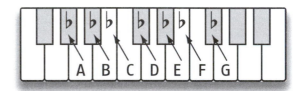

Playing Tune Fragments That Use Sharp, Flat, and Natural Signs

Study and play the following tunes written for either RH or LH at a moderate tempo. Locate the starting note by studying the landmark notes (C, F or G). Some start on the landmark note. Others start from a note near a landmark note. Chant letter names in rhythm. Slur marks (⌣) indicate connection of one note to another. This enhances smooth or *legato* playing. Place each hand in a 5-finger pattern according to the fingering. Sharps, flats, or naturals introduced at the beginning of a measure last through the remainder of the measure.

from a **British Tune**

from a **French Tune**

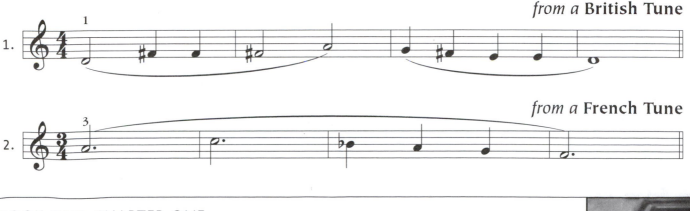

from a **Polish Tune**

3.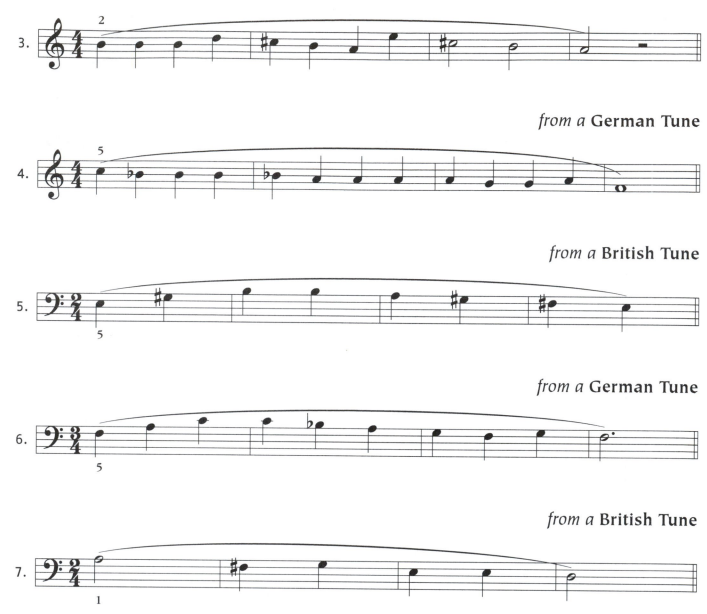

from a **German Tune**

4.

from a **British Tune**

5.

from a **German Tune**

6.

from a **British Tune**

7.

Tied Notes ♩‿♩

Tied notes consist of a curved line joining two (or more) notes of the same pitch. The duration of the tied notes is the combined values of the connected notes. Count out loud as you play the following example.

Irving Berlin

Combining FGAB and CDE

The following melody combines 𝄢 FGAB with 𝄞 CDE. Observe the slur marks. Say the note names as you play and keep a steady rhythm.

Adding F, G, and A to the Right Hand (RH)

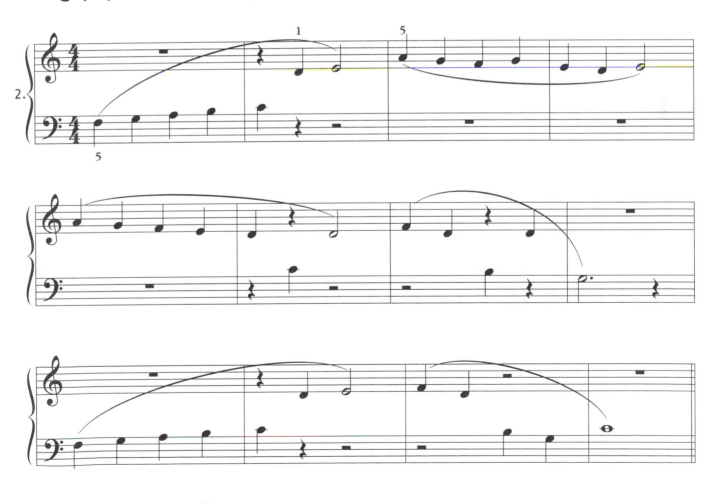

Intervals (Unison – 5th)

An interval represents the distance in pitch between two tones. Study the intervals below as they look on both the staff and on the keyboard.

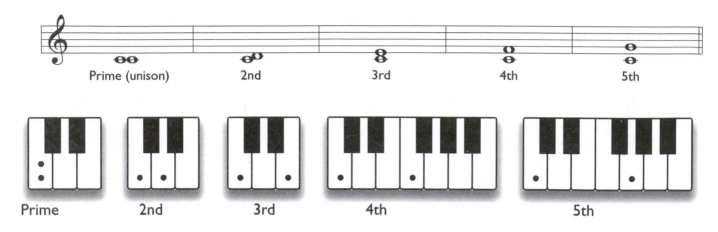

Prime (unison)   2nd   3rd   4th   5th

Prime   2nd   3rd   4th   5th

Interval Reading

The following melodies encompass either a CDE group or an FGAB group (with a few notes added). Some melodies are for RH; others are for LH. A variety of time signatures and note values is used. Observe the fingering and count. Analyze the intervals that are bracketed. Chant note names in rhythm. You have played these intervals. Now you have a specific designation, e.g., 2nds, 3rds, etc. Write the correct interval within each bracket as shown in measure 2 of No. 1.

Melodies for Sight Reading

Before sight reading the following studies, establish the following procedures. Identify landmark notes
(𝄢 F, middle C and 𝄞 G). Then place the hands in the patterns suggested by the fingering (given at the
beginning). Find CDE groups and FGAB groups. Count and play at reasonable tempos (speeds). Do NOT
go back to correct errors. In beginning reading it helps to chant letter names of notes. For example, in
No. 1, chant E G C E | C A G – 2 | etc. Dynamic marks are used in the tunes for reading: *f* = loud, *p* =
soft, *mf* = medium loud, and *mp* = medium soft.

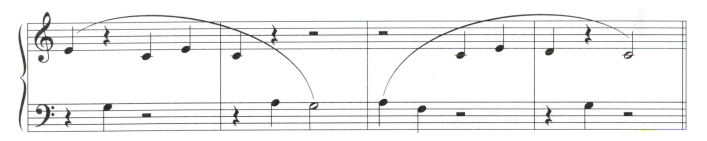

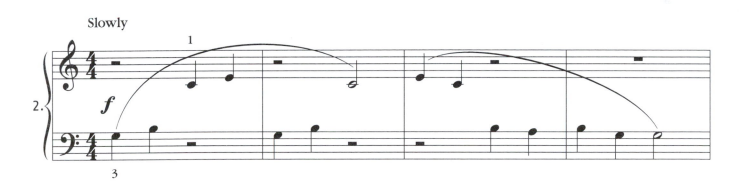

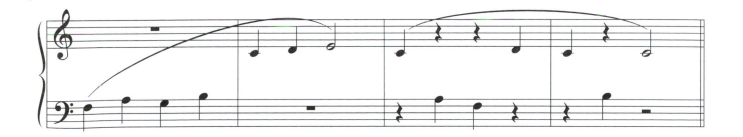

Moderately

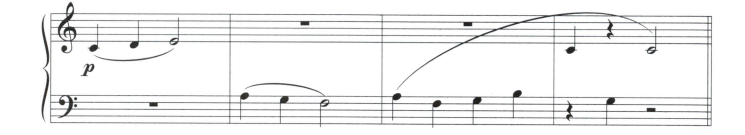

Brightly

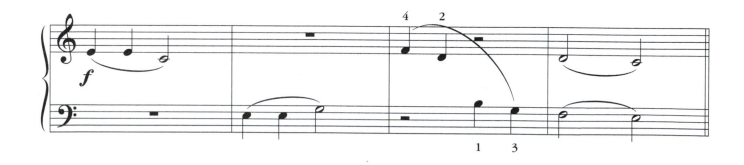

Moderate waltz time

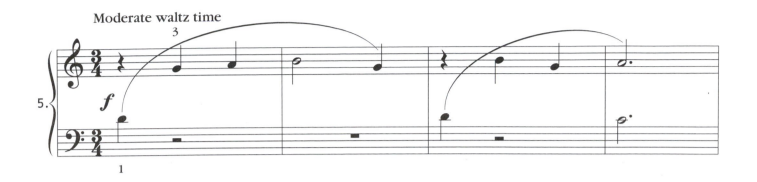

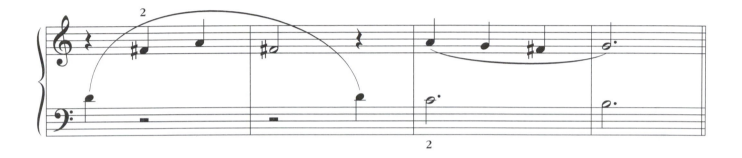

March tempo

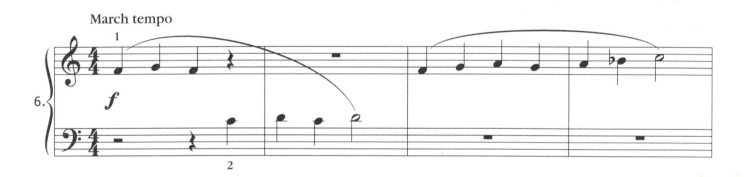

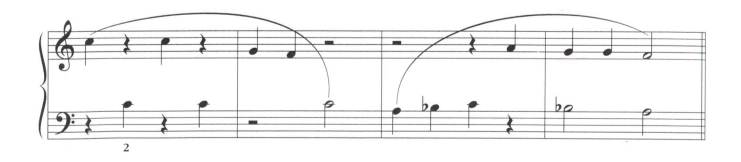

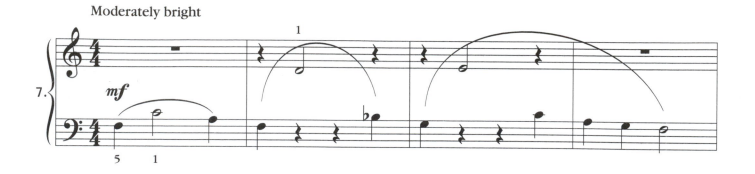

Identify the RH and LH intervals in the following sight reading excercise.

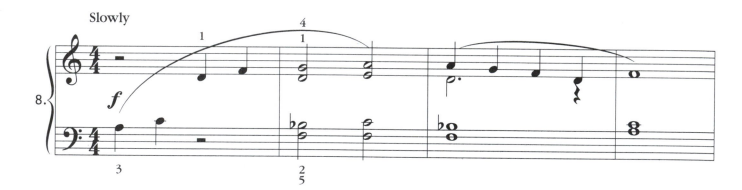

One-Hand Reading in 5-Finger Patterns (Pentachords)

Play the following melodies at an easy tempo (rate of speed). The starting notes should be determined from land mark notes and from CDE / FGAB groupings. Observe the repeat signs (:||). Say the note names as you play in a steady rhythm. Remember that sharps, flats, or naturals introduced at the beginning of a measure last through the remainder of the measure.

RIGHT HAND MELODIES

LEFT HAND MELODIES

MELODIES BY GREAT AMERICAN SONGWRITERS

The following melodies are extracts from songs by American Songwriters. Be attentive to the starting fingers in each hand.

Jerome Kern

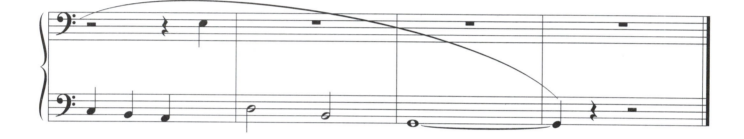

Walter Donaldson

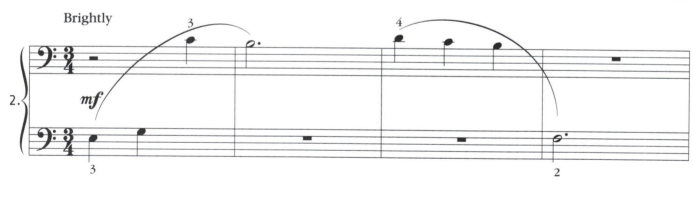

George Gershwin

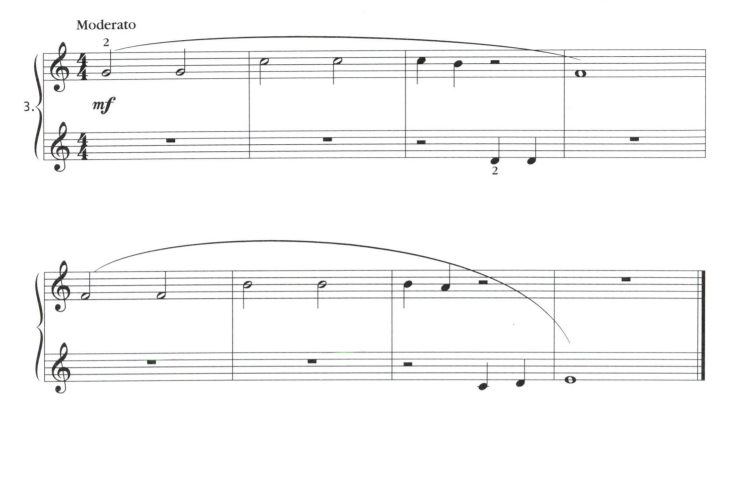

George Gershwin

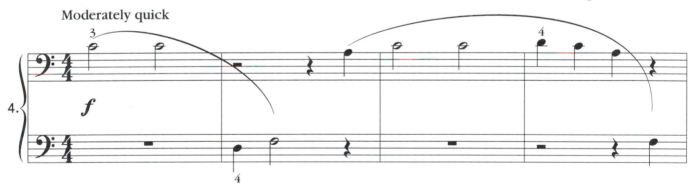

ACCOMPANYING

Play the accompanying part (**S**) to *Shoo Fly*. Your teacher (**T**) will play the melody. The combination of LH bass notes and RH intervals creates chords. Study the fingering in the opening measures and maintain this fingering throughout the song. TEACHER: Double the melody one octave higher.

SHOO FLY

American
arr. **James Lyke**

NOTE TO STUDENT

D.C. is an abbreviation for *Da Capo* meaning go back to the beginning and play until the *Fine* (the end).

STUDENT: Pay attention to the fingering.
TEACHER: Double the melody one octave higher.

SEA CHANTY

arr. James Lyke

ENSEMBLE REPERTOIRE

ITALIAN FOLK SONG

Secondo – Teacher

arr. **James Lyke**

STUDENT: Play both hands *8va* when joined by the secondo at one piano.

ITALIAN FOLK SONG
Primo – Student

arr. **James Lyke**

Medium tempo

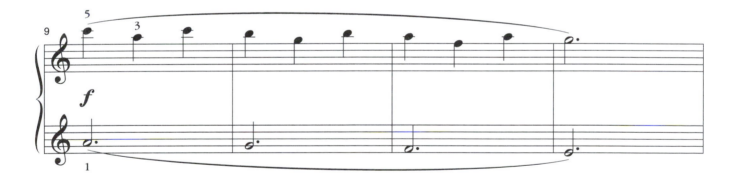

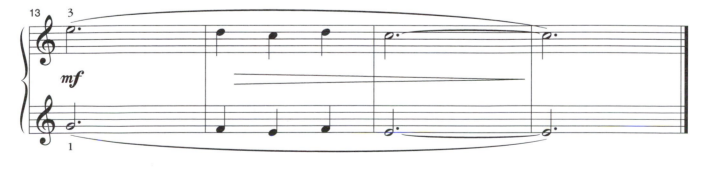

< A *crescendo* mark means gradually become louder.

\> A *decrescendo* mark means gradually become softer.

BOOK ONE, CHAPTER ONE

CRADLE SONG

Secondo – Student

Franz Schubert
arr. James Lyke

Cantabile ♩ = 88

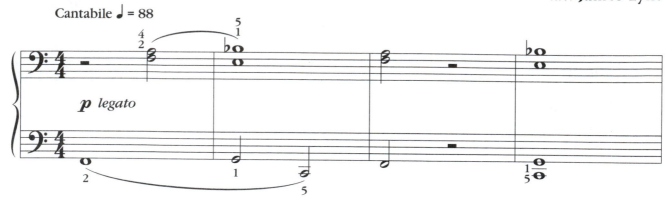

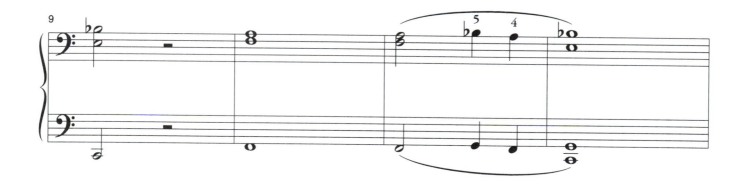

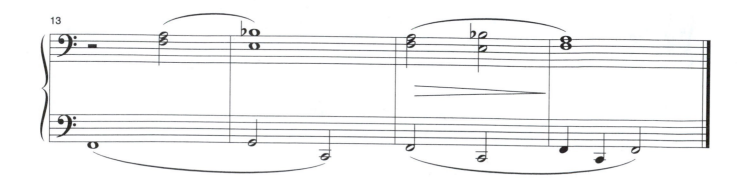

CRADLE SONG

Primo – Teacher

Franz Schubert
arr. **James Lyke**

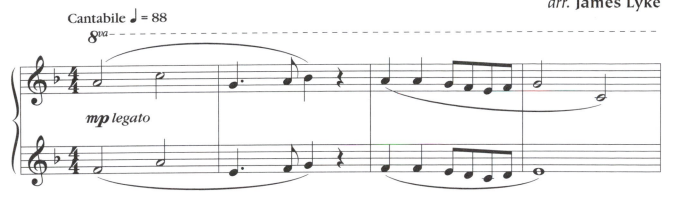

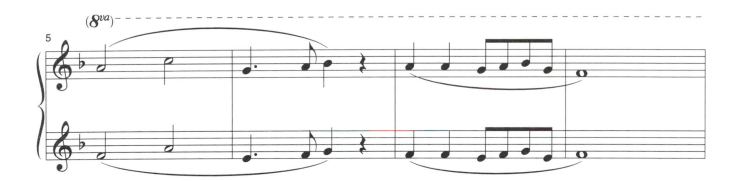

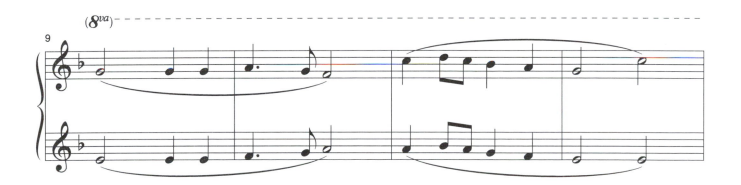

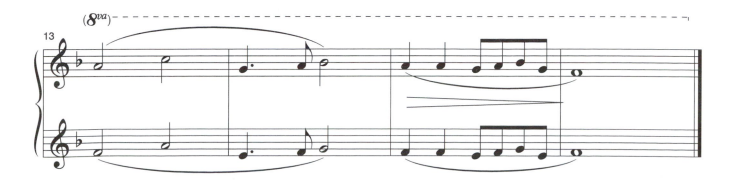

BOOK ONE, CHAPTER ONE

White Key Groups – A Review

Knowing how to locate FGAB and CDE groups will help you learn the names of lines and spaces on each staff. Moreover, it will help you place your hands in the proper position for playing. Study the groups below. Play each group in the proper register.

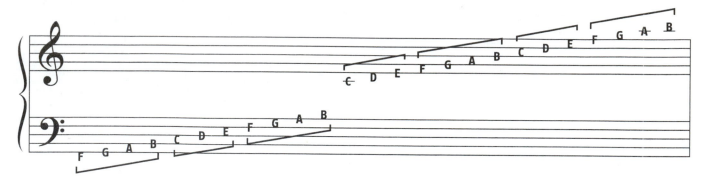

Intervals – A Review

You will recall that an *interval* is the distance between two notes. In your pieces so far, you have played all the intervals shown below. Study these intervals that are pictured as *blocked*, or *harmonic* intervals. Play the intervals with the LH, also.

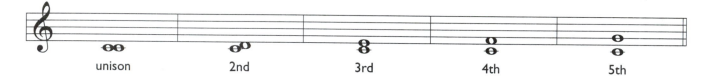

| unison | 2nd | 3rd | 4th | 5th |

SOLO REPERTOIRE

Before beginning to learn solo selections, review white key groups, intervals, and sharps, flats and naturals. Pay close attention to dynamic marks and slurs. A few new elements will be introduced in this section.

Smooth Thirds presents a few fingering challenges and shifts to different positions. Follow the fingering with care.

SMOOTH THIRDS

James Lyke

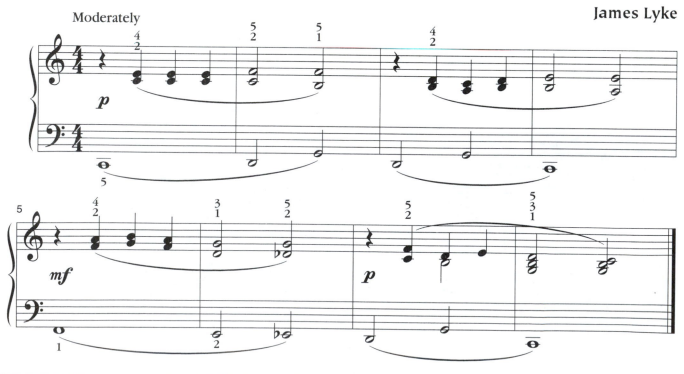

Staccato Touch (·)

A dot placed above or below a note indicates that the note is to be played short (half of the time value).
Learn *Fifth Frolic* slowly and calculate the shifts of position (up and down) in both hands.

FIFTH FROLIC

James Lyke

Tied Notes ♩–♩ 𝅗𝅥–𝅗𝅥 – A Review

Tied notes consist of a curved line joining two or more notes of the same pitch. The duration is that of
the combined note values.

IF YOU ONLY CARE ENOUGH

melody by **Jerome Kern**
arr. **James Lyke**

CLIPPED SECONDS

James Lyke

MOSTLY FOURTHS

James Lyke

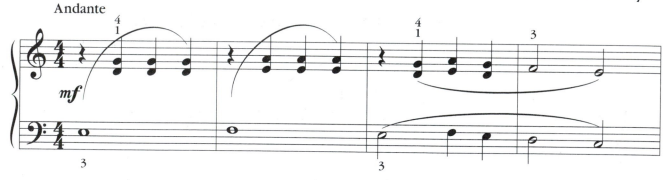

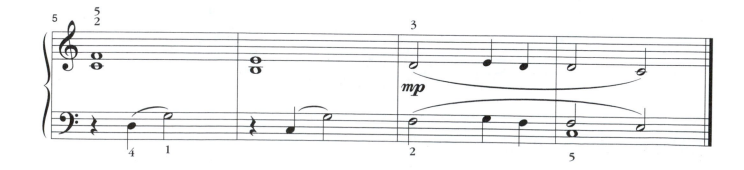

In *Imitation* the LH maintains a C – G 5-finger pattern. However, the RH dips below a 5-finger pattern in bar 11. Keep a smooth *legato* feel.

IMITATION

Fritz Spindler

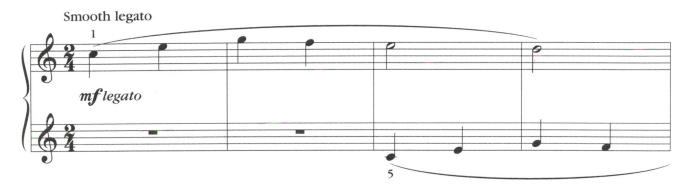

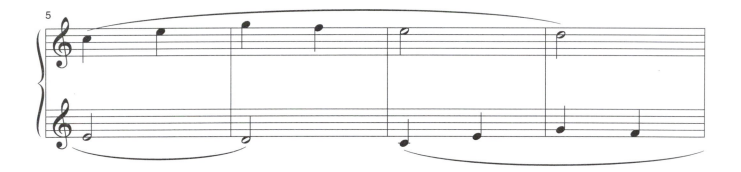

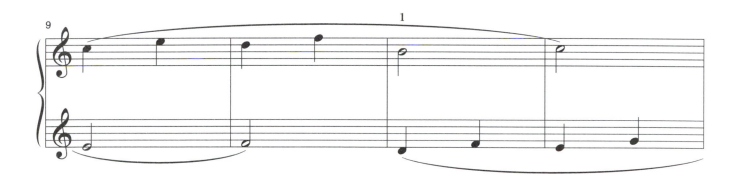

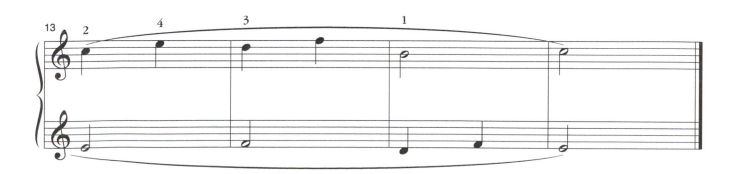

Modal Memory requires shifting to new 5-finger positions. Practice hands separately with careful attention to fingering.

MODAL MEMORY

Tony Caramia

With a gentle lilt

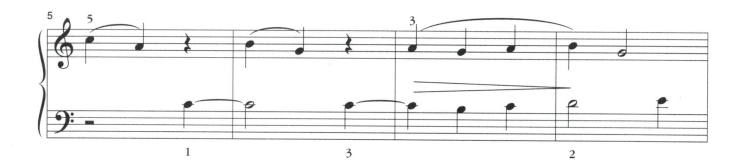

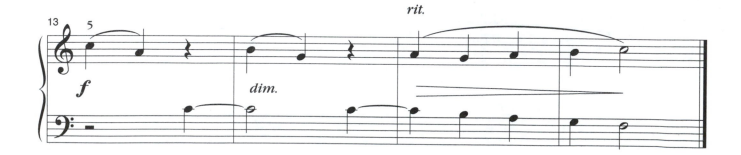

MUSICIANSHIP ACTIVITIES

Harmonic and Melodic Intervals

unison   2nd   3rd   4th   5th   6th   7th   octave

Intervals may also be played as *melodic* intervals, i.e., one tone follows another. Study and identify the melodic intervals below. Notice the sound of each melodic interval.

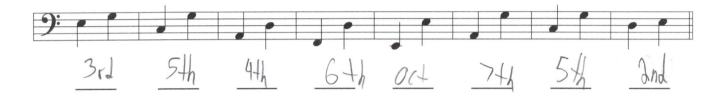

3rd   5th   4th   6th   oct   7th   5th   2nd

Study and identify the harmonic intervals below. Notice the sound of each harmonic interval.

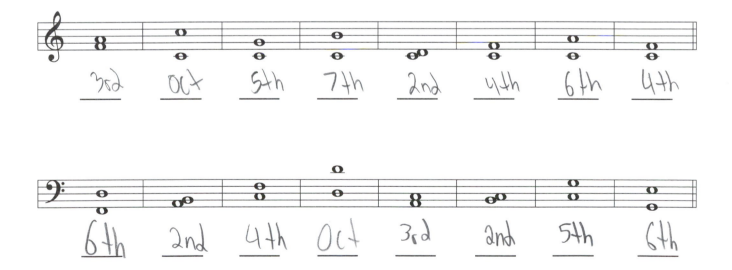

3rd   Oct   5th   7th   2nd   4th   6th   4th

6th   2nd   4th   Oct   3rd   2nd   5th   6th

Ear Training
As your teacher plays various intervals in the treble and bass clef, see if you can identify them.

Improvising

Improvise melodies using the black key pentatonic scales shown below. Note the fingering of each pattern. The teacher accompaniments stress various moods. Use elements of repetition, sequence (same idea on different pitches) and contrast (change in the melody). Use ♩, ♩, ♩., and o notes. Develop four-bar phrases in the beginning. Later, expand the length of the improvisation.

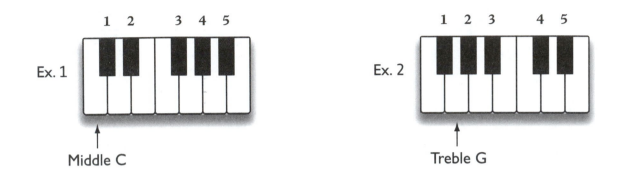

Teacher Patterns (will work for either Ex. 1 or Ex. 2)
Keep repeating each pattern until the improvisation comes to a logical conclusion.

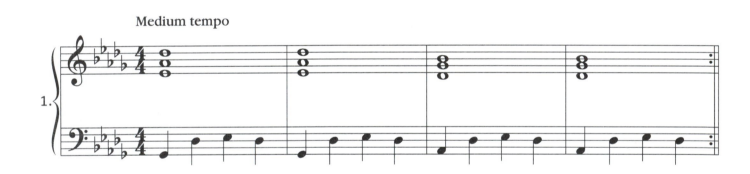

Technical Studies

The following exercises emphasize ease in playing. Avoid any tension. Drop into the keys with a natural follow-through (slight drop) of the wrist.

RIGHT HAND ALONE

Repeat with 12321 and 34543

LEFT HAND ALONE

Repeat with 12321 and 34543

SUGGESTED PLAYING EXAM TOPICS
CHAPTER ONE

1. Play any sight reading study or melody by great American songwriters with good accuracy, pages 11–14 and 16–17.

2. Play at least one accompaniment fluently. Select from pages 18 or 19.

3. Play one duet with good ensemble skills. Select from pages 20–23.

4. Play a selected piece from the *Solo Repertoire* section found on pages 24–28. (Two short pieces on one page count as one piece.)

5. Play the harmonic intervals from *Technical Studies* on page 31.

6. Improvise a short melody using the black key pentatonic scale on page 30.

2 chapter | *Major Pentachords, Major Triads, Eighth Notes (♫, ♩. ♪), Scale Building, Harmonization, Pedaling, Reading Studies, Repertoire, Musicianship Activities, and Technical Studies*

The Major Pentachord (Major 5-Finger Pattern)

Play the following two examples that illustrate an important structure called the *major pentachord*, or *major 5-finger pattern*. Chant the letter names in rhythm as you play each example.

C Major Pentachord – RH

G Major Pentachord – LH

Whole Steps and Half Steps

The *major pentachord* consists of a certain step arrangement of piano keys. A *half step* is the distance from one key to the very next key. A *whole step* consists of two half steps, with one key skipped. Study the diagrams below. H = half step; W = whole step.

A major pentachord (major 5-finger pattern) consists of the following arrangement of steps: whole step, whole step, half step, whole step. Memorize this pattern. Each pentachord starts with a keynote which names the pattern (C major pentachord, G major pentachord, etc.).

The major scale always contains half steps between scale degrees 3-4 and 7-8.

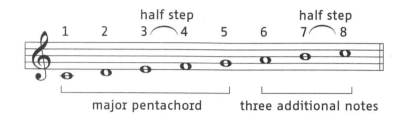

Scale Fingering – C Major Scale

Observe the descending RH scale and ascending LH scale below. Crossing over onto finger 3 enables each hand to play an additional three notes to complete the scale. Memorize the fingering in each hand.

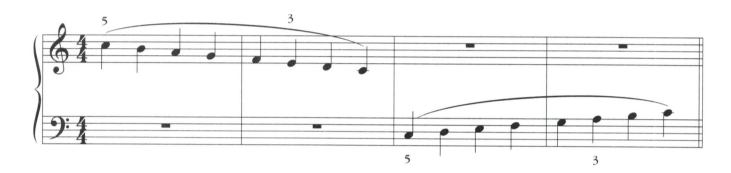

The quarter note that begins *A Danish Tune* is another illustration of an upbeat. Identify the pentachord used in this tune. Tap the rhythm in each hand and chant the letter names before playing.

A DANISH TUNE

Before playing each of the following tunes, name the keynote, check the arrangement of whole and half steps, tap and chant letter names in rhythm, then set a moderate playing tempo. Identify the pentachord used in *A Hungarian Tune*. What sharp is used? Why?

A HUNGARIAN TUNE

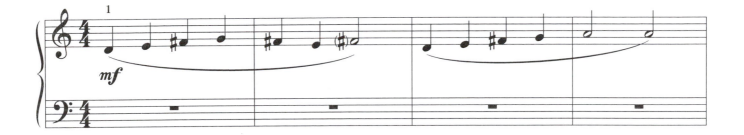

Identify the pentachord used in *A French Tune*. What flat is used? Why?

A FRENCH TUNE

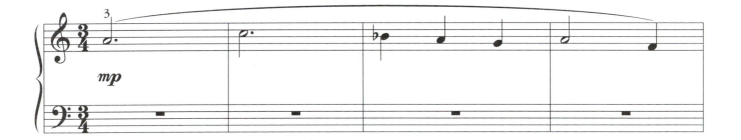

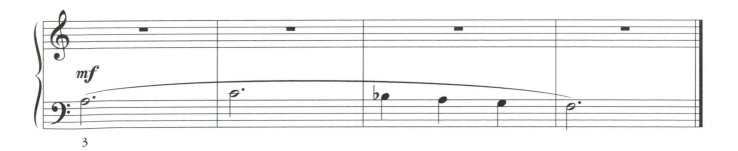

Major Triads (Chords)
In a major pentachord, the first, third, and fifth tones form a major triad.

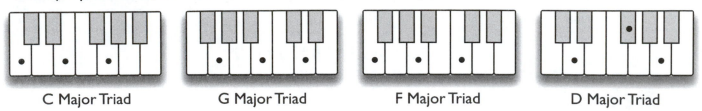

C Major Triad   G Major Triad   F Major Triad   D Major Triad

Triads may be outlined in melodies, or may be "blocked" (all tones sounding at once). A triad is a three-note *chord*. Triads are added to enrich the melody.

AMERICAN MELODY

FOLK MELODY

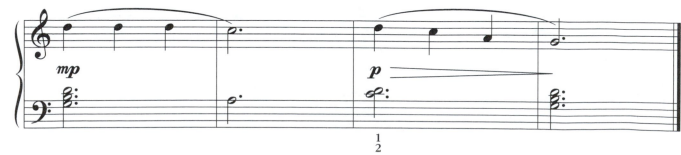

In *American Melody* and *Latin Melody* lighten your touch on the chords so that the melody sings out.

AMERICAN MELODY

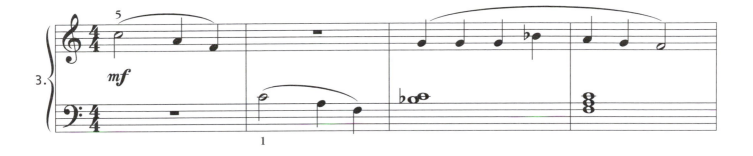

LATIN MELODY

Unison Playing

Freight Train illustrates both hands playing in *unison*. You will notice that the LH plays the same tones an octave lower than the RH. Follow the fingering. Hands are in various 5-finger patterns.

FREIGHT TRAIN

American Folk Song

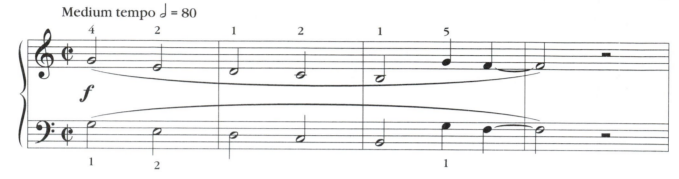

Additional 5-Finger Melodies in Unison with Occasional Triads

Play the following melodies that feature unison playing (both hands playing the melody) and the use of triads at the ends of phrases. Before playing, tap the rhythm and chant the note names.

RUSSIAN MELODY

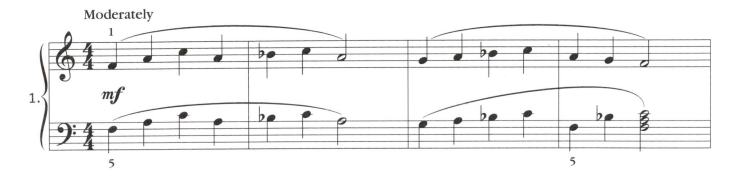

DUTCH MELODY

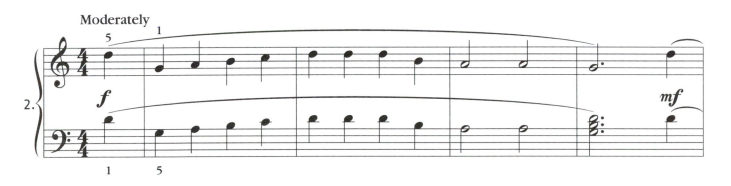

BRITISH MELODY

In *French Melody* circle the chord outlines.

FRENCH MELODY

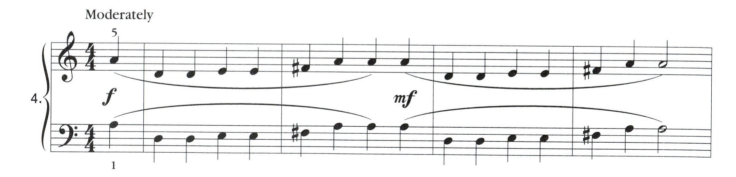

FOLK MELODY

AUSTRIAN MELODY

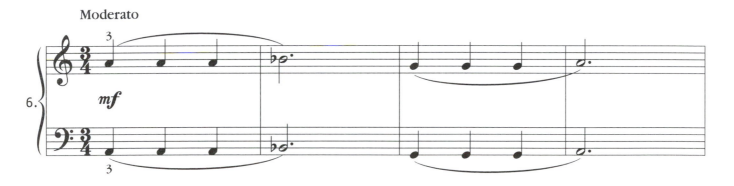

Eighth Notes

In meters with a **4** as the bottom number, eighth notes (♫ or ♪♪) are grouped two to a beat (♫ = ♩). Tap the rhythms of each hand found in *Casey Jones* directly below. Note that the hands come together at the end and outline the major pentachord. Chant eighth notes as "1 – a" or "1 – and."

CASEY JONES

U.S. Railroad Song

In *A Schubert Melody*, practice the shifts of position silently. Start with LH triads, then practice the melody alone. Put the hands together slowly, then increase the tempo.

A SCHUBERT MELODY

AUSTRIAN MELODY

WHO'S THAT TAPPING AT MY WINDOW?
(version 1)

Virginia

Dotted Quarter Note Followed by an Eighth Note

A dotted quarter note lasts as long as a quarter note tied to an eighth note (♩.=♩⌣♪). Tap the following rhythms found in *Ode To Joy*.

ODE TO JOY

Ludwig van Beethoven
arr. James Lyke

MICHAEL ROW YOUR BOAT ASHORE

U.S. Spiritual

RISE UP SHEPHERD AND FOLLOW

(Chorus)

U.S. Spiritual

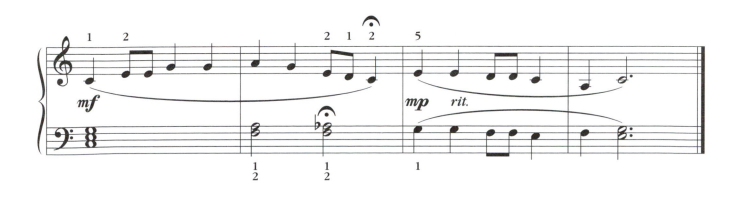

Using the Pedals*

Damper Pedal: When the right pedal on an acoustic piano is depressed, the dampers are lifted from the strings. This allows the strings to continue to vibrate – and the tones to sound – even after the fingers have left the keys. The *damper* pedal produces a sustained *legato* effect between melody notes and chordal figures. On digital pianos, the same effect is created electronically.

Sostenuto Pedal: The middle pedal is called the *sostenuto* pedal (*sost.* or *s.p.*). This pedal catches and holds any dampers that are raised at the moment it is depressed. While this pedal is held down, it doesn't interfere with any other dampers raised while playing their notes or using the damper (right) pedal. On moderately priced upright pianos, this pedal may not function.

Una Corda Pedal: The left pedal is called the *una corda* pedal (*u.c.*). It is somethimes referred to as the soft pedal. Depressing this pedal shifts the hammers so that only two of the three strings are struck. The release of this pedal is indicated by the words *tre corde* (*t.c.*) which mean that three strings are sounded again.

Syncopated Pedal: Chordal music is easier to pedal than purely melodic music because both melody and accompanying chords are based on the same chord formation. When passing from one tone or chord to the next we use the *syncopated* or *legato* pedal in order to achieve an unbroken, *legato* effect. Play the tone first, then quickly change the pedal. The pedal is depressed *after* the tone begins to sound, and connections are made without a blur. As each change is indicated, the pedal is released and depressed immediately after the key goes down. This stops the sound of the preceding tone. Change quickly in order to retain the sustained *legato* effect.

Melodic Pedaling

Brace RH finger 2 with the thumb behind it while playing the following pedal exercise.

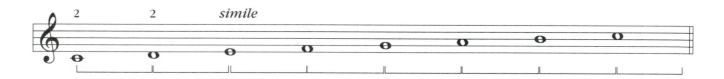

Pedal Markings

Pedal markings are indicated in several ways.

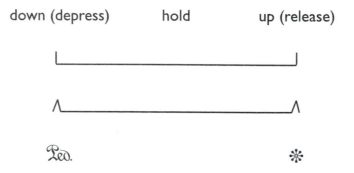

down (depress)   hold   up (release)

* In addition to the two pedal studies on the next page, there are several pieces in the Solo Reprtoire section that require the use of the damper pedal.

Two Pedal Studies
Both pedal studies employ the damper (right) pedal. At first, practice each piece without using the pedal.

PEDAL STUDY NO. 1

Tony Caramia

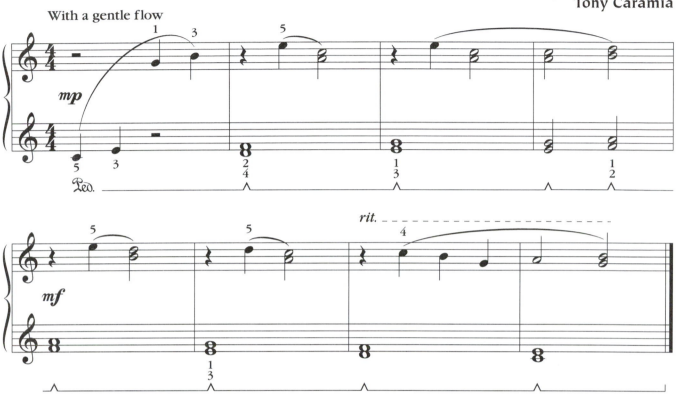

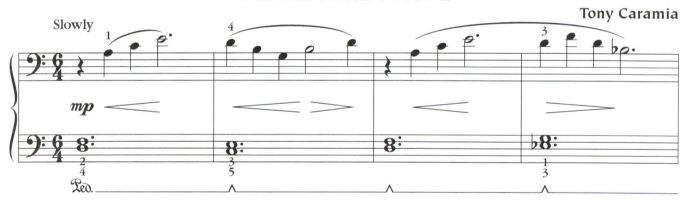

Pedal Study No. 2 uses a new time signature, $\frac{6}{4}$. Count 6 beats to a measure.

PEDAL STUDY NO. 2

Tony Caramia

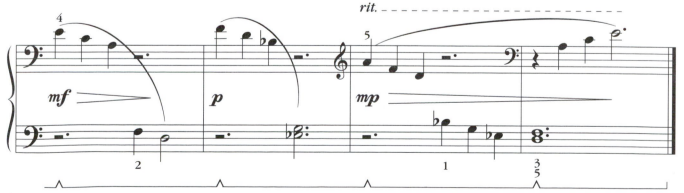

BOOK ONE, CHAPTER TWO

Music for Sight Reading and Transposing

The following tunes feature ♫ and ♩. ♪. Be sure to observe the starting fingering. Sometimes there will be shifts of position. Before playing, tap the rhythms and name notes and chords.

melody by **Henry Tierney**

melody by **Jerome Kern**

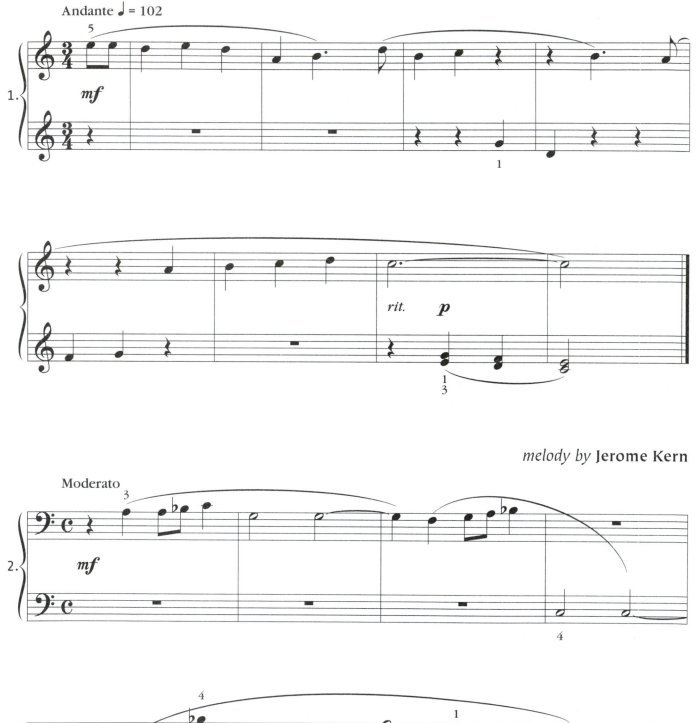

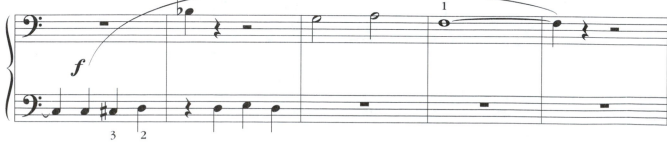

DUTCH MELODY

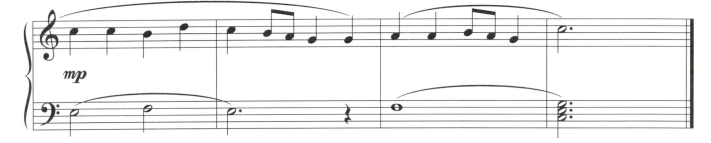

Transpose to D.

POLISH MELODY

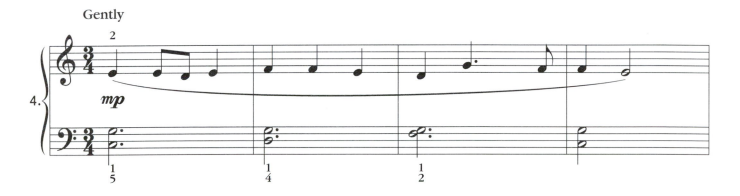

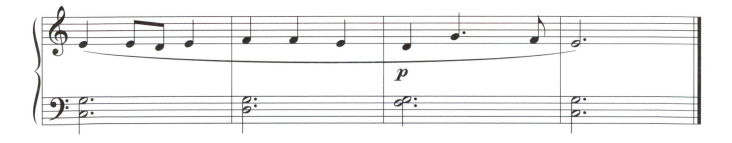

Transpose to D.

BOOK ONE, CHAPTER TWO

SANDY LAND

Folk Tune

Transpose to G.

CRADLE SONG

Franz Schubert

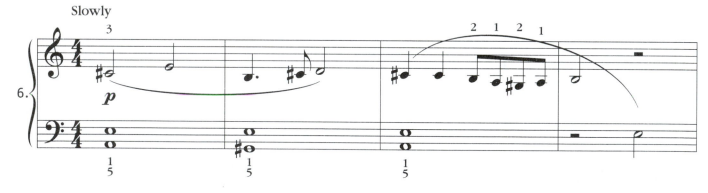

Transpose to G.

Notice the new pentachord built on E in *Who's That Tapping at My Window?*

WHO'S THAT TAPPING AT MY WINDOW?

(version 2)

Virginia

Transpose to F.

GERMAN FOLK SONG

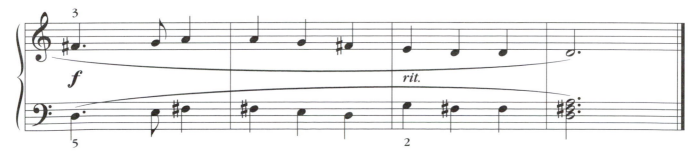

Transpose to C.

ACCOMPANYING

Examine the "**S**" part and practice the two main chords to become familiar with the fingering. Move from a slow tempo to a medium tempo. TEACHER: Double the melody with the RH playing one octave higher.

THE STREETS OF LAREDO

arr. **James Lyke**

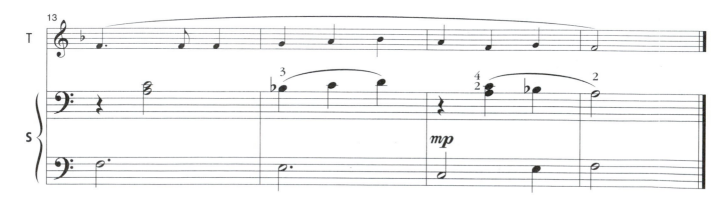

Before playing the *Loch Lomand* accompaniment, practice the following chord pattern until the fingering is memorized. Play each chord four times before moving on to the next chord. Try to memorize the chord pattern so it becomes automatic. These chords will be studied in upcoming chapters.

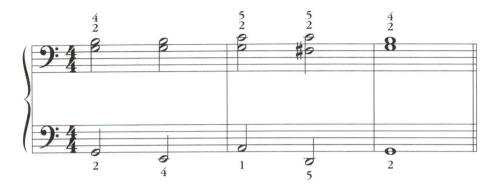

TEACHER: Double the melody with the RH playing one octave higher.

LOCH LOMAND

arr. **James Lyke**

AMERICAN SONG REPERTOIRE

Beginning in Chapter Two, works of the great classic American Songwriters will appear. Composers such as Jerome Kern, Irving Berlin, Cole Porter, George Gershwin, and Richard Rodgers will be featured. Their melodies are fashioned into easy-to-play arrangements. As you move through the book, typical jazz rhythms and harmonies will be introduced in these pieces. Play hands alone until the fingering is mastered.

PLAY A SIMPLE MELODY

Irving Berlin
arr. James Lyke

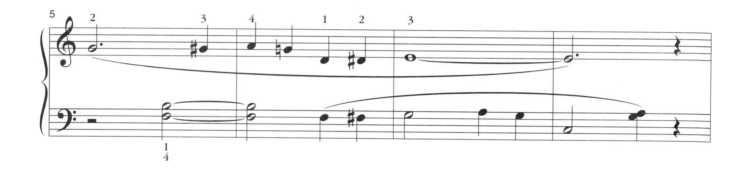

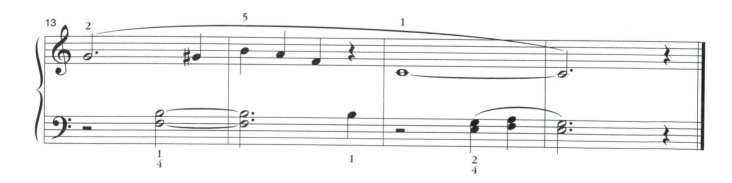

SOME LITTLE GIRL

Jerome Kern
arr. James Lyke

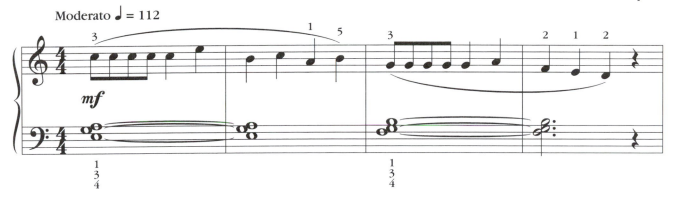

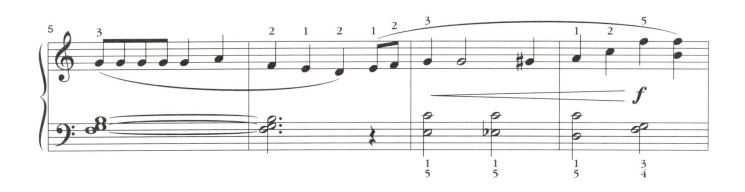

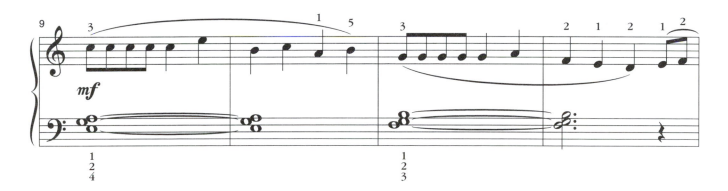

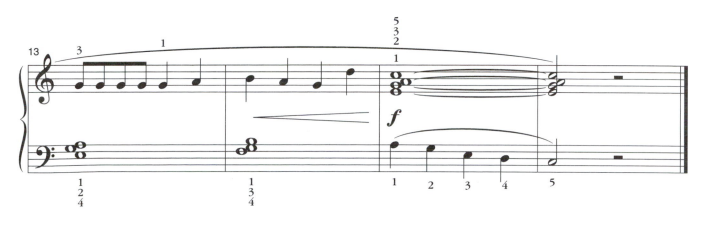

ENSEMBLE REPERTOIRE

WHEN THE CURTAIN FALLS
Secondo – Teacher

music by **Irving Berlin**
arr. **James Lyke**

Moderately slow

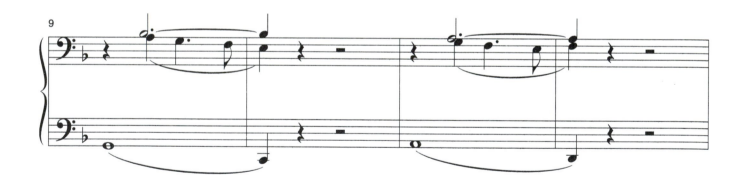

WHEN THE CURTAIN FALLS

Primo – Student

music by **Irving Berlin**
arr. **James Lyke**

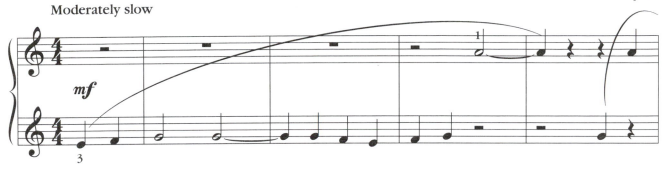

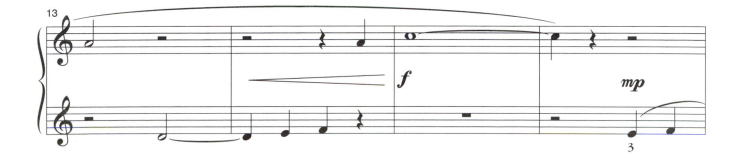

NOTE TO STUDENT

The primo part of *When the Curtain Falls* is good practice for bass clef readers. Sing or say the notes in rhythm when first learning: E, F, G-2, G-2, tie, etc.

Secondo

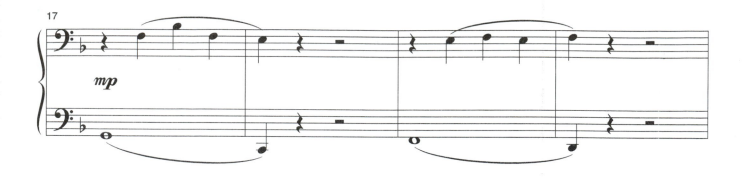

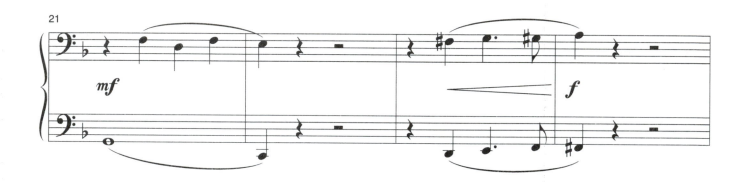

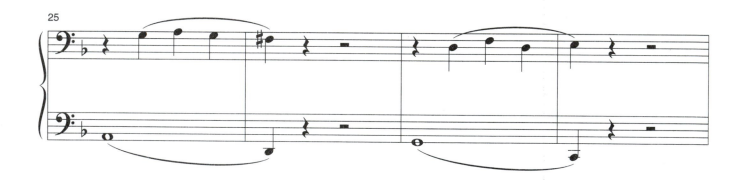

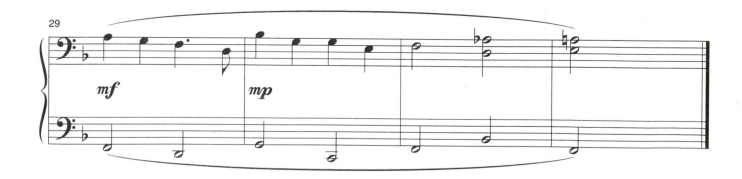

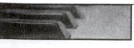

Primo

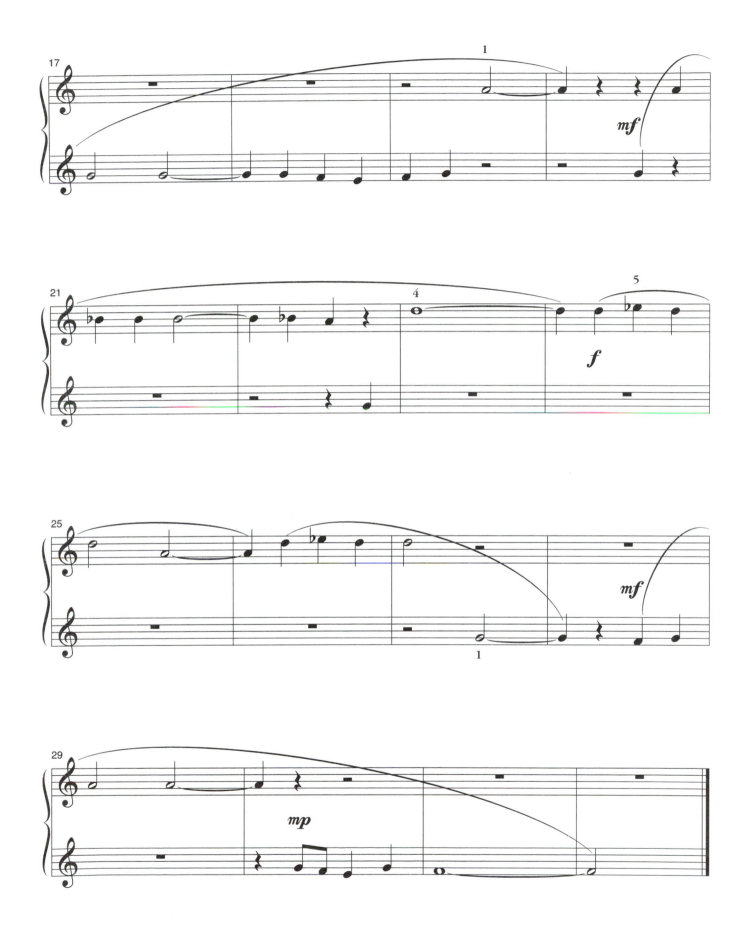

WALKING HOME WITH ANGELINE

Secondo – Student

music by **George Gershwin**
arr. **James Lyke**

NOTE TO STUDENT

The secondo part to *Walking Home with Angeline* is good practice for treble clef readers. Sing or say the notes in rhythm when first learning this piece: D, C, B, A, D, C, B, A, D, A, B, C, D, etc.

WALKING HOME WITH ANGELINE

Primo – Teacher

music by **George Gershwin**
arr. **James Lyke**

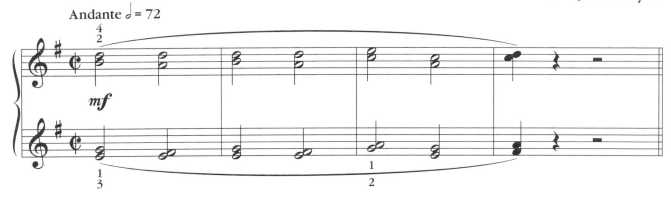

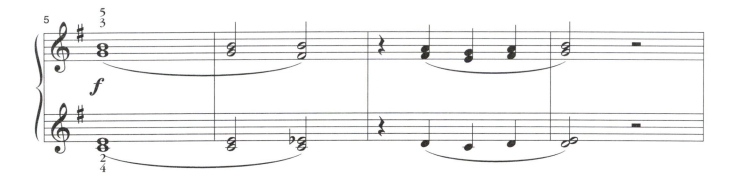

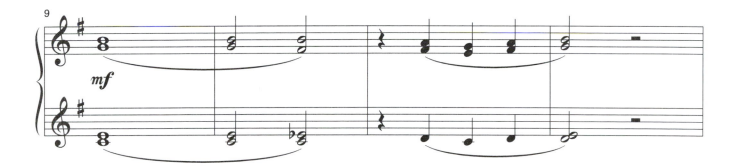

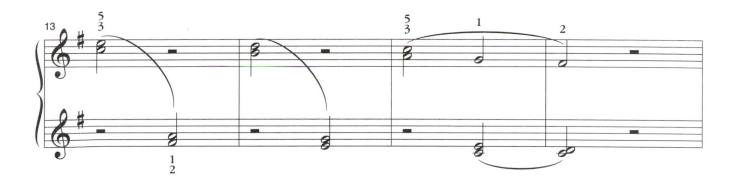

BOOK ONE, CHAPTER TWO

Secondo

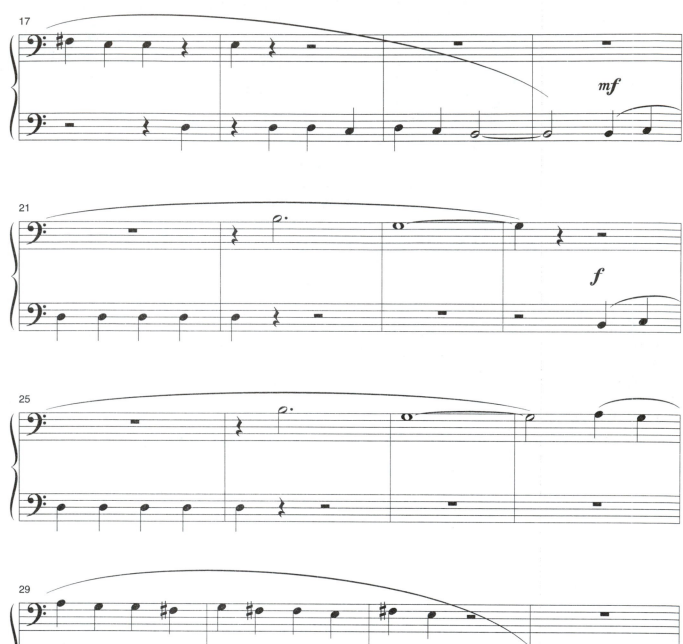

Primo

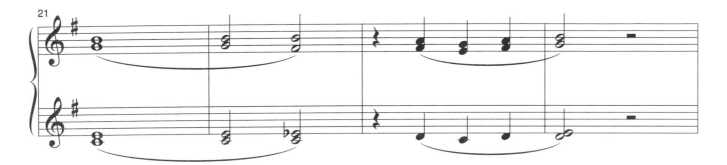

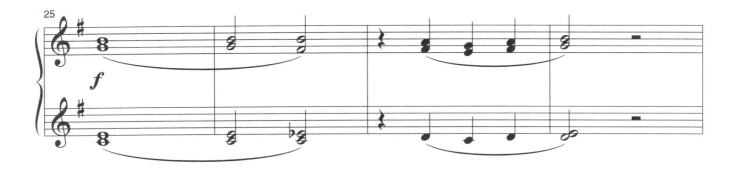

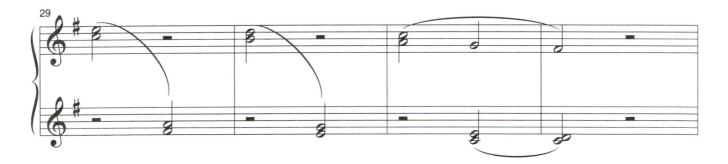

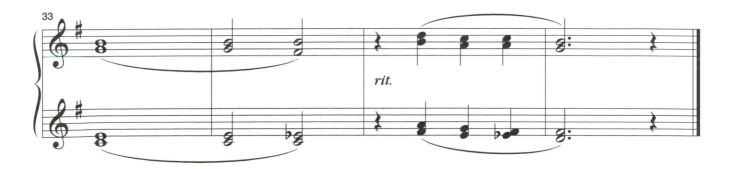

SOLO REPERTOIRE

In learning the following pieces, develop an effective practice plan with the help of the teacher. Isolate difficulties, such as shifts and problem fingerings, for special study. Block figures, observe expressive markings, and play evenly. Smooth playing may require a *slow* tempo until everything comes together. Above all, *listen* and make judgments about your own playing. Find various sections of a piece and study their similarities and differences. Several pieces will require hands alone practice before combining hands. This will ensure secure fingering, proper position, and details of touch and sound.

Practice Plan: Perform eighth notes evenly. Practice the final three measures slowly in order to achieve the correct coordination.

from "FIRST TERM AT THE PIANO"

Béla Bartók

Practice Plan: Exaggerate RH *staccato* and *legato* touches. Strive for even eighth notes.

DRONE PIECE

Jan Valastan Dolinsky

This piece is an example of "mirror composition," a popular 20th-century idiom. Notice that the LH is a mirror pattern of the RH; intervals in the RH are "mirrored" in the LH. Play hands alone singing or saying the notes in rhythm.

FIVE-FINGER PIECE

Halsey Stevens

(without pedal)

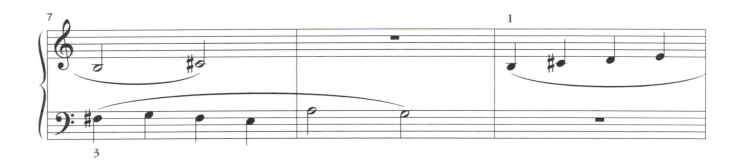

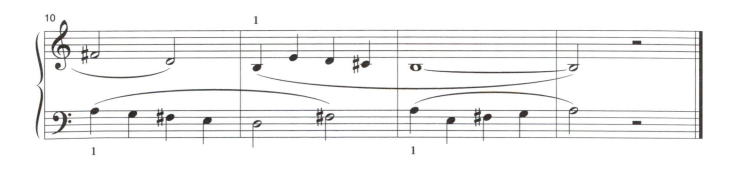

(Used by permission of Helias Music Edition.)

Practice Plan: Practice the LH first, especially the shift (4 to 1) in bars 12 to 13. The RH lies mostly within the G five-finger pattern and shouldn't present any problem. Put the hands together moving from a slow tempo to a quicker one.

DANCE

Daniel Gottlob Türk

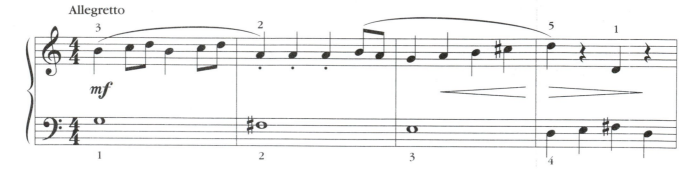

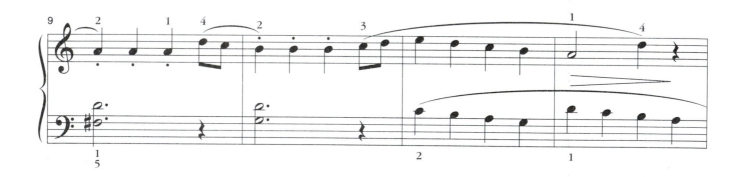

Practice Plan: Practice hands alone until a steady pulse is achieved. Isolate measure 13 striving for even eighth notes while holding the thumb note. Take note of the change of meter in measures 9–10.

This "white key" piece has an austere sound due to the interval combinations of seconds, fourths and fifths. In the second section, practice the left hand alone until the thumb can hold its tone while the other voices move.

FIVE FINGERS

Igor Stravinsky

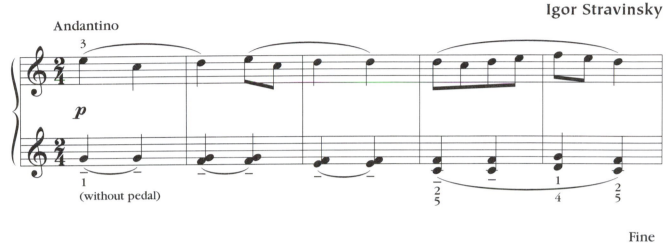

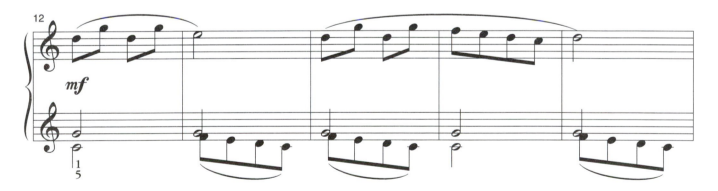

Practice Plan: Isolate the bars with pedal markings and play each 4 times. Next play the LH part (easy), then the RH part without the pedal. Finally, play hands together (HT) without the pedal, then with the pedal.

HI, THERE!

James Lyke

MUSICIANSHIP ACTIVITIES

Complete the following exercises that review various topics introduced in Chapter Two.

Major Pentachord Review

Build the major pentachords indicated below by drawing letters on the correct keys. Number one serves as an example. Then spell the major triad outlined by the 1st, 3rd, and 5th note of each pentachord.

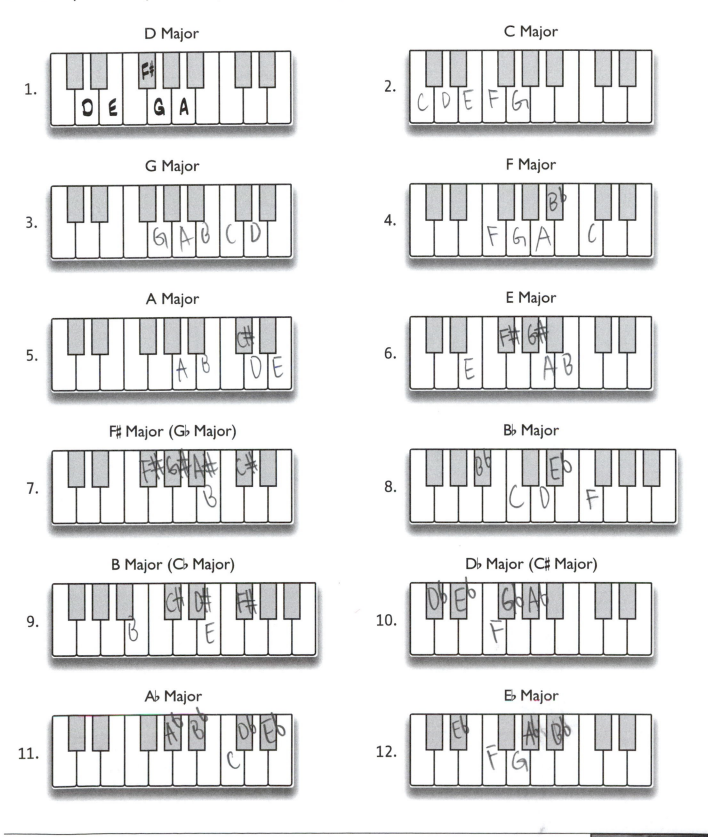

Technical Studies – Major Pentachord Exercise

Play the following major pentachords in sharp keys and flat keys. As you move through the keys, the top note of the triad becomes the bottom note of the new pattern. Remember the W W H W pattern.

Sharp Keys (C through C♯)

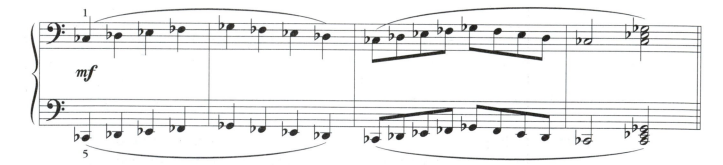

Continue on to D, A, E, B, F♯, and C♯.

Flat Keys (C♭ through C)

Continue on to D♭, A♭, E♭, B♭, F, and C.

Major Triad Exercise

Play the following major triad studies in sharp keys and flat keys. The top note of the triad beomes the bottom note of the new pattern.

Sharp Keys

Continue on to E, B, F♯, and C♯.

Flat Keys

Continue on to E♭, B♭, F, and C.

Two-Note Slur Exercises

Lift the wrist gently after each two-note group. Roll the wrist toward the fallboard.

Transpose to all white key pentachords.

SUGGESTED PLAYING EXAM TOPICS
CHAPTER TWO

1. Build and play major pentachords with keynotes beginning on any key. Use the example below in C. Then transpose to all other keynotes.

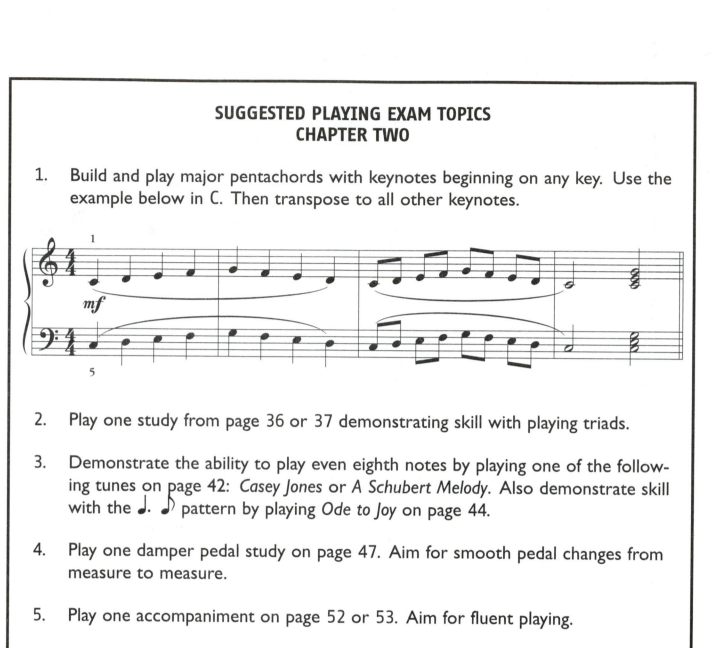

2. Play one study from page 36 or 37 demonstrating skill with playing triads.

3. Demonstrate the ability to play even eighth notes by playing one of the following tunes on page 42: *Casey Jones* or *A Schubert Melody*. Also demonstrate skill with the ♩. ♪ pattern by playing *Ode to Joy* on page 44.

4. Play one damper pedal study on page 47. Aim for smooth pedal changes from measure to measure.

5. Play one accompaniment on page 52 or 53. Aim for fluent playing.

6. Perform one American Song on page 54 or 55.

7. Play one ensemble piece found on pages 56–63.

8. Perform one or two pieces from the Solo Repertoire section, pages 64–68.

3 chapter

Major Scales, Key Signatures, 6ths, 7ths and Octaves, Primary Chords, Dominant 7th Chords, Harmonization, Reading Studies, Accompanying, Ensemble, Repertoire, Musicianship Activities, and Technical Studies

The Major Scale – A Review

Recall the major scale introduced in Chapter 2. A major scale adds 3 tones to the major pentachord (major 5-finger pattern). Remember the *cross-over* fingering in the descending RH scale and ascending LH scale (below). The ascending RH scale and descending LH scale makes use of *thumb-under* fingering. Review the arrangement of half and whole steps on page 34. Also review the fingerings in each hand.

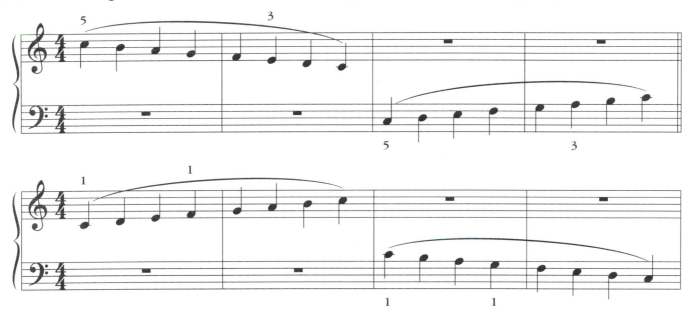

Practice Plan: Play *Scale Song* hands separately before putting the hands together. Note the thumb-under fingering from 3 to 1 in the LH, the thumb on the G (measure 4) needs special attention. In the RH note the cross-over fingering in measure 6, the third finger on the E. Finally, put the hands together (HT) using a slow to moderate tempo.

SCALE SONG

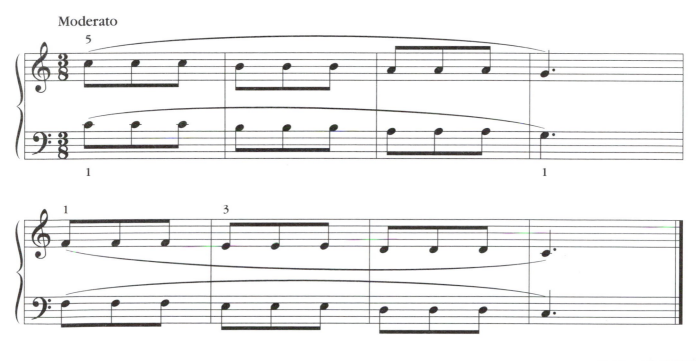

Recall the major scale step pattern that you learned in Chapter 2. Remember that the major scale always contains half steps between scale degrees 3-4 and 7-8.

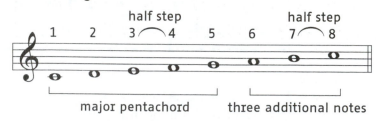

Key Signatures

If we try to build a major scale on other tones, the same whole step and half step arrangement (as in C major) must be maintained. Try playing the D major scale by ear. You will find that an F♯ and C♯ become necessary to maintain half steps between scale steps 3-4 and 7-8. The discovery of the step arrangement of the major scale brings us to the reason for *key signatures*.

In written or printed music, the sharps or flats required to build the various scales are assembled at the beginning of the staff, rather than appearing before the notes. This combination of sharps or flats indicates the key in which the piece of music is written and is called the *key signature*. It tells which notes are to be sharped or flatted throughout the piece in order to preserve the whole step and half step arrangement for the key.

From the key signature it is possible to determine the *keynote* or first note in the scale. In sharp keys, count up one half step from the last sharp (on the right) in the key signature to find the keynote. In flat keys, the next to the last flat in the key signature is the keynote. Remember that the key of F major has only one flat.

Identify the following major keys from the key signature.

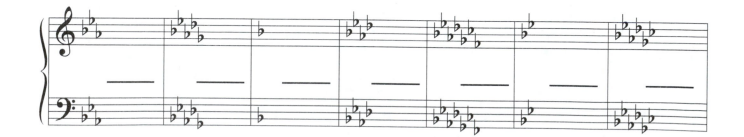

Tetrachord Scales

Scales may be divided between the hands into two *tetrachords* (four-note patterns). Two fingering choices are shown in the example below. Tetrachord scale practice in all keys appears in Musicianship Activities at the end of the chapter. Learn tetrachord scales in C and in all sharp keys. Then learn them in all flat keys.

The A Major Scale Divided Into Tetrachords

Forming Major Scales

If three more tones are added to the major pentachord (5 + 3), a major scale is formed. Added are two whole steps and one half step. Simply remember that half steps in the major scale occur between tones 3–4 and 7–8. Here are four major scales formed from the familiar C, G, D, and A pentachords.

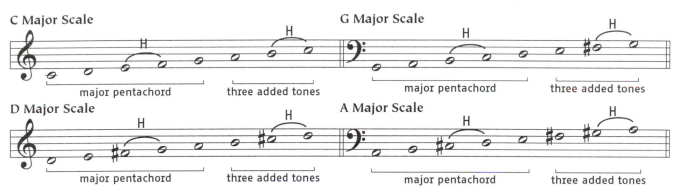

Introduction to Scale Fingering

Study the following traditional fingerings for the scales of C, G, D, and A (all use the same fingering). Play these scales hands alone ascending and descending using the given fingerings. Your instructor will point out the *thumb-under* and *cross-over* (3rd finger) fingering patterns. Scale study will have increasing importance throughout the text. Play each scale firmly and slowly. Memorize the fingering patterns. All major scales and fingerings may be found in Appendix B.

76

D Major Scale

A Major Scale

Playing RH and LH Melodies in the Keys of C, G, D, and A

For the following melodies review the scale fingerings on pages 75 and 76.

BRITISH MELODY (RH)

MELODY IN G (LH)

BRITISH MELODY (LH)

BRETON MELODY (RH)

Practice Plan: Play *English Folk Tune* hands separately before playing hands together (HT).

ENGLISH FOLK TUNE (HT)

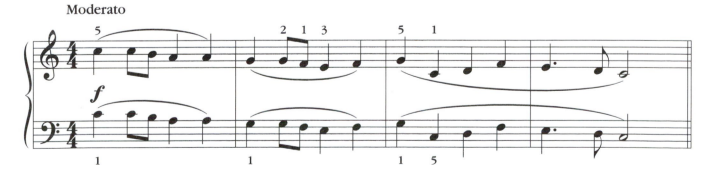

Building 6ths, 7ths, and Octaves

Previously you blocked unisons, 2nds, 3rds, 4ths, and 5ths. Now that you've studied how a scale is formed, you need to block 6ths, 7ths, and octaves. Play the intervals shown below starting with a 5th and stretching to the octave. Then move from the octave back to the 5th in each hand.

Play the following fragments from folk melodies. Identify the circled intervals. See the example.

1.

2.

3.

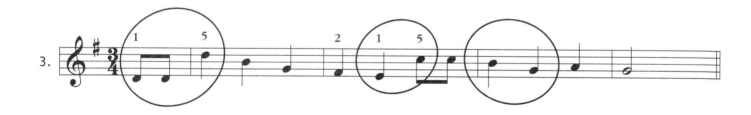

4.

5.

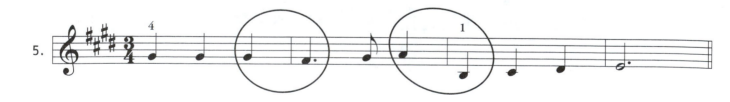

Find 6ths, 7ths, and octaves in *Stretches*. They are all fingered alike (1–5).

STRETCHES

James Lyke

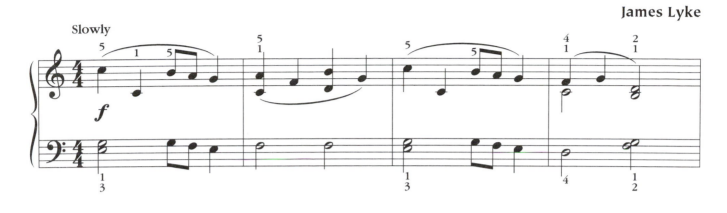

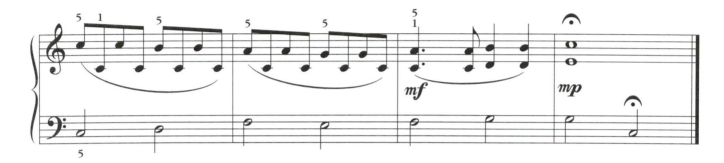

Take care with pedal changes in *A Pleasant Dream*.

A PLEASANT DREAM

James Lyke

BOOK ONE, CHAPTER THREE

Tonic and Dominant Triads

A *tonic* triad is built on the first degree of a scale. A *dominant* triad is built on the fifth degree of the scale. The dominant triad, like the tonic, is often outlined in melodies. Study the following examples.

The dominant chord has a strong tendency to move to the tonic. You have already used tones of the dominant chord to harmonize non-tonic tones. Study the tonic and dominant outlines in the following melody.

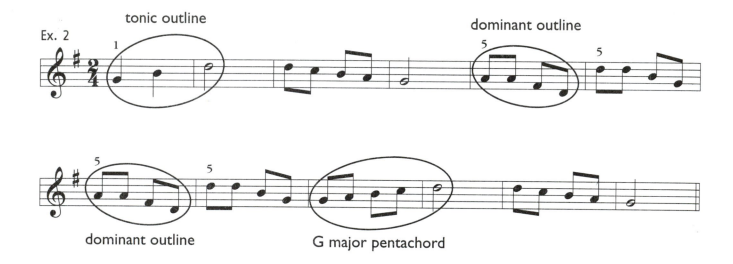

Study the following harmonization that uses the tonic and dominant chords. Capital letter names (G, D) indicate major chords. The capital letter refers to the root of each chord. (See Ex. 1 above.)

Folk Song

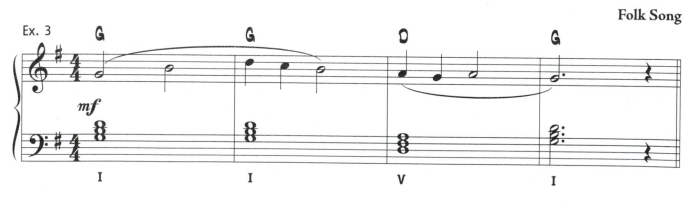

Transpose to F and A.

The Dominant Seventh Chord: Root Position and First Inversion

Study the first four bars of the German folk song below. Note the four circled tones. Spelling from bottom to top (D, F#, A, C), this four-note chord is called a *dominant 7th*. It is built on the fifth degree of the scale and adds one more third to the dominant triad. *Seventh chords* (there are many types) contain four notes built in 3rds. The essential tones of a seventh chord are the root, third, and seventh.

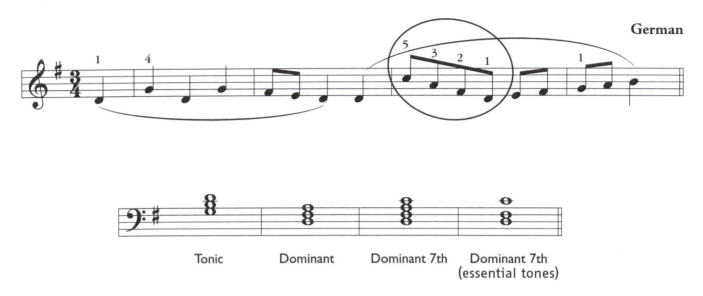

German

Tonic · Dominant · Dominant 7th · Dominant 7th (essential tones)

For ease in playing this chord, the essential tones may be rearranged, or inverted. For now, the first inversion will be useful.

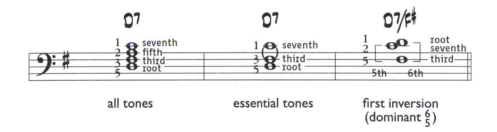

all tones · essential tones · first inversion (dominant $^6_5$)

The "7" appearing after the capital letter D in the example above identifies this chord as a *dominant seventh*. There are many types of seventh chords which will be explored at a later time. The D^7/F# chord means that F# is the lowest tone. A letter following a slash normally indicates the chord tone in the bass.

Dominant Seventh Chord Drill

Write the letter name (i.e., chord symbol) in the box above each chord.

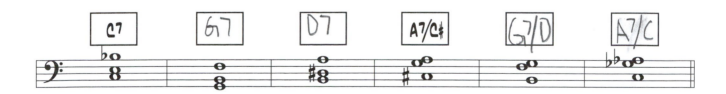

C7   G7   D7   A7/C#   G7/D   A7/C

The Subdominant (IV) Chord in Major Keys – Primary Chords I-IV-V

In one measure of the *Norwegian Melody* below, the subdominant, or IV chord, is outlined.

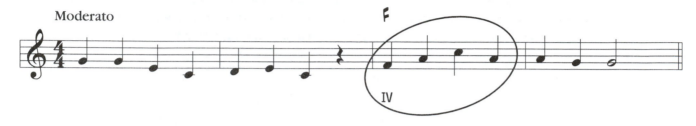

The subdominant chord is built on the 4th scale degree as shown below. It is major in quality and generally moves to V (dominant) or I (tonic).

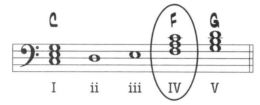

The three most common chords, in music are the I, IV, and V. These chords are known as *primary* chords. Chords built on other tones of the scale (ii, iii, vi, etc.) are called *secondary* chords.

As you learned when dealing with V^7 in root position as opposed to V^7 in first inversion (V_5^6), inversions help the hand assume a more comfortable position and create smoother voice leading. In LH style harmonization, it is easy to move from I to V_5^6 and return to I. $I-V^7-I$ is less smooth. The same holds true for $I-IV-I$ and $I-IV_4^6-I$. Study and play the examples below.

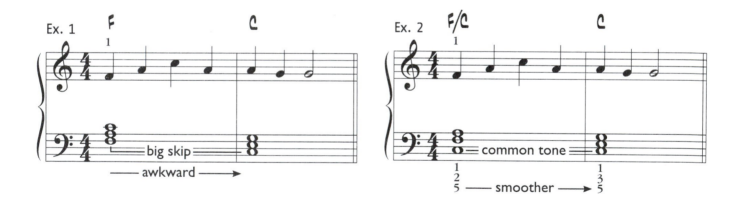

$I-IV_4^6-I-V_5^6-I$ Chord Pattern

Practice the following chord pattern and transpose it to all white keys (C, D, E, F, G, A, and B). Place letter name chord symbols above each chord as shown in the C major example. Pedal as indicated.

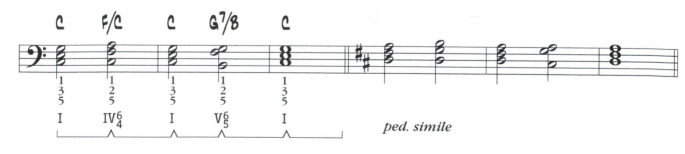

Harmonization Using I, IV$_4^6$, and V$_5^6$ in Major Keys

MINUET
(Block Chords)

W.A. Mozart

MELODY
(Broken Chords)

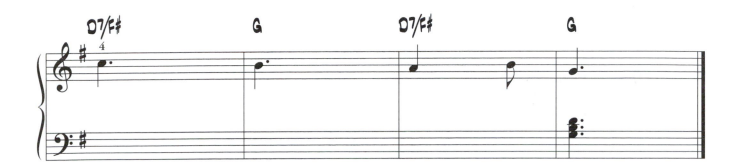

FOLK MELODY
(Waltz Accompaniment)

MICHAEL ROW THE BOAT ASHORE
(Rolled Chords)

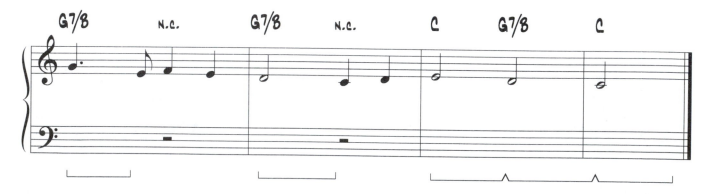

NOTE TO STUDENT

A wavy line in front of a chord (𝄕) means to roll the notes of the chord quickly from bottom to top. **n.c.** means no chord. Observe all pedal markings.

HUNGARIAN FOLK SONG
(after beat chords)

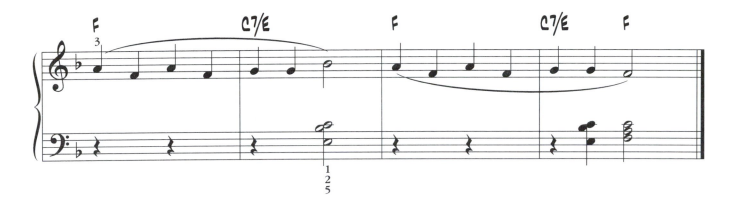

GERMAN FOLK SONG
(Block Chords)

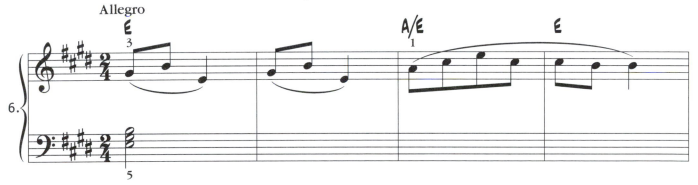

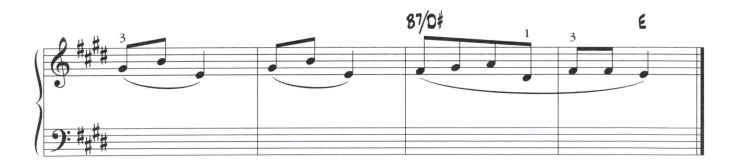

NOTE TO STUDENT
When no chord symbol is given, continue with the harmony from the previous measure.

Music for Sight Reading and Transposing

Before sight reading the following studies, establish the habit of 1) identifying the key signature, 2) chanting and tapping the rhythms in each hand (or both hands together), 3) locating beginning pitches and fingerings, and 4) playing slowly to avoid halting at any point in the study. Analyze errors after the first reading. *Trust your hands.* Transpose selected studies to the keys indicated.

ENGLISH FOLK SONG

Transpose to G.

AMERICAN GAME SONG

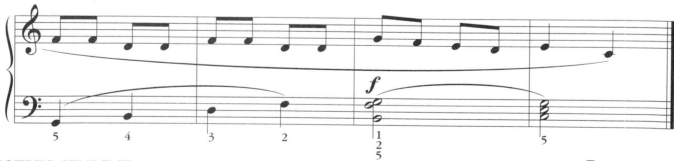

Transpose to D.

NOTE TO STUDENT

Notice the left hand V^7 chord (inverted) in measure 7 of *American Game Song*.

BRITISH MELODY

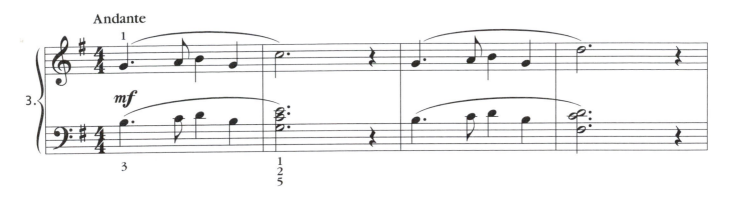

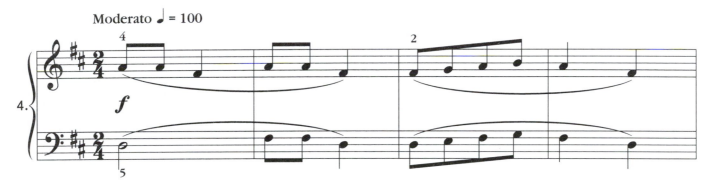

Transpose to A.

CZECH FOLK MELODY

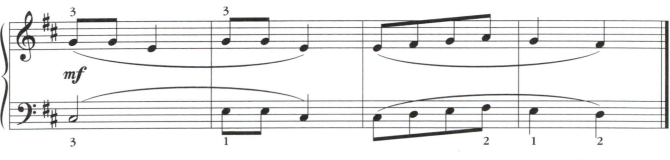

Transpose to C.

BOOK ONE, CHAPTER THREE

88

SLOVAKIAN FOLK TUNE

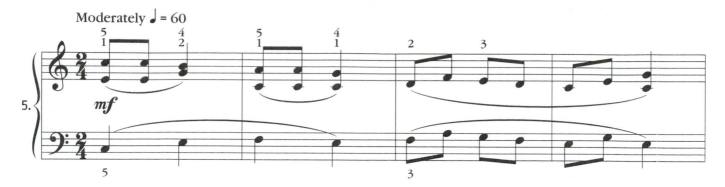

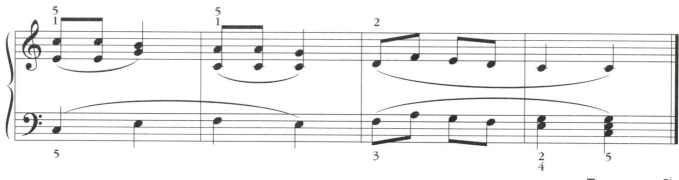

Transpose to B♭.

BRITISH FOLK SONG

Transpose to C.

THEME BY BEETHOVEN

Transpose to D.

GERMAN FOLK SONG

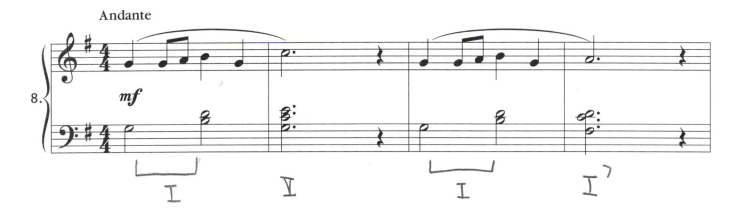

Transpose to F.

ACCOMPANYING

TEACHER: Double the melody one octave higher.

LONE STAR TRAIL

Cowboy Song
arr. James Lyke

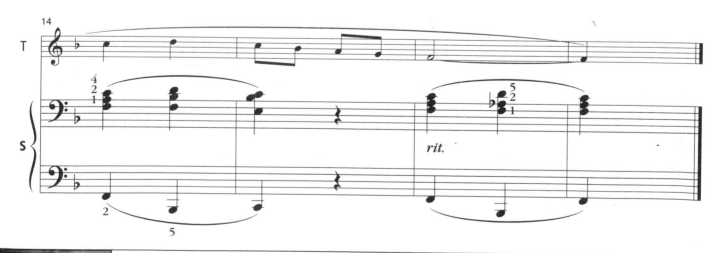

STUDENT: Find the bars with subdominant chords (IV). TEACHER: Double the melody one octave higher.

RUSSIAN FOLK SONG

arr. James Lyke

Moderato ♩ = 112

BOOK ONE, CHAPTER THREE

AMERICAN SONG REPERTOIRE

THEY CALL IT DANCING

music by **Irving Berlin**
arr. **James Lyke**

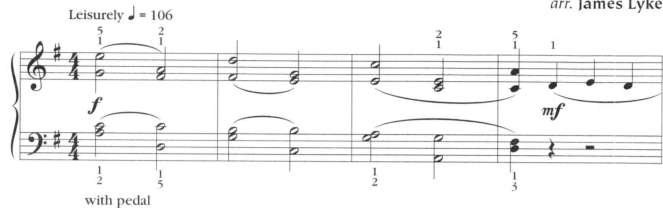

with pedal

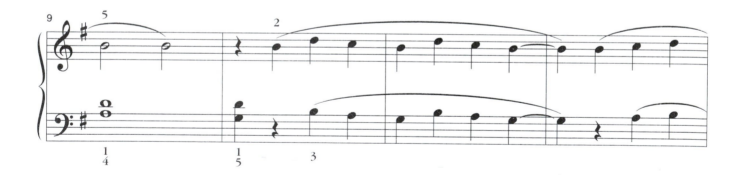

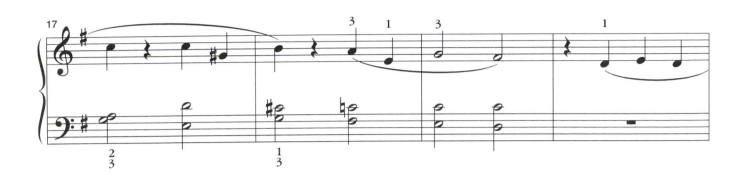

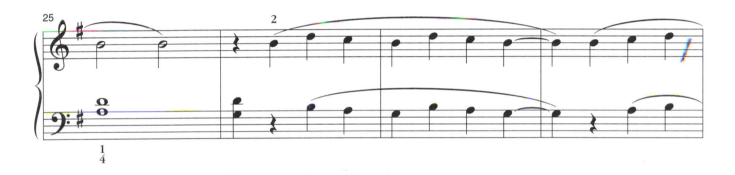

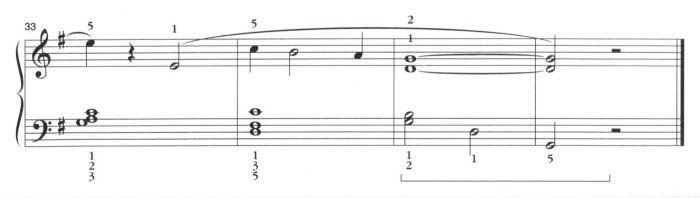

AIN'T WE GOT FUN

Richard Whiting
arr. **James Lyke**

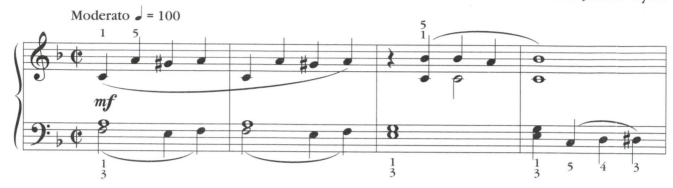

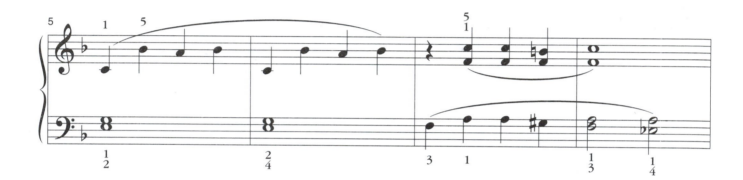

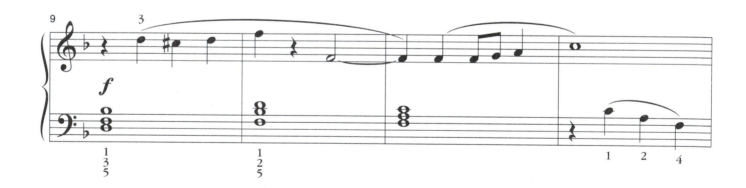

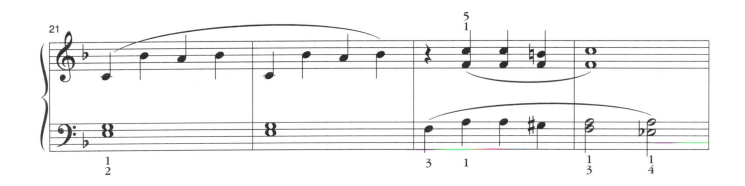

ENSEMBLE REPERTOIRE

RUMBA

Secondo – Teacher

James Lyke

RUMBA

Primo – Student

James Lyke

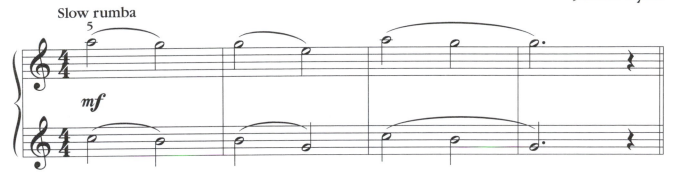

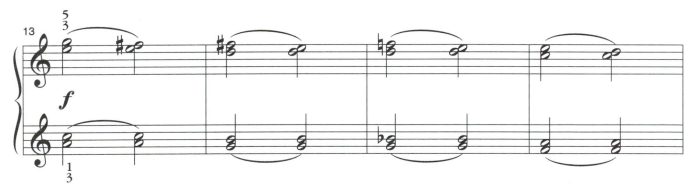

THEME FROM POLOVETZIAN DANCES

Secondo – Teacher

Alexander Borodin
arr. **James Lyke**

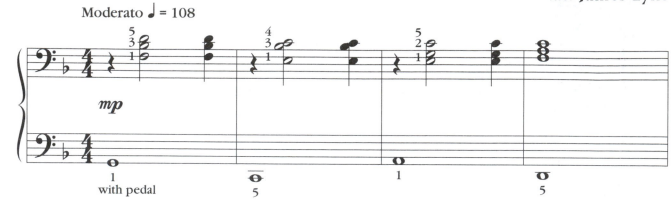

THEME FROM POLOVETZIAN DANCES

Primo – Student

Alexander Borodin
arr. **James Lyke**

Reminder: *8va* - - - - - - means to play the melody one octave higher than written.

Theme from Polovetzian Dances contains a recurring four chord pattern. Practice the following LH progression until it becomes fluent. Transpose the primo part one octave lower and you will have an effective solo! Add pedal.

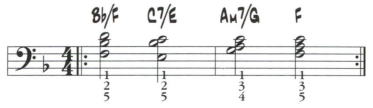

SOLO REPERTOIRE

In Chapters 3 – 8, consult Appendix A for definitions of unfamiliar terms and signs.

Practice Plan: Practice hands alone, as usual, to make fingering very secure. Perform cleanly with no pedal. Feel the shifts of position without looking at your hands.

TWO CLASSIC PIECES

No. 1

Daniel Gottlob Türk

Transpose to G.

No. 2

Daniel Gottlieb Türk

Transpose to F.

Practice Plan: Exaggerate the RH two-note slurs (drop, lift). Find examples of root position dominant seventh chords in the LH. In the second section, take note of the descending chromatic thirds. Isolate this passage for special practice.

MARIE DORT
(MARIE SLEEPS)

Darius Milhaud

Practice Plan: Practice hands alone and be attentive to touches (*legato, staccato*). Measures 9–16 require special work with changes of position and hand-over-hand arpeggiation. What patterns are suggested by the title? Analyze the triads and triad outlines,

PATTERNS

Tony Caramia

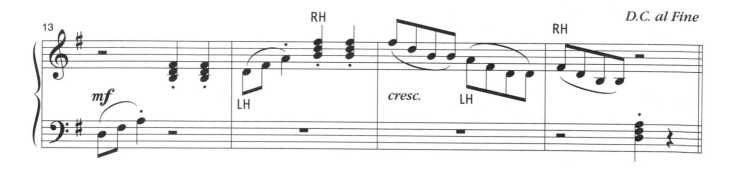

Reminder: *D.C. al Fine* means go back to the beginning and play to the place marked *Fine*.

Practice Plan: Block intervals in both hands before performing as written. Take note of the *fermata* 𝄐 in bar 8 and the change of clef in measure 16, RH.

SEVENTH INNING STRETCH

Tony Caramia

QUIET HOUR

Louis Gordon

Andante (but with a steady beat)

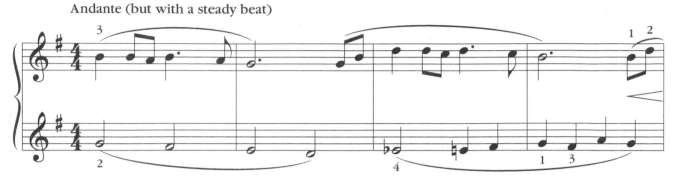

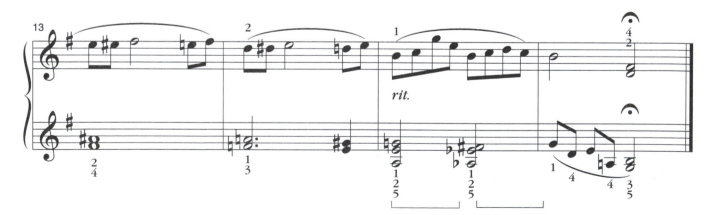

From *Junior Jazz*. Copyright Edward B. Marks, Music Corporation. Used by permission.

NOTE TO STUDENT

Sometimes jazz tunes are soft and slow. In *Quiet Hour* the piano sings. There is a feeling of four-to-the-bar. Analyze the seventh chords in the last two bars. Consider the tones in *both* hands.

KEYBOARD MUSICIANSHIP

Practice Plan: At first, practice without the pedal. Pay close attention to the fingering.

DREAMING

James Lyke

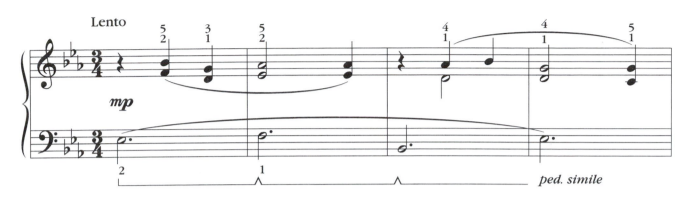

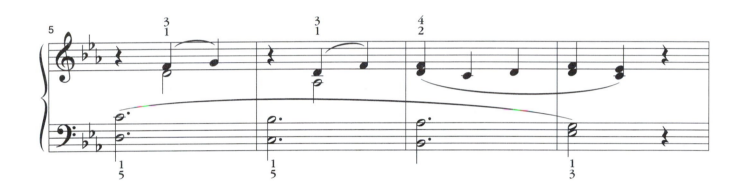

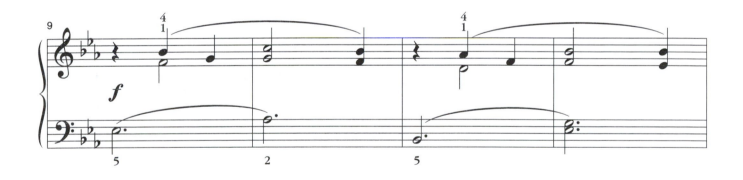

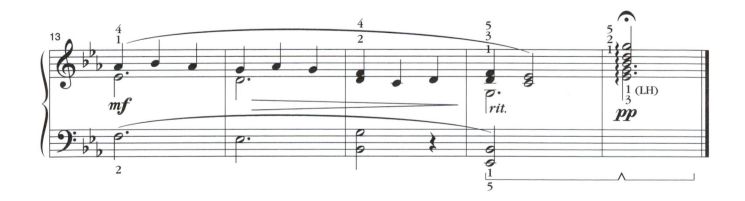

Practice Plan: In early practice, play *Scale Etude* without pedal, striving for a smooth *legato*. Then add pedal as indicated in the score. As usual, start slowly and then increase the speed. Analyze LH chords (G^7/D, G/B, etc.).

SCALE ETUDE

Jean Louis Gobbaerts

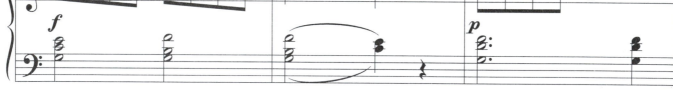

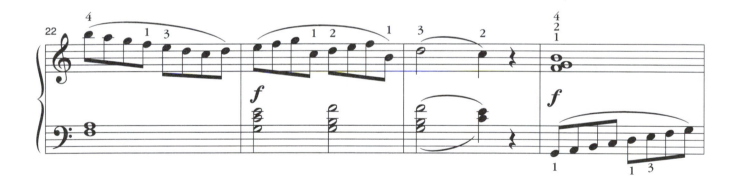

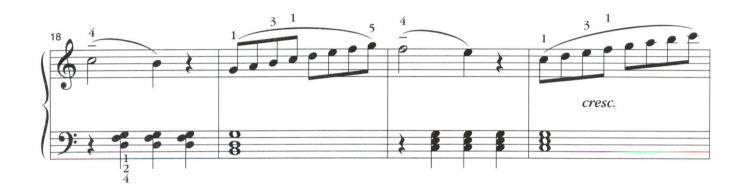

MUSICIANSHIP ACTIVITIES

Tetrachord Scales: C and Sharp Keys via the Circle of 5ths

This study divides the scale of C (and the sharp keys that follow) into *tetrachords* (four-note scales in each hand). Each new scale starts a 5th above the previous scale. Follow the practice suggestions.

Practice Suggestions: When moving to a new scale, lift the LH for the new pattern. Arrange the RH to cover the new 4 note tetrachord.

count:
1 2 3,
2 2 3

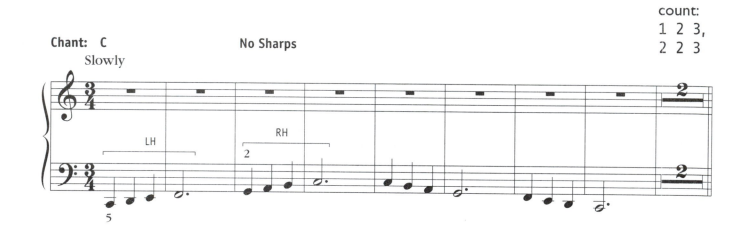

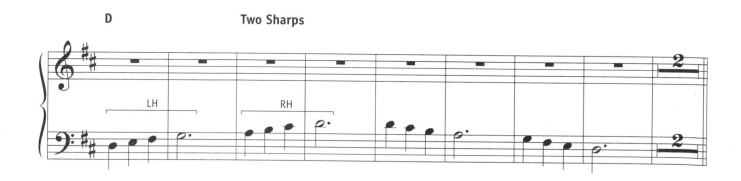

Chant: **A**   **Three Sharps**

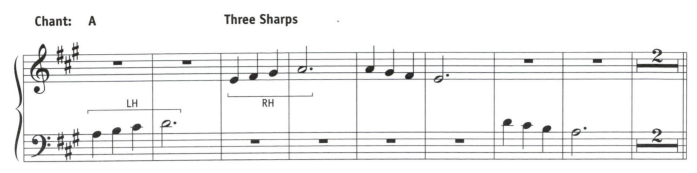

E   **Four Sharps**

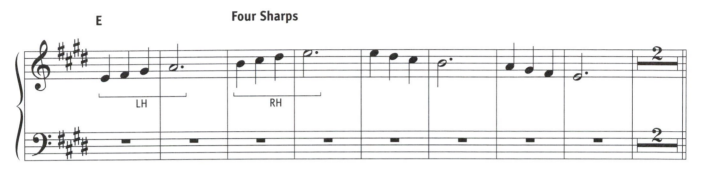

B   **Five Sharps**

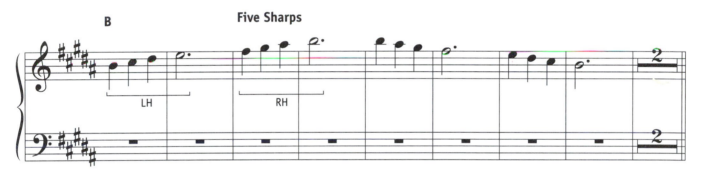

F♯   **Six Sharps**

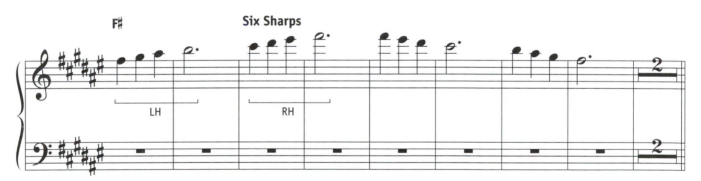

C♯   **Seven Sharps**

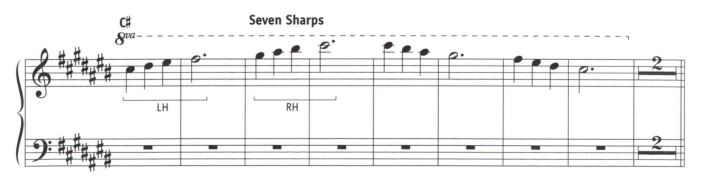

Tetrachord Scales: Flat Keys and C via the Circle of 5ths

This study divides the flat scales and C into *tetrachords* (four-note scales in each hand). The study begins with Cb (7 flats) and progresses by 5ths to C (no flats). Follow the practice suggestions on page 108.

Chant: Cb   **Seven Flats**

Gb   **Six Flats**

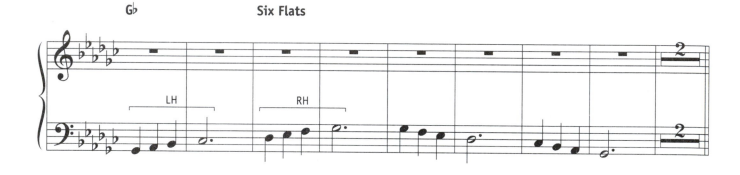

Db   **Five Flats**

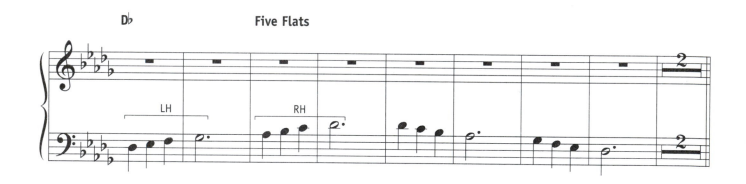

Chant: Ab   **Four Flats**

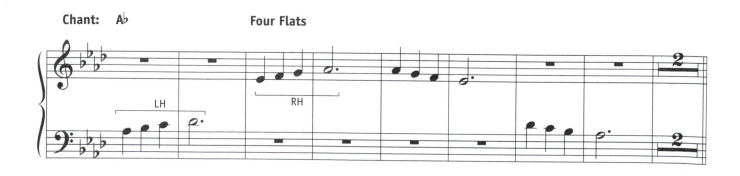

Eb **Three Flats**

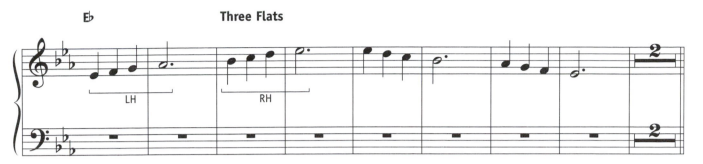

Bb **Two Flats**

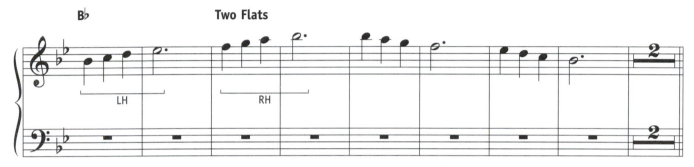

F **One Flat**

C **No Flats**

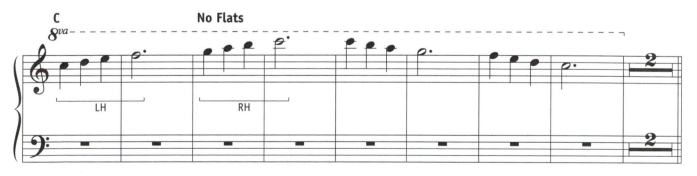

BOOK ONE, CHAPTER THREE

Reviewing the Subdominant Chord (IV)

The IV chord was presented earlier in this chapter both in root position and inverted form IV_4^6. Observe both tonic chord (C) and subdominant chord (F) outlined in the melody of *My Home's in Montana*.

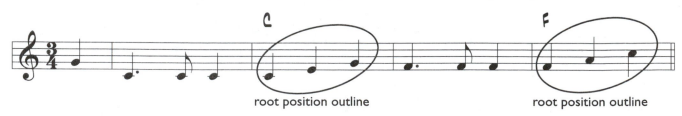

The subdominant chord is built on the 4th scale degree as shown below. It is major in quality and generally moves to V (dominant) or I (tonic).

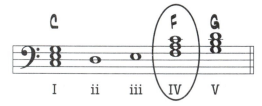

The three most used chords in music are the I, IV, and V. These chords are known as *primary* chords. Chords built on other tones of the scale (ii, iii, vi, etc.) are called *secondary* chords.

$I–IV_4^6–I$ Chord Pattern - LH

Practice the following chord pattern and transpose it to all white keys. Place letter name chord symbols above each chord as shown in the C major example. Also, place Roman numeral chord symbols below each chord as shown.

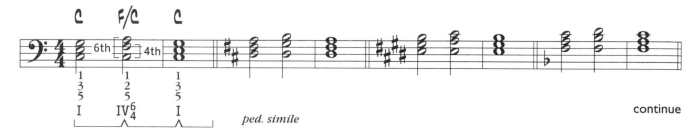

An Essential Chord Pattern: $I–IV–I_4^6–V^7–I$ (Four Voices)

First, review playing the $I–IV_4^6–I–V_5^6–I$ progression with each hand. Note the RH fingering on the tonic which simplifies the movement to the subdominant chord. Practice both of the two-handed style versions with LH playing roots of chords and RH playing the harmony.

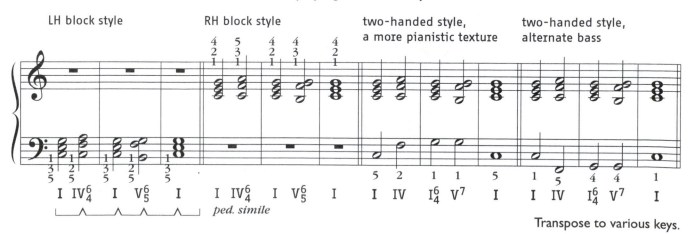

Triplets

An eighth note triplet $\overset{3}{\sqcap}$ fills the time of one quarter note.

Triplet Chord Study

Practice the following chord study (I–IV$_4^6$–V$_5^6$–I). Transpose to several keys such as G, F, D, E, etc.

Practice Plan: First block chords without the pedal. Identify inversions (ex. bar 2 – F/C). Then play *Pedal Study* as written, observing the pedal markings.

PEDAL STUDY

Louis Köhler

SUGGESTED PLAYING EXAM TOPICS
CHAPTER THREE

1. Play one of the major scales found on pages 75–76 hands together (HT) with the correct fingering.

2. Play one of the harmonization studies from pages 83–85.

3. Play one of the accompaniments from pages 90–91.

4. Perform one of the American Songs found on pages 92–95.

5. Perform the primo part of one of duet on page 97 or 99.

6. Perform one (or two) solos from the Solo Repertoire collection found on pages 100–107.

7. Play any tetrachord scale from pages 108–111 suggested by your instructor.

4 chapter

Minor Pentachords, Minor Triads, ⁶⁄₈ Meter, Sixteenth Notes, Reading Studies, Harmonization, Repertoire, Musicianship Activities, and Technical Studies

NOTE TO TEACHER: Now is a good time to begin working in Appendix C (Holiday Music).

Compare the C major scale with the most common form of the minor scale, the *harmonic minor*. Scale steps 3 and 6 are lowered one half step in this minor scale. All minor scales share a key signature with a major scale. The lowered third step of the minor scale is "borrowed" from the major scale which best fits its structure. Other forms of the minor scale are explored in a later chapter.

The Minor Pentachord (5-Finger Pattern)

We have learned the construction of the pentachord in major as: whole step, whole step, half step, whole step. This particular order of steps forms the first five notes of the major scale. *Major* is a quality and its sound is associated with brightness. The *minor* quality, by contrast, is associated with mournfulness or sadness. It differs from the major pattern in only one way: its third note is one half step lower.

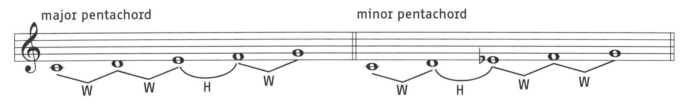

The Minor Triad

Play the ascending and descending major pentachord in the 1st measure below. Repeat it (measure 2), lowering the 3rd tone by one half step. Then play the minor triad as shown.

Transpose to all white keys, then to all black keys, then play chromatically: C, D♭, D, E♭, etc.

Minor 5-Finger Pattern Reading

Sight read the following melodies that lie within the minor five-finger pattern in each hand. Determine the minor key from the key signature. For example, No. 1 has a key signature of C major. Count down one and one half steps from C to establish the key of Am. Transpose each melody as indicated. The instructor can provide simple accompaniments using the chord symbols above the melody.

Bulgarian

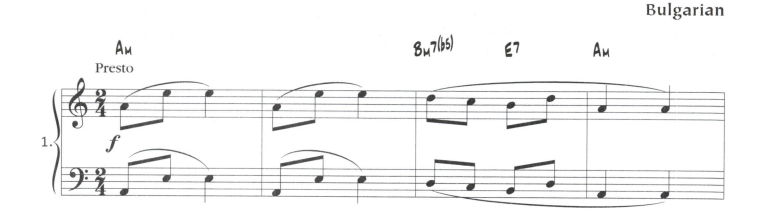

Transpose to G minor.

Lettish

Transpose to C minor.

Russian

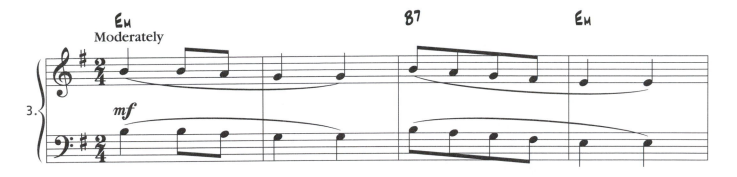

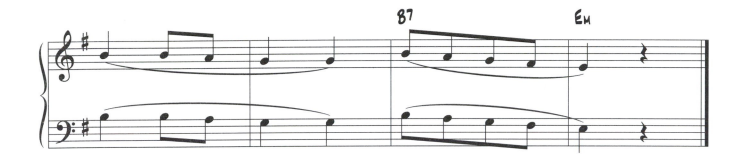

Transpose to D minor.

Hungarian

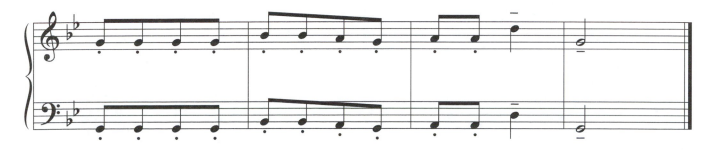

Transpose to F minor.

French

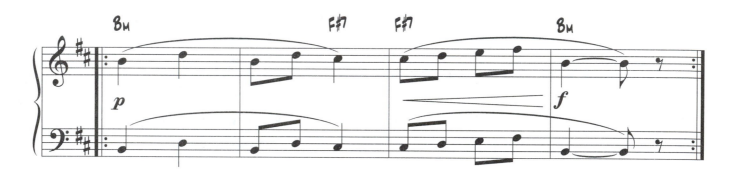

Transpose to A minor.

Russian

Transpose to F minor.

Harmonizing in Minor Keys Using the Tonic and Dominant $\frac{6}{5}$ Chords

Harmonize melodies 1–4 using the I, V^7, and V^6_5 chords. Complete the LH according to the examples given. Write the chord symbols in the boxes.

Russian

British

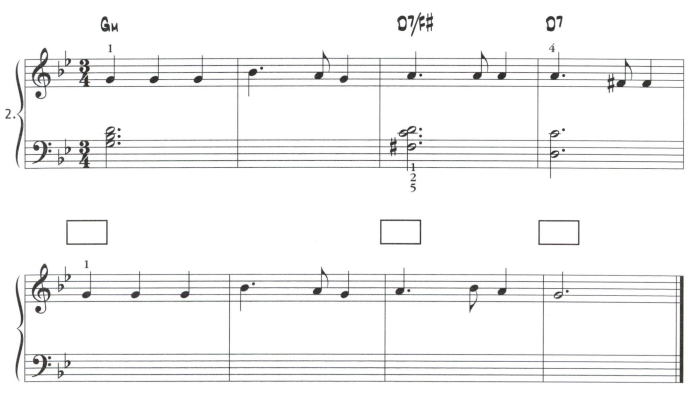

Czech

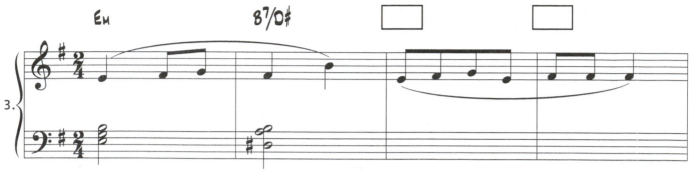

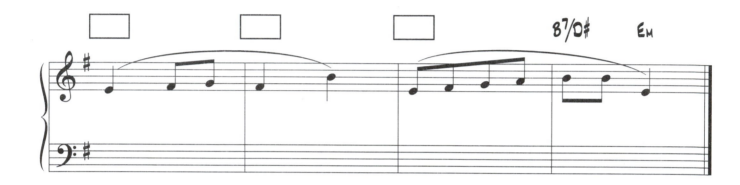

Latvian

The Tonic–Dominant $\frac{6}{5}$–Tonic Progression – A Review

The dominant $\frac{6}{5}$ chord was introduced in Chapter Three. Practice the tonic–dominant $\frac{6}{5}$–tonic progression starting on all white keys. The $\frac{6}{5}$ refers to the intervals measured from the bottom note to the two top notes. Remember that the LH thumb plays the dominant tone (or root of the chord), 2nd finger plays the seventh, and 5th finger plays the third of the chord.

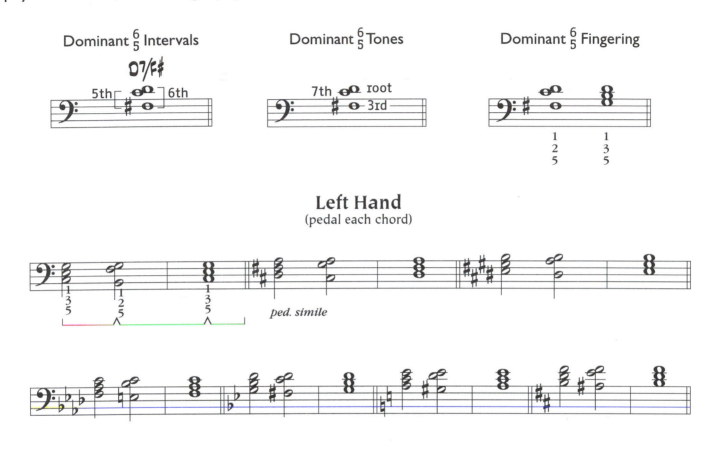

Left Hand
(pedal each chord)

For accompanying and harmonizing purposes, it is necessary to put the chords in the RH, while LH bass notes supply fundamental tones and rhythm. Learn all of the RH I–V$\frac{6}{5}$–I patterns below.

Right Hand
(pedal each chord)

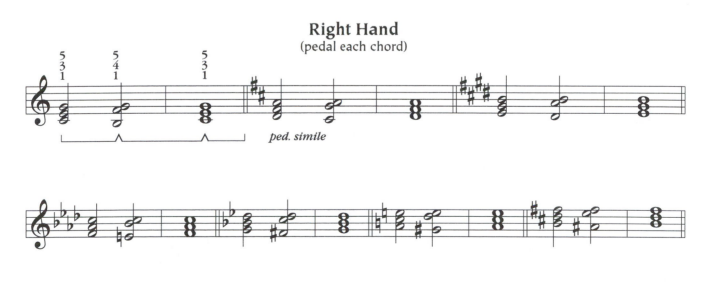

I–V⁷–I: Four-Voice Texture in Major and Minor Keys

You have used the chords shown on the next page in various LH accompaniments. Now we will examine how these RH chords plus a bass note form a *four-voice texture*. It is important to remember that the lowest tone (bass note in LH) determines how the chord is labeled. For example, a C$_5^6$ chord in the RH plus a bass note C would be labeled C⁷. The four-voice texture becomes useful in chording accompaniments. Review and practice the following examples. Change the pedal with each chord as indicated.

Chording a LH Accompaniment

There are many styles of LH accompaniment. Below are various accompaniment styles used with the melodies that begin on the following page. The Fm chord is used to illustrate the various styles.

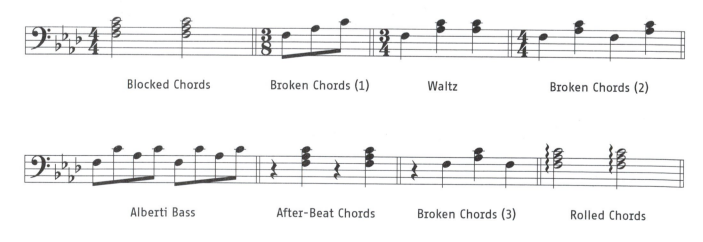

Blocked Chords   Broken Chords (1)   Waltz   Broken Chords (2)

Alberti Bass   After-Beat Chords   Broken Chords (3)   Rolled Chords

Harmonizing Using Chord Symbols in Both Major and Minor Keys

Harmonize the following four melodies according to the chord symbols. Only tonic triads and dominant $\frac{6}{5}$ chords are used. Notate the LH parts. *Take note of various LH styles of harmonization.*

LH: Block Chord Style

Folk Song

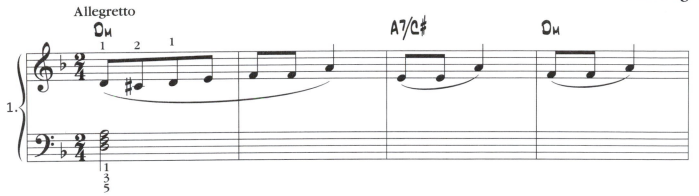

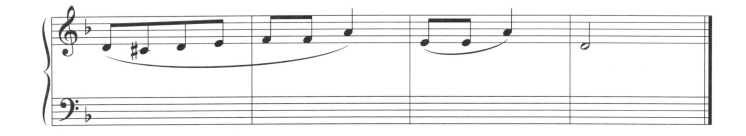

LH: Waltz Style

Bohemian

LH: Alberti Bass Style

Czech

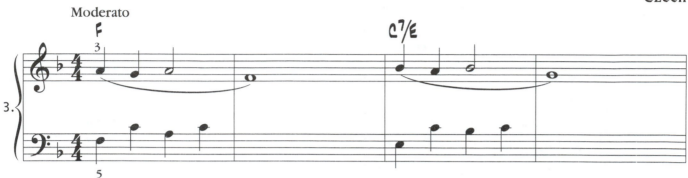

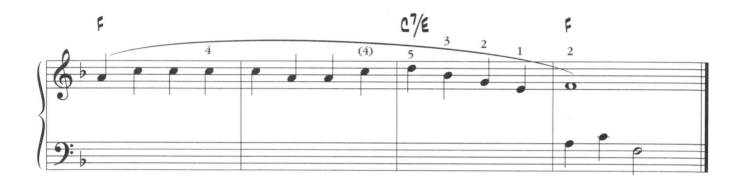

LH: Broken Chord Style

British

Harmonize *Melody No. 5* with tonic and dominant $^6_5$ chords, blocked style. Determine the harmony from the melodic structure and from what sounds agreeable. Play one chord per measure. Notate the LH and put chord symbols above the melody.

Czech

Harmonize *Melody No. 6* with tonic and dominant $^6_5$ chords. Use a waltz style accompaniment. Determine the harmony from a close examination of the melody. Non-tonic tones suggest the dominant $^6_5$. Notate the LH and write chord symbols above the melody.

Czech

Sixteenth Notes

Four sixteenth notes are grouped to the beat in meters with **4** as the bottom number. Two sixteenth notes fill the time of one eighth note. Dotted eighth notes followed by a sixteenth note may be felt as an eighth note tied to the first of two sixteenth notes that follow. Study the example below.

⁶⁄₈ Meter

In ⁶⁄₈ meter, the top number shows how many eighth notes are in a measure. In ⁶⁄₈ meter it is important to feel the pulse as *two to the bar*. In other words, ♩. becomes the pulse. ⁶⁄₈ is a *compound meter* because the subdivision of the pulse is three eighth notes. Other compound meters include ⁹⁄₈ and ¹²⁄₈. Tap and count the following rhythmic patterns.

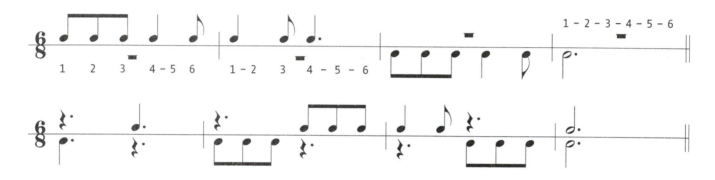

Rhythm Patterns to Tap

Tap the following rhythm patterns that include sixteenth notes and ⁶⁄₈ meter.

Tunes to Study and Play that Incorporate ⁶⁄₈ Meter and Sixteenth Notes

Study and play the following folk song arrangements in ⁶⁄₈ and ²⁄₄ meter that use various combinations of eighth and sixteenth note figures (♫♪, ♩♪, ♪♩, ♫♫, ♫♫, etc.).

French

Dalmation

Italian

Spanish

Sea Chantey

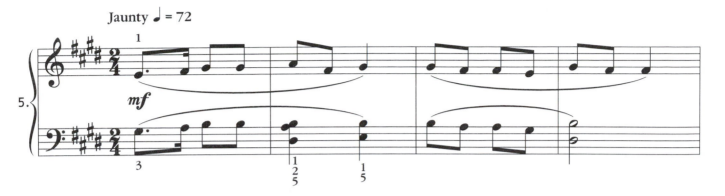

Croatian

BOOK ONE, CHAPTER FOUR

The Subdominant (iv) Chord in Major Keys

In the circled measures of *Russian Melody*, the notes form the subdominant, or **iv** chord.

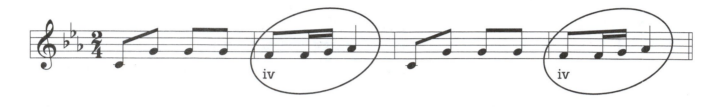

The subdominant chord (**iv**) is built on the 4th scale degree of the minor scale as shown in the circle below. It is minor in quality and moves to the dominant (**V**) or tonic (**I**) chord.

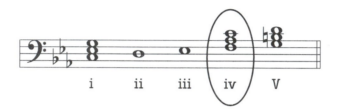

As you learned with the **IV** chord in major, smoother voice leading occurs when the **iv** chord (in minor) is inverted to the iv_4^6. Study the example below.

Ex. 1   Ex. 2

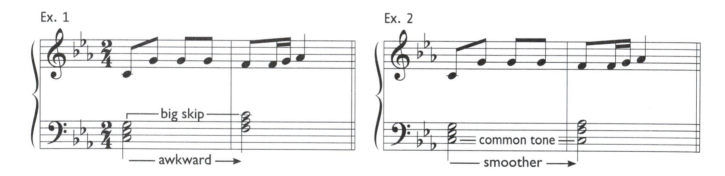

$i–iv_4^6–i–V_5^6–i$ Chord Pattern

Practice the following chord pattern and transpose it to all white keys. Place letter name symbols above each chord and Roman numerals below as shown in the C minor example below. Pedal as indicated.

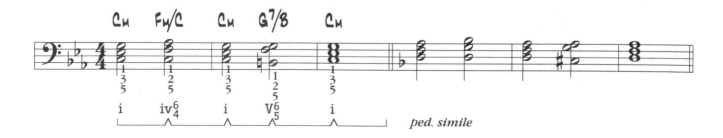

Music for Sight Reading and Transposing – Minor Keys

Determine the minor key from each key signature. As always, tap the rhythm of each hand separately before playing. You will find tunes that include sixteenth note figures and tunes in $\frac{6}{8}$ meter. After reading, transpose each arrangement to the indicated minor keys. Identify the LH accompaniment styles.

CROATIAN FOLK SONG

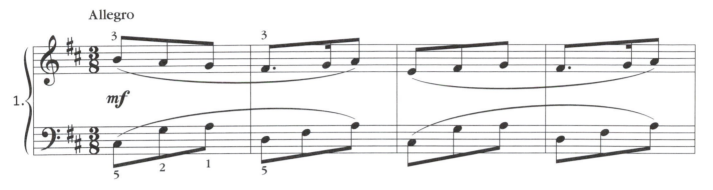

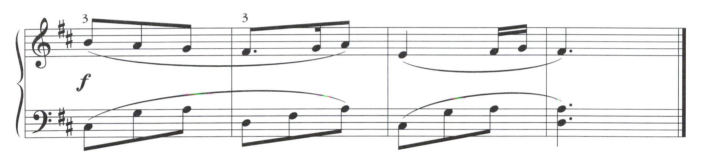

Transpose to C minor.

ITALIAN FOLK SONG

Transpose to C minor.

BOOK ONE, CHAPTER FOUR

FRENCH CANADIAN FOLK SONG

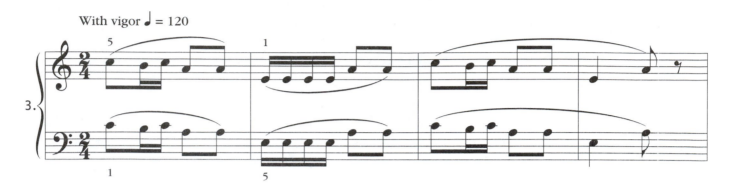

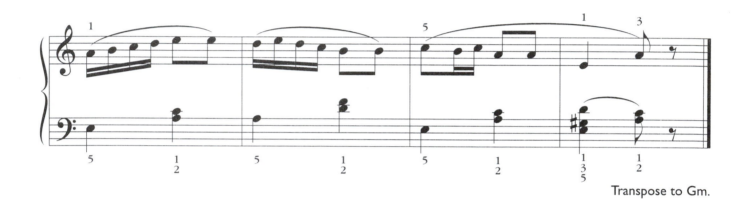

Transpose to Gm.

OLD KING COLE

Transpose to Dm.

ITALIAN FOLK SONG

Transpose to B♭m.

RUSSIAN FOLK SONG

Transpose to Cm.

ACCOMPANYING

The accompaniment to *Italian Folk Song* makes use of broken chord style and the minor i-iv-V^7 progression.

TEACHER: Double the melody one octave higher.

ITALIAN FOLK SONG

arr. **James Lyke**

LATIN TANGO

South American
arr. **James Lyke**

AMERICAN SONG REPERTOIRE

EVERY DAY

Jerome Kern
arr. James Lyke

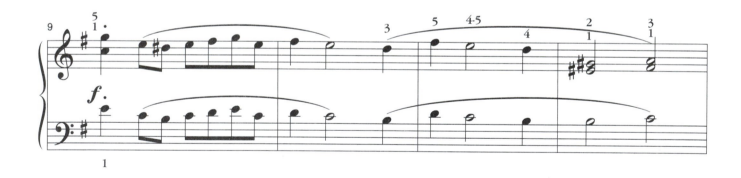

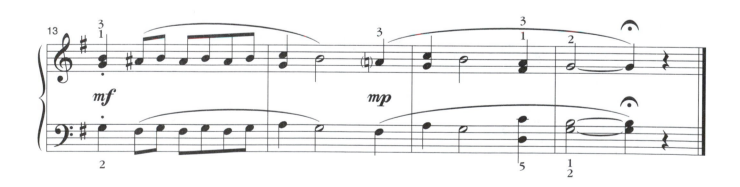

K-K-K KATY

music by **Geoffrey O'Hara**
arr. **James Lyke**

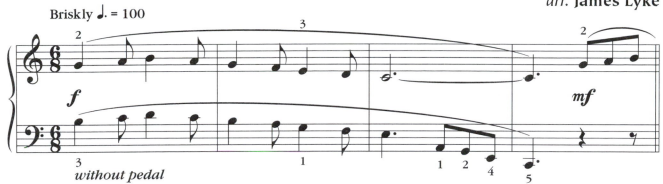

ENSEMBLE REPERTOIRE

WAVES OF THE DANUBE

Secondo – Teacher

Josef Ivanovici
arr. Lee Evans

WAVES OF THE DANUBE

Primo – Student

Josef Ivanovici
arr. Lee Evans

Secondo

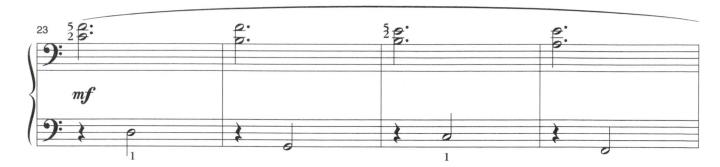

D.S. al Coda
with repeat

✠ Coda

Primo

TRA–LA–LA

Secondo – Teacher

George Gershwin
arr. **James Lyke**

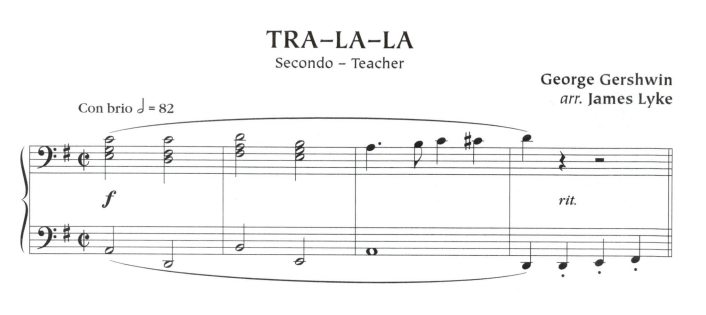

TRA–LA–LA

Primo – Student

George Gershwin
arr. **James Lyke**

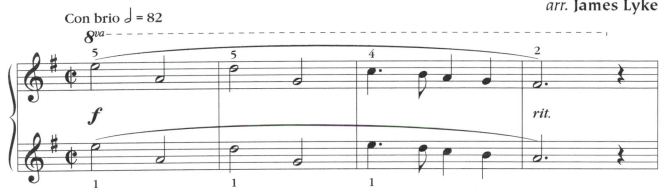

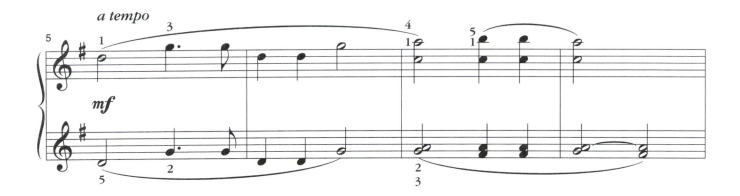

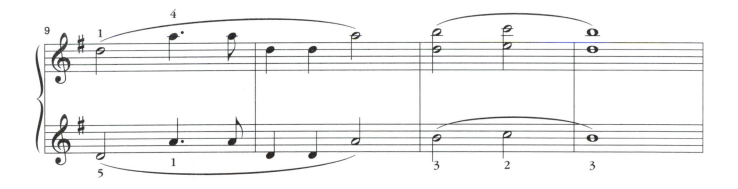

Secondo

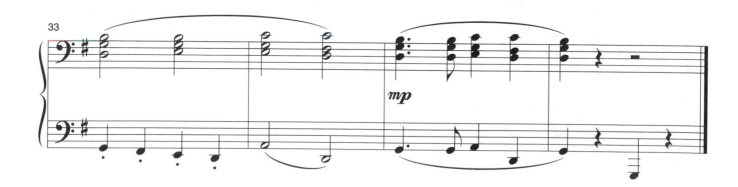

SOLO REPERTOIRE

Practice Plan: In *Etude in A Minor*, first play the LH alone, paying attention to the fingering. Next, play the RH, paying attention to the § feel. Then play hands together (HT), slowly at first, gradually picking up speed until you can play at the indicated tempo.

ETUDE IN A MINOR

Stephen Heller

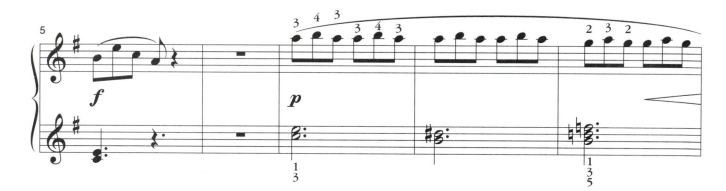

Practice Plan: The LH in *Hopak* presents no problems. The RH is chock full of sixteenth-note figures: ♪♫, ♪♩, and ♫♫. Tap the rhythm of the RH before playing. Start slowly, then increase the tempo. Play the RH alone before adding the LH 5ths.

HOPAK

Alexander Goedicke

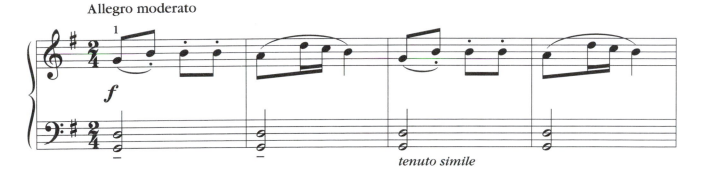

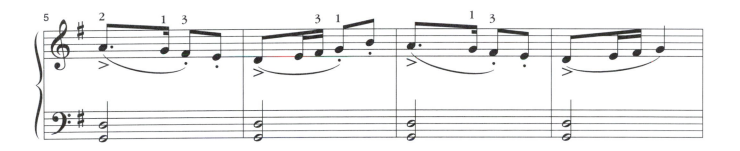

Practice Plan: In Spindler's *Song*, block the LH chords and intervals. Identify the chords and inversions. Play the RH alone with attention to fingering, especially the stretches in bars 9–12. Play without the pedal, working towards a beautiful *legato*.

SONG

Fritz Spindler

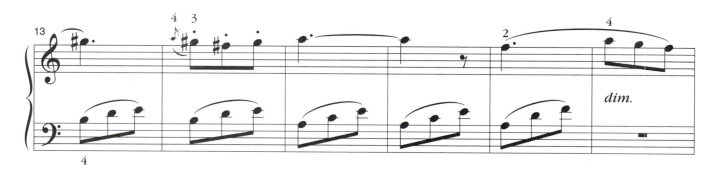

Practice Plan: Play *Minuetto* without pedal. Pay attention to the phrasing, gently lifting at the end of each slur. As usual, play hands alone at first. When putting the hands together, strive for a smooth *legato* touch.

MINUETTO

Domenico Scarlatti

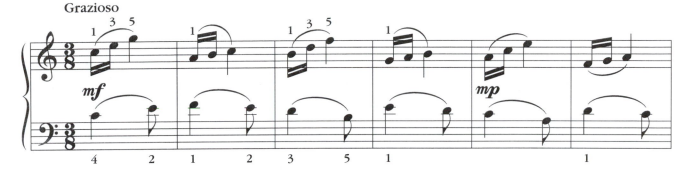

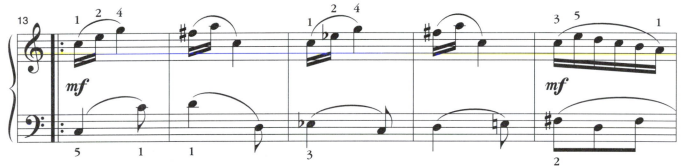

Practice Plan: Play the LH first and identify the chords (A_M, D_M/A, etc.). Then play the RH and notice the sequences of ♪♪♪ notes that begin on the 2nd beat of bar 1. At first, play at a slow tempo and exaggerate the various touches. Play without pedal.

TARANTELLA

Frank Lynes

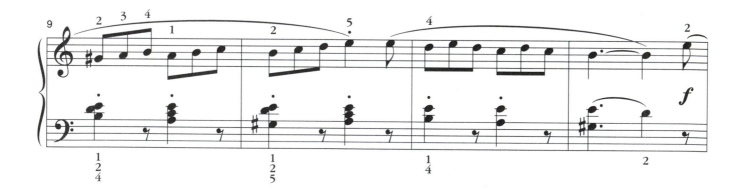

Practice Plan: Practice the LH first, detaching (clipping) all *staccato* eighth notes. The RH *staccato* ♫
notes followed by the ♫♫♫ ♪ figure require good finger work. Isolate bars 2, 6, 8, 10, 12, and 14 for
special work. Play *The Fifes* many times to perfect the rhythm.

THE FIFES

Jean François Dandrieu

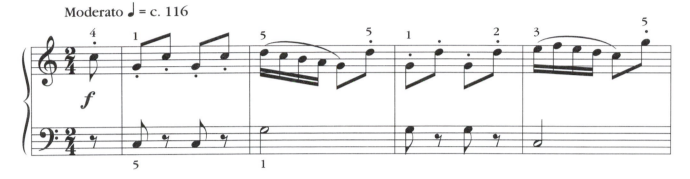

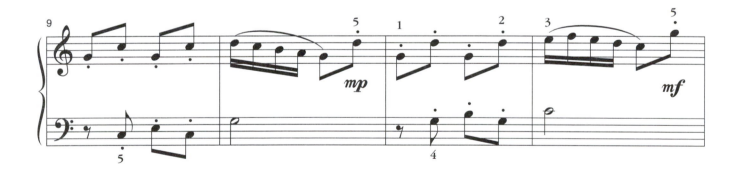

Practice Plan: In *Scale Etude for the Left Hand*, first play the easy RH part paying attention to the slurs. Then practice the LH slowly, being careful with the cross-overs and thumb-unders. Gradually increase the tempo. Work towards a clean performance. No pedal!

SCALE ETUDE FOR THE LEFT HAND

August Damm

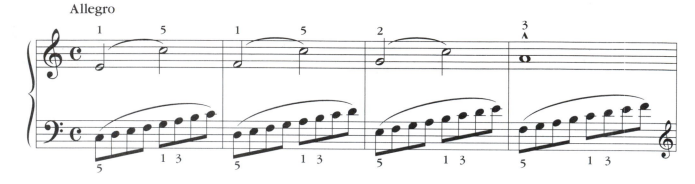

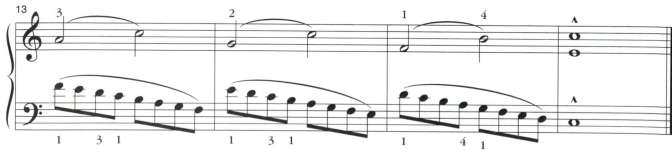

Practice Plan: *Lullaby* calls for nicely connected 3rds in the RH. Work on bars 3–5, 7–9, 12–13, and 15–17. Practice LH alone, holding finger 5 down while playing the upper notes.

LULLABY

Norman Dello Joio

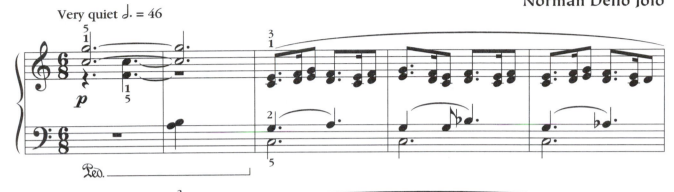

From *Suite for the Young*. Copyright Edward B Marks Music Corp. Used by permission.

Practice Plan: In *Celebration*, first play the LH being careful with the (♫ ♩) touch and clef changes. Then practice the RH alone (without pedal). Watch out for time signature changes. Put the hands together at a slow tempo. Count carefully and gradually increase the tempo.

CELEBRATION

John Cacavas

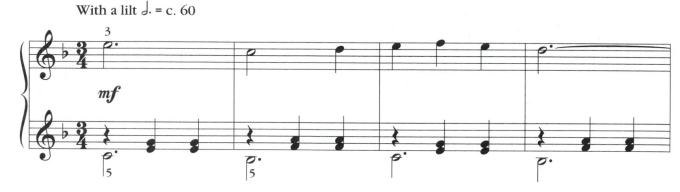

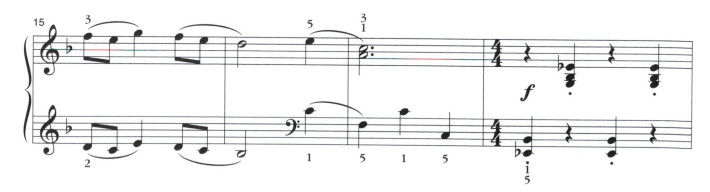

From Three Miniatures for Piano. *Reprinted by permission of Willis Music Company.*

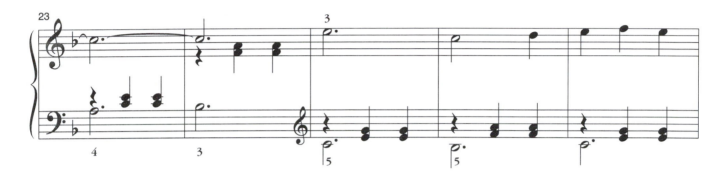

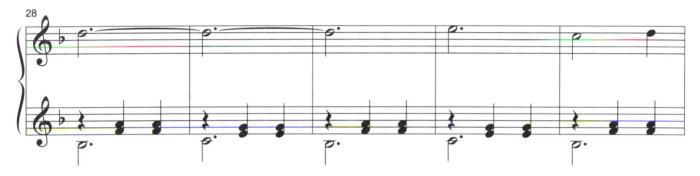

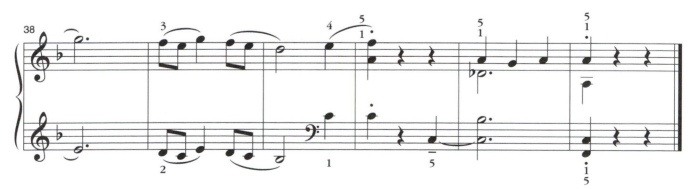

BOOK ONE, CHAPTER FOUR

MUSICIANSHIP ACTIVITIES

Improvisation

Play the adapted version of *Menuet* as written. Then improvise new melodies over the LH accompaniment. Be guided by your ear to avoid clashes with the harmony.

MENUET
(adapted)

Leopold Mozart

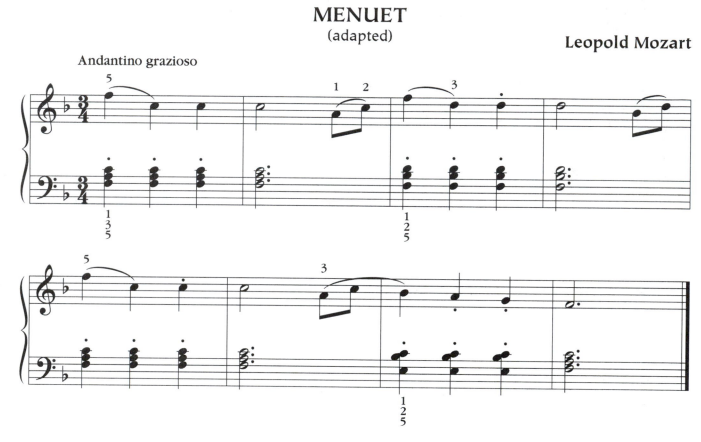

TECHNICAL STUDIES

Broken Chord Studies: Develop a feel for 1st and 2nd inversion triads. Practice using various major and minor triads.

Major Scales: Perform the following major scales in two octaves, hands alone at first, then together.

C, G, D, A, E
G♭ (F♯), D♭ (C♯), C♭ (B)

Consult Appendix B for a thorough presentation of all scales and fingerings.

Practice Plan: Before adding the pedal to *Pedal Study*, practice blocking each outlined chord. Then without the pedal, play and try to achieve a smooth *legato*. After this step, incorporate the pedal.

PEDAL STUDY

Ludvig Schytte

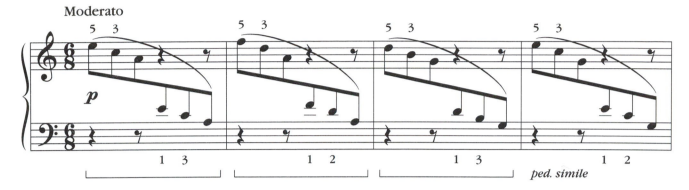

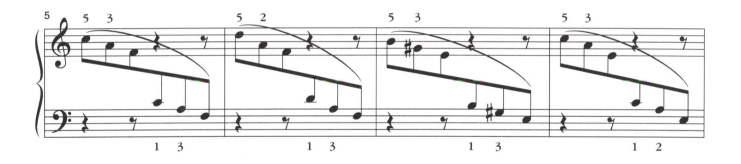

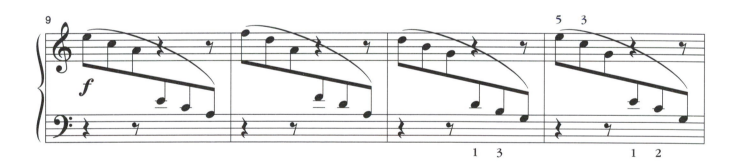

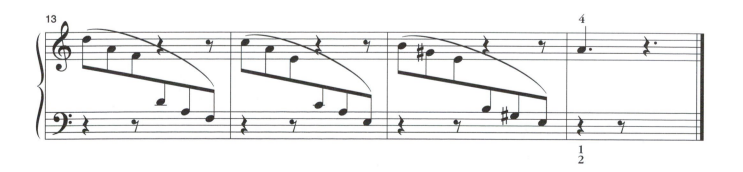

SUGGESTED PLAYING EXAM TOPICS
CHAPTER FOUR

1. Play one or two harmonization examples from pages 119–120 (minor melodies) and pages 123–125 (accompaniment styles).

2. Demonstrate facility with sixteenth note figures (♩♪, ♪♪♪, ♪♪♩, ♪♪♪♪, etc.) and $\frac{6}{8}$ meter by playing examples on pages 127–129.

3. Play the LH chord pattern found on the bottom of page 130 in the following minor keys: Cm, Dm, Em, Fm, Gm, and Am.

4. Play one sight reading example found on pages 131–133. Transpose as indicated.

5. Perform one of the accompaniments found on page 134 or 135.

6. Play one of the American Song arrangements on page 136 or 137.

7. Perform one Ensemble Repertoire piece from pages 138-145.

8. Perform one or two solos from the Solo Repertoire section, pages 146–155.

5
chapter

Chord Inversion Review, Substitute Chords (ii, iii, vi), I-IV-V⁷ Review in Major/Minor Keys, Syncopation, Harmonization with RH Chords, Single LH Bass Notes, Triplets, Reading Studies, Repertoire, Musicianship Activities, and Technical Studies

Read the melody of *American Folk Song* and notice the chord outline of the tonic in bars 1 and 2. All of the tones of the C major triad are present, but the lowest tone is G instead of C. Block this chord. In the 2nd inverstion, the fifth is on the bottom, root in the middle, and third on the top.

AMERICAN FOLK SONG

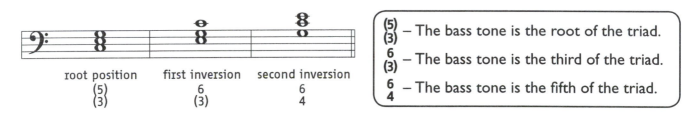

Chord Inversion

The rearrangement of chord tones results in a *chord inversion*. Study the following chord in root position, first inversion, and second inversion. Any triad may be inverted.

root position	first inversion	second inversion
(5)	6	6
(3)	(3)	4

(5)
(3) — The bass tone is the root of the triad.

6
(3) — The bass tone is the third of the triad.

6
4 — The bass tone is the fifth of the triad.

A kind of musical shorthand known as *figured bass*, or *thorough bass*, flourished in the seventeenth and the first half of the eighteenth centuries. In this system, chords were represented by Arabic numerals that related the upper tones to the bass. These numbers delineated intervals above the bass tone, but not necessarily in any particular vertical order. In figured bass playing, the numbers in parentheses were taken for granted and not included. The absence of numerals meant the triad was in fundamental or root position (the root of the triad is in bass).

Pop Song and Jazz Chord Symbols – A Review

In folk and popular music, another system is used. The letter names of the chords appear above the melody line. Often letter names will appear with a slash mark. The letter following the slash identifies which chord tone should be in the bass (the lowest note).

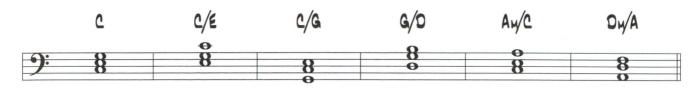

Read the melody of *American Folk Song* again, this time studying the chord outline in bars 5 and 6. Here, the dominant seventh chord is completely formed.

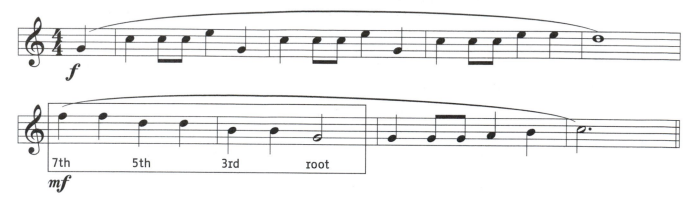

You will recall from Chapter Four that seventh chords contain four tones, the most important being the root, third, and seventh. It is common to omit the 5th. Study the root position and inversions of the dominant seventh chord in the key of C. Then play the I-V^7-I and the I-V$^6_5$-I voicings in the LH as shown.

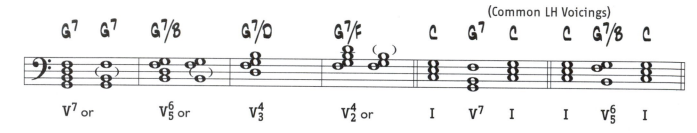

Voice Leading – A Review

To avoid awkward sounds (and awkward fingerings), it is important that tones of successive chords move smoothly to the nearest chord tones, or to common tones. Study the examples below to understand how inversions help chord voices move smoothly and create good voice leading.

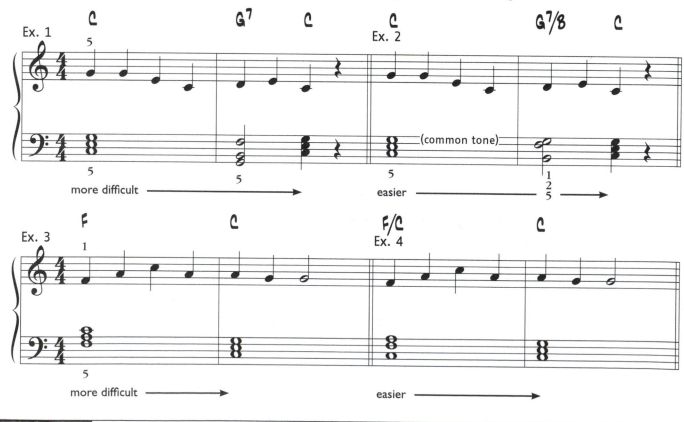

Two Styles of Harmonization

Compare the LH harmonization of *Skip to My Lou* to the harmonization of *German Carol*. *German Carol* puts the harmony in the RH with single bass notes (chord roots) in the LH creating a richer texture.

SKIP TO MY LOU

American

In *German Carol*, put the harmony in the RH and single bass tones in the LH (chord roots).

GERMAN CAROL

BOOK ONE, CHAPTER FIVE

Study and play *No. 3*. Here, the RH incorporates a two-voice texture and the LH plays bass notes approximately two octaves lower. This style is one we will work with in future harmonization exercises, one that is more pianistic and has a richer texture.

Italian

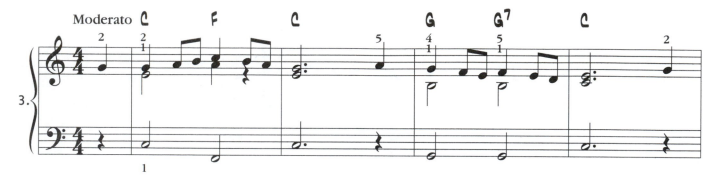

The four-voice texture in *Study No. 4* works well with slower melodies. Write a comfortable fingering above the melody.

English

Completion Studies

Complete the next two studies using the harmonization texture suggested in the first measure.

Study No. 5 continues with a RH two-voice texture and LH bass notes approximately two octaves lower. Notate the alto voice (mostly in 6ths with some 3rds) and the LH bass voice.

British

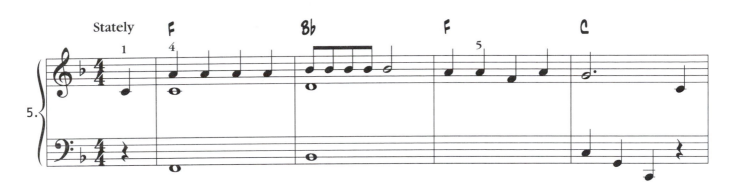

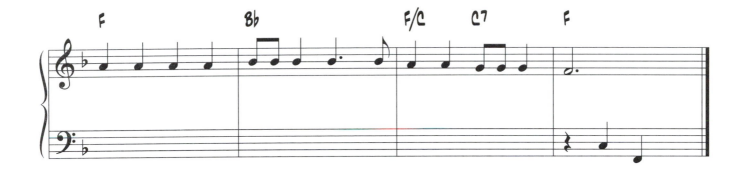

In *Study No. 6*, complete the alto and bass voices, relying mostly on 3rds and 6ths in the RH.

Folk Song

Substitute Chords (ii, iii, and vi)

Three minor chords (ii and vi) are often used for harmonization purposes in major keys. The ii chord substitutes for the IV chord, the iii chord substitutes for the V chord, and the vi chord substitutes for the I chord. In each instance, two of the notes in a substitute chord are found in the major chord for which it is a substitute. In C major, F and A are common to the ii and IV chords; G and B are common to the iii and V chords; and C and E are common to the vi and I chords.

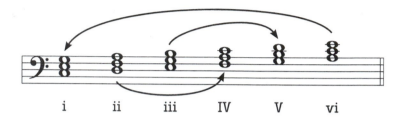

The ii chord is often found in first inversion (ii^6) as it approaches the V chord. See, play, and study the two examples below.

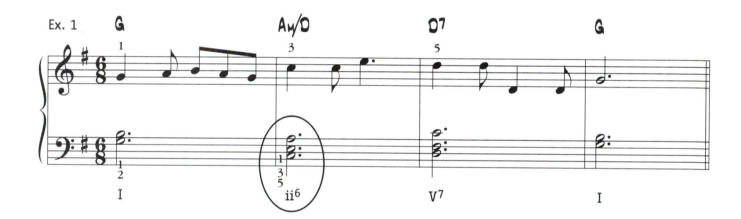

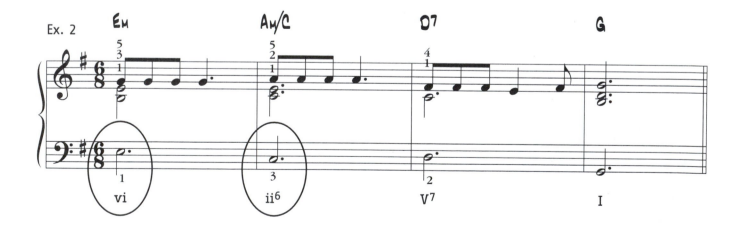

Two Tunes Using Substitute Chords

Study and play the two tunes below that use substitute chords ii and vi. When no chord is indicated, continue the harmony (chord) from the previous measure.

United States

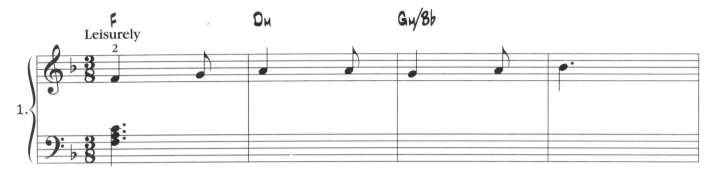

Calypso

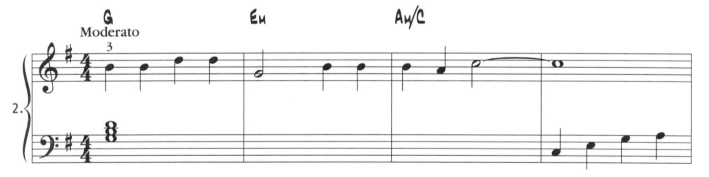

Triplets

An eighth note triplet  fills the time of one quarter note. Practice tapping and clapping the following rhythmic pattern.

Triad Triplet Study

The following study outlines triads and the dominant $^6_5$ in triplet figures. Practice this study and transpose to various major and minor keys suggested by your instructor.

Song Arrangements That Include Triplets

Sometimes triplets are notated as  (without brackets). Study and play the following song arrangements.

SALLY GO ROUND THE SUNSHINE

South Carolina

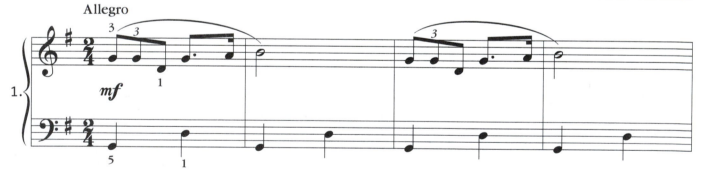

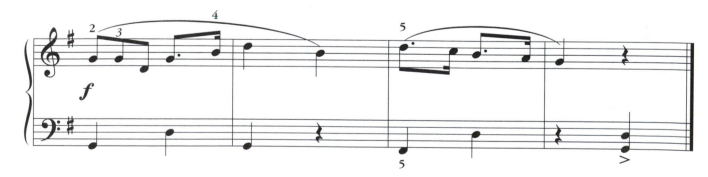

POLISH FOLK SONG

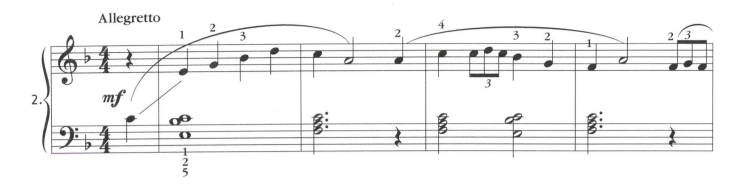

GERMAN MELODY

Syncopation

When a weak beat, or a weak part of a beat is stressed, *syncopation* occurs. Practice the rhythmic pattern below before studying and playing *Hello Ma Baby* and *Mr. Banjo*.

HELLO MA BABY

music by **Joe Howard**
arr. **James Lyke**

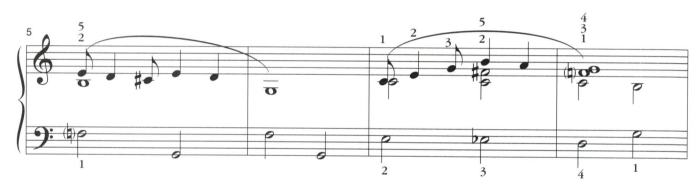

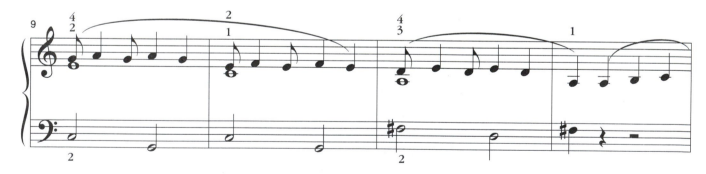

MR. BANJO

Louisiana Creole
arr. **James Lyke**

Andantino

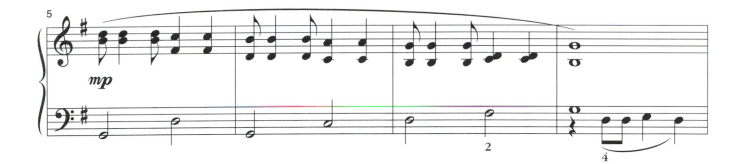

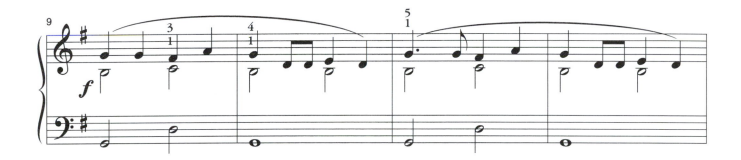

Music for Sight Reading and Transposing

Reading studies in Chapter Five include review material as well as new elements: chord inversion, voice leading, the subdominant chord, triplets, and syncopation. Continue the routine established earlier, i.e., tap rhythms, identify the tonality, find patterns such as chord outlines, and so on. In addition, pay attention to elements beyond notes and rhythm such as touch, dynamics, phrasing, tempi, and fingerings.

FOR HE'S A JOLLY GOOD FELLOW

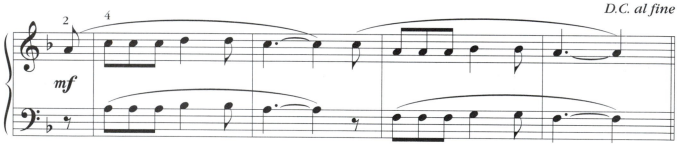

Transpose to G major.

British

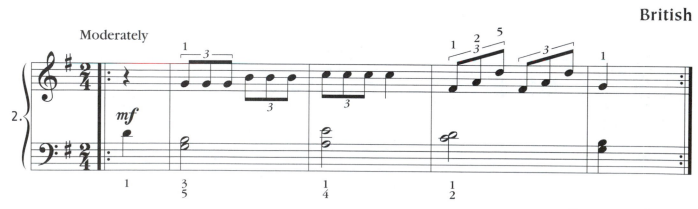

Transpose to A major.

COTTON-EYED JOE

Tennessee Folk Song

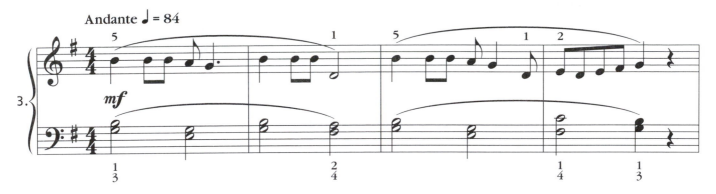

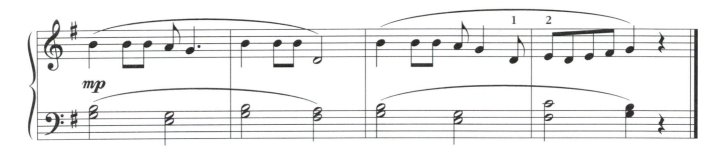

Transpose to G♭ major.

RUSSIAN DANCE

Transpose to D major.

U.S. Spiritual

5.

Transpose to A♭ major and G major.

Italian

6.

Transpose to C major.

German

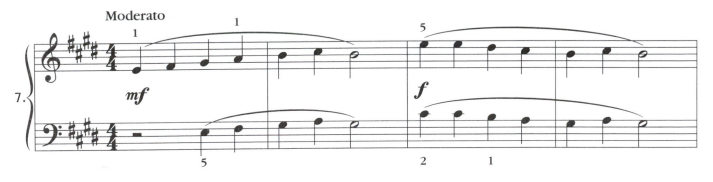

Transpose to D major.

Hungarian

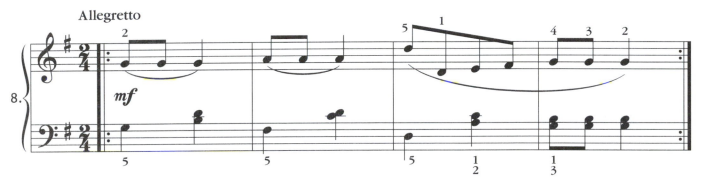

Transpose to F major.

ACCOMPANYING
TEACHER: Double the melody two octaves higher.

LONELY ACCORDIAN

B. Mokrousov
(Russian)
arr. **James Lyke**

Before playing *Wearing of the Green*, practice the following chord progression from a slow to fast tempo. Take note of the fingering.

TEACHER: Double the melody one octave higher.

WEARING OF THE GREEN

Traditional
arr. **James Lyke**

TEACHER: Double the melody one octave higher.

IN THE VALLEY

Russian Folk Song
arr. **James Lyke**

AMERICAN SONG REPERTOIRE

YANKEE DOODLE BLUES

music by **George Gershwin**
arr. **James Lyke**

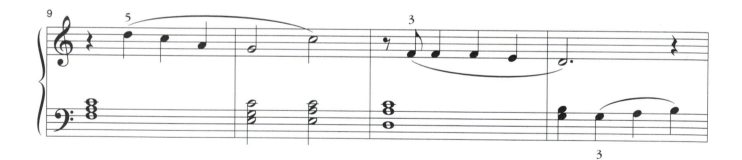

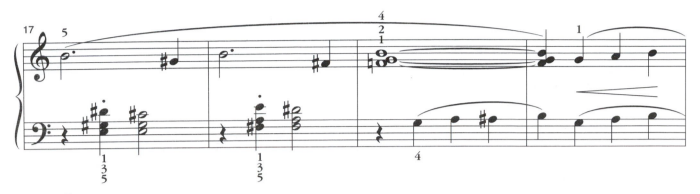

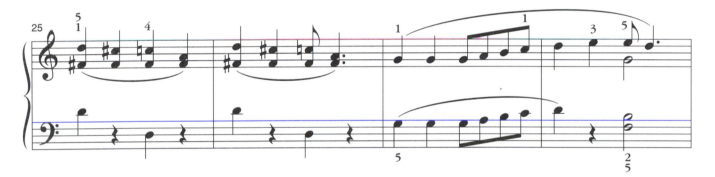

BOOK ONE, CHAPTER FIVE

TIRED OF ME

Walter Donaldson
arr. James Lyke

Slow waltz ♩ = 92

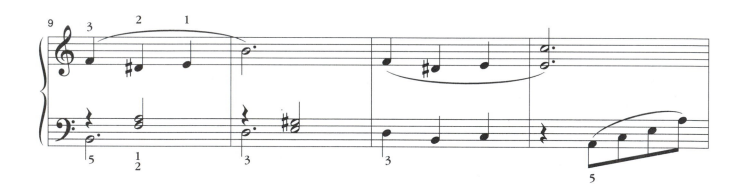

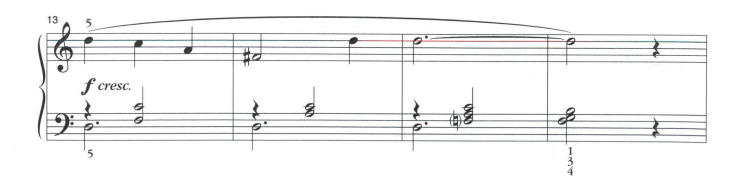

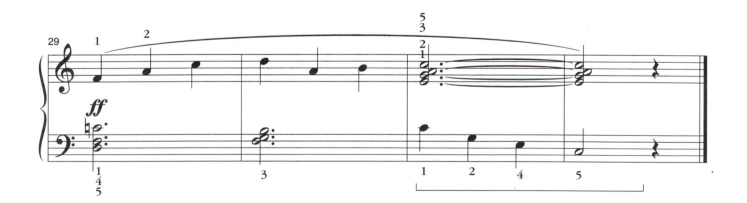

ENSEMBLE REPERTOIRE

EVERYBODY LOVES SATURDAY NIGHT

Secondo – Teacher

Nigerian Folk Song
arr. **James Lyke**

EVERYBODY LOVES SATURDAY NIGHT

Primo – Student

Nigerian Folk Song
arr. **James Lyke**

PLAY A SIMPLE MELODY

Piano II – Teacher

words and music by **Irving Berlin**
arr. **Geoffrey Haydon**
and **James Lyke**

Medium Rag Tempo

PLAY A SIMPLE MELODY

Piano I – Student

words and music by **Irving Berlin**
arr. **Geoffrey Haydon**
and **James Lyke**

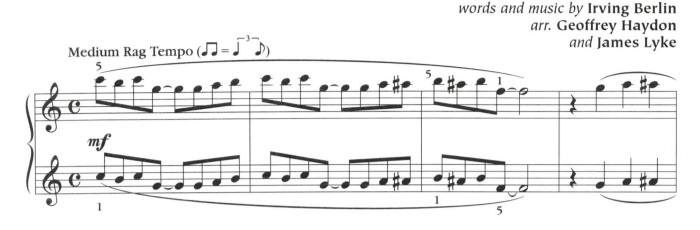

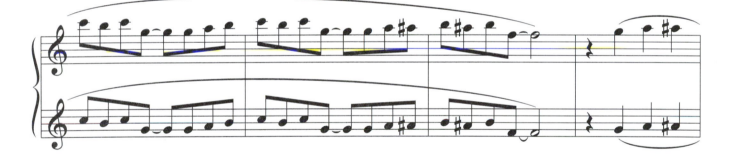

The "Jazz Feel"

When jazz flavored pieces "swing", three elements are present: (1) the beat is divided into three parts so that ♫ = ♫♫♫ or ♩ ♪, (2) the third part of the beat is stressed ♩ ♪, and (3) the articulation, or touch, is *legato*. "Swing" is indicated at the beginning of a piece (after the tempo indication) as follows: ♫ = ♩ ♪. Sometimes directions give the following: ♫ = ♫ meaning to play "straight" even eighth notes instead of "swinging" eighth notes. Occasionally ♫ (swing eighths) are written as ♫.

SOLO REPERTOIRE

Practice Plan: Practice *Menuet in C Major* hands alone, isolating shifts of position. Feel the octave stretches in the LH. Maintain proper fingering and precise rhythmic execution.

MENUET IN C MAJOR

Carl Philipp Emanuel Bach

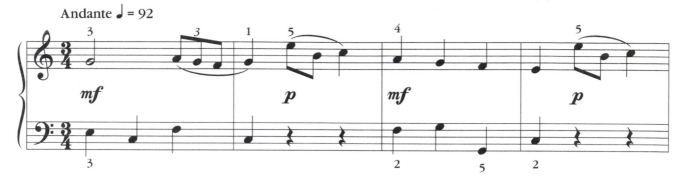

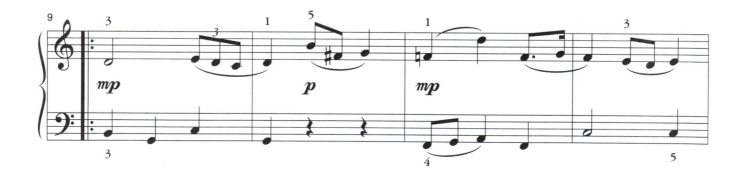

Practice Plan: In the Haydn *Minuet*, practice the LH alone to attain good finger crossings and detached playing. Practice the RH alone and find chord outlines. Master the mixture of *legato* and *staccato* touch. Combine the hands (HT) at a slow and steady tempo and gradually increase the speed.

MINUET IN G MAJOR

Franz Joseph Haydn

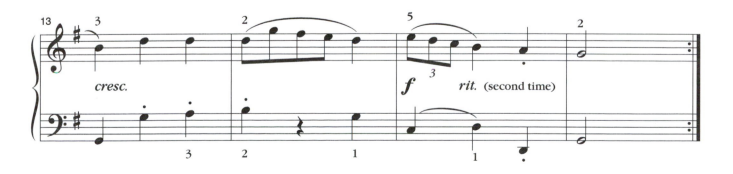

Practice Plan: In *Sonatina*, play the LH alone being attentive to fingering. Play the RH alone making a clear distinction between triplet figures (♩♩♩) and eighth notes (♩♩♩♩). Then play HT, beginning slowly and gradually increasing the tempo. (HT = hands together)

SONATINA

William Duncombe

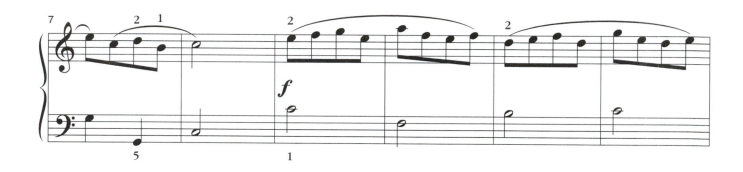

Practice Plan: *The Great Lawn* is based almost entirely on triads and inversions (RH), and octaves (LH). Careful fingering of the chords is necessary. Listen for clear, connected pedaling.

THE GREAT LAWN

James Lyke

Practice Plan: In *Elegy*, first practice the LH part (easier than the RH) and become familiar with all of the moves. Practice RH alone and be cautious with the fingering. Play very slowly hands together without pedal. When all is in place, add the pedal and listen carefully to the colors. Follow the pedal markings strictly.

ELEGY

Tony Caramia

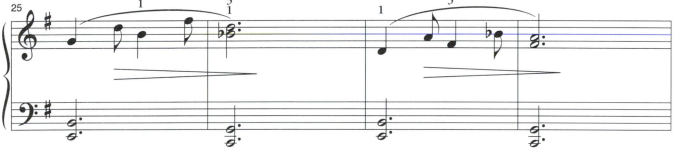

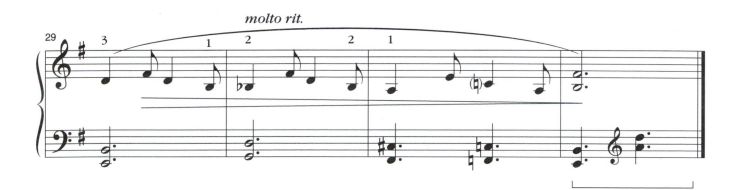

Practice Plan: The RH melody in *Serene Lagoon* should be heard over the LH accompaniment throughout. Shape the RH phrasing, taking note of the dynamic markings.

SERENE LAGOON

Geoffrey Haydon

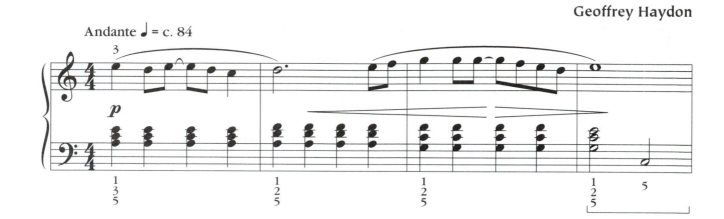

Practice Plan: *A Bag of Rags* should have a nice, gentle flow. Be sure to notice the fingering suggestions, as well as changes in touch between the short *staccato* notes and the smooth *legato* phrases.

A BAG OF RAGS

Tony Caramia

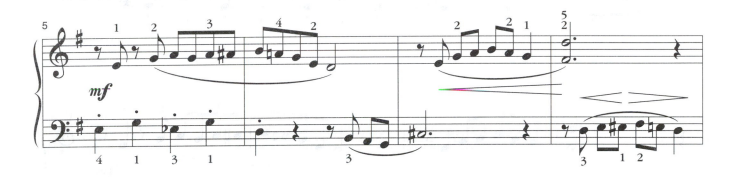

MUSICIANSHIP ACTIVITIES

Complete the following exercises that review various topics introduced in Chapter Five.

I–IV$\frac{6}{4}$–I–V$\frac{6}{5}$–I LH Progression Review

Notate this progression for the LH in the indicated keys. Follow the example.

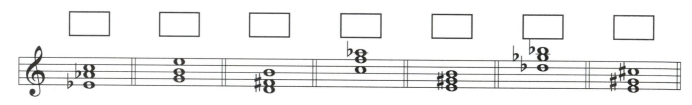

Chord Inversion Review

Use letter-name symbols to label the following root position and inverted triads.

Notate the following chords on the staff. Be aware of the clef.

Improvising RH Melodies

Play the following LH chord patterns while improvising RH melodies. Use tones from the keynote major scales. Make use of sequences and add some syncopations to the RH.

TECHNICAL STUDIES

Major Scale Review: C, G, D, A, E, G♭(F♯), D♭(C♯), C♭(B)

Two octaves. Hands together.

NEW Major Scale: F

RH	1	2	3	4	1	2	3	1	etc.
LH	5	4	3	2	1	3	2	1	etc.

Major Arpeggios: Up to this point, arpeggios have been performed within one octave, and hand-over-hand. Practice the following steps, first hands alone, then hands together (HT). Transpose to F, G, D, E, A, and B. **Consult Appendix B for a thorough presentation of all scales AND arpeggios.**

Step 1: BLOCKING Play the 3rd and 5th of the chord together.

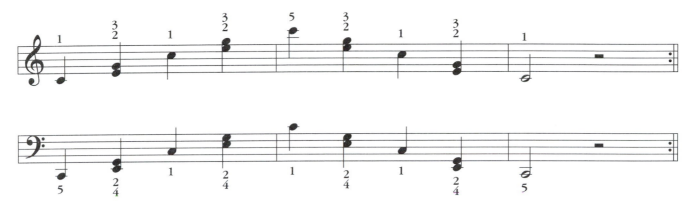

Step 2: THUMB TO THUMB Gently pass under and/or roll over with the thumb. Allow the thumb to be flexible and loose.

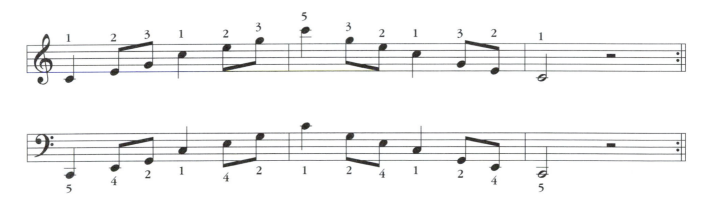

Step 3: TWO OCTAVE ARPEGGIO HANDS TOGETHER Strive to make all notes connected and even.

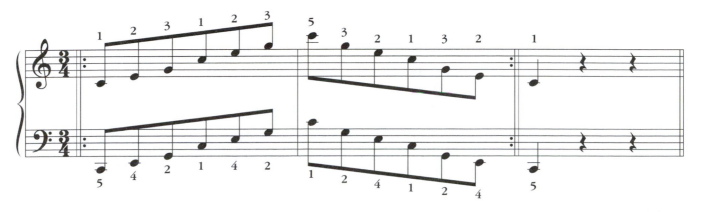

Broken Chords: Practice each pattern four times, twice slow and twice fast. Exaggerate the rotation to the outside of the hand. At the end of each repetition, lift the hand from the keyboard and let it hang loosely from the wrist.

Black Key Arpeggio Preparation: Gently "roll over" your thumbs with either 2 or 4. Relax your thumbs. Hold the fermatas and take time preparing the next arpeggio pattern.

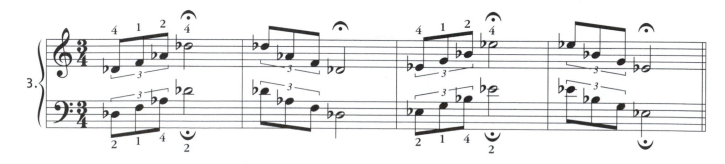

Practice Plan: Practice the LH slowly at first and keep in mind it must sing out while the RH is more subdued in sound. The RH should be rhythmic and played with a loose wrist. Put the hands together slowly at first. Gradually increase the tempo until *Allegro non troppo* (fast but not too fast) is achieved.

ETUDE IN D MINOR

Cornelius Gurlitt

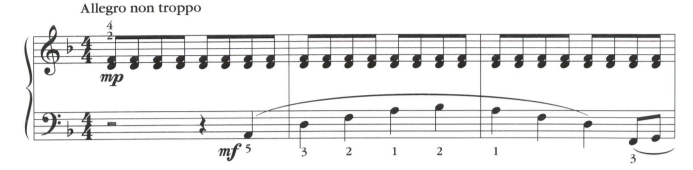

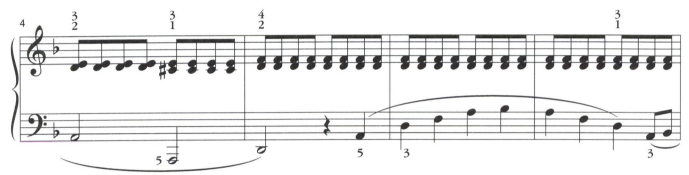

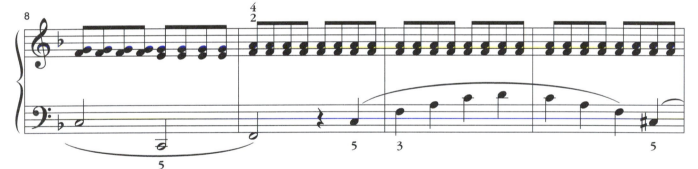

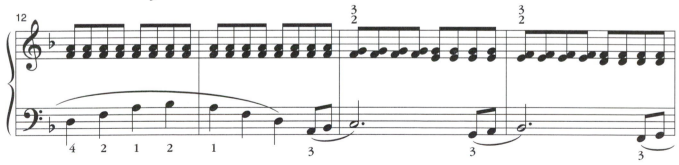

SUGGESTED PLAYING EXAM TOPICS
CHAPTER FIVE

1. Perform two harmonization studies from pages 161-163 and page 165.

2. Demontrate an understanding of syncopation by playing an arrangement chosen from page 168 or 169.

3. Perform two sight reading studies selected from pages 170-173 with the suggested transposition.

4. Play the accompaniment to *Lonely Accordian* (pages 174-175), *Wearing of the Green* (page 176), or *In the Valley* (page 177).

5. Play a selection from American Song Repertoire: Gershwin's *Yankee Doodle Blues* (pages 178-179) or Kern's *Tired of Me* (pages 180-181).

6. Play the student part of one ensemble piece: *Everybody Loves Saturday Night* (page 182-183) or *Play a Simple Melody* (page 184-185).

7. Perform one or two solos from the Repertoire section (pages 186-193).

8. Demonstrate the ability to play the LH stronger than the RH in *Etude in D Minor* found on page 197. Do this by playing bars 1–9.

6

chapter

Augmented and Diminished Triads, New Scale Forms, Reading Studies, Harmonization, Accompanying, Repertoire, Musicianship Activities, and Technical Studies

Using Substitute Chords (Secondary Chords)

Play the opening bars of Kern's *Look For The Silver Lining*. The harmony is spread between the hands in "piano style." Examine the harmony on the second beat of bar one (Dm) and the first beat of bar 2 (Gm) discounting the tied notes. These chords are known as secondary chords. Another way to label these chords is with Roman numerals. In this system, the Dm chord (built on the 6th scale degree in F major) is vi and the Gm chord (built on the 2nd scale degree) is ii – both of them minor chords in a major key. These chords, introduced in Chapter 5, are also known as *substitute chords*: vi substitutes for I and ii substitutes for IV. Dm shares two notes with the F major triad. Similarly, Gm shares two notes with the Bb major triad.

LOOK FOR THE SILVER LINING

music by **Jerome Kern**

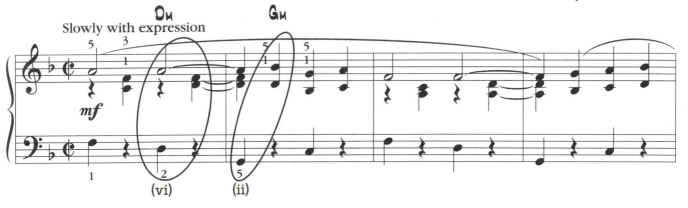

Reviewing Substitute (Secondary) Chords

We have analyzed, played, and used the primary chords, I, IV, and V in various ways. Secondary chords, ii, iii, and vi, *substitute* for primary chords. Secondary chords are also known as *subordinate* triads. Study the boxed substitute chords below. ii is also called the *supertonic* chord; iii is known as the *mediant* chord; and vi is the *submediant* chord. All are minor in quality.

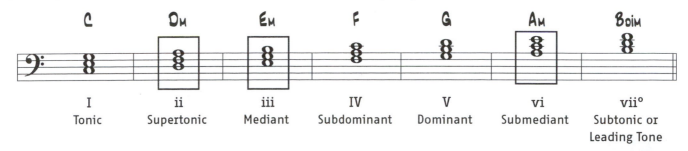

C	Dm	Em	F	G	Am	Bdim
I	ii	iii	IV	V	vi	vii°
Tonic	Supertonic	Mediant	Subdominant	Dominant	Submediant	Subtonic or Leading Tone

As *Look For The Silver Lining* continues, another important substitute (secondary) chord is used: Am or iii in the key of F major.

I–vi–IV–ii–I$_4^6$–V^7–I Chord Progression

This useful progression adds substitute chords to the familiar I–IV–V^7–I pattern. Gradually work toward mastering this progression in several keys. Play this progression and study the voice leading. Only one voice changes in the RH from I to vi and from IV to ii. Then a typical cadence (closing chords) of I$_4^6$–V^7–I ends the progression. Minor triads are symbolized with lower case Roman numerals.

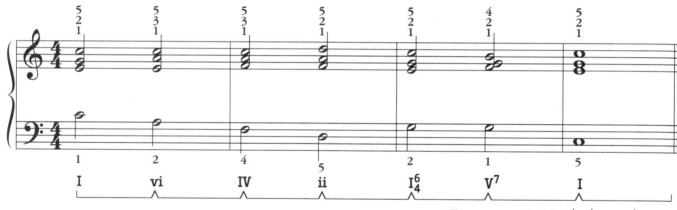

Transpose to G, F, D, B♭, E♭, and A♭ major.

I–vi–ii(or ii^7)–V^7–I Chord Progression

This "formula" progression is often used in American popular music. The ii^7 chord, formed by adding another third to the ii chord, becomes important in our study of American popular songs. Work out and practice this progression in several keys.

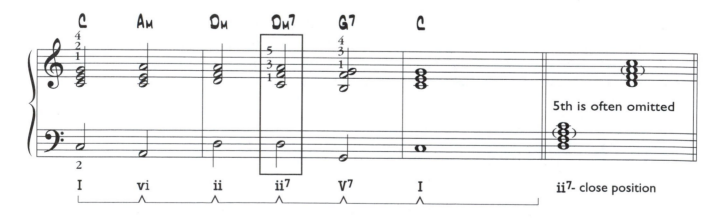

Folk Song Study Pieces Using Substitute Chords ii, vi, and iii

Study and play the following folk song arrangements containing substitute chords. Analyze each chord with a letter name symbol and Roman numeral symbol. Note that ii is frequently found in first inversion ii^6. Fill in the blank squares above selected chords with letter name symbols.

DANISH FOLK SONG I

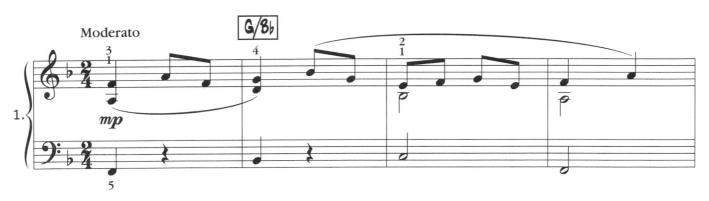

DANISH FOLK SONG II

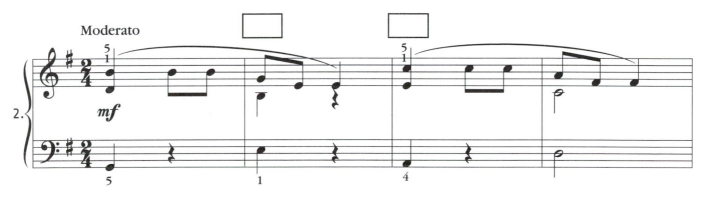

STOMPING DANCE

Czech

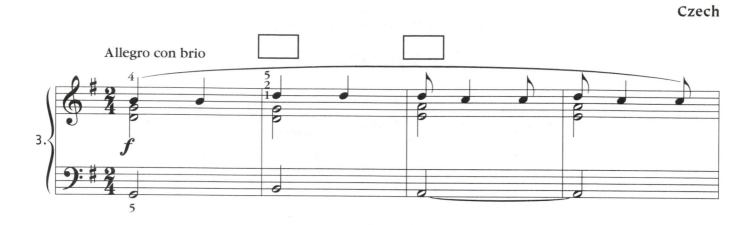

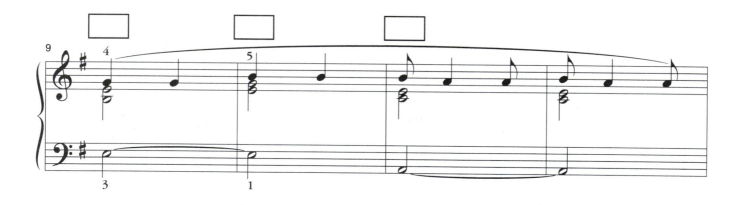

GERMAN FOLK SONG

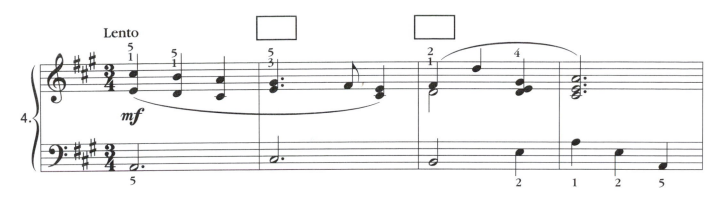

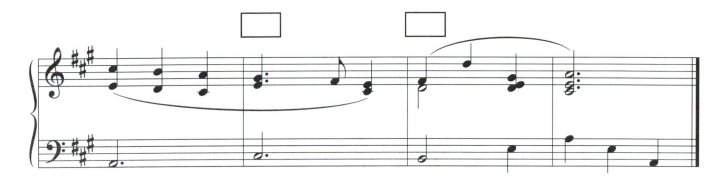

ENGLISH FOLK SONG

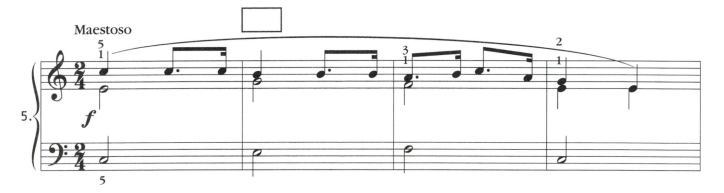

Harmonization Studies

In the following studies the RH texture includes both the melody and harmony. The bass line plays roots and occasional inversions. Study the styles suggested in the first bar or two of the following examples and complete the harmonization.

MELODY

Giovanni Paisiello

(do not double the 3rd)

(do not double the 3rd)

ITALIAN FOLK SONG

dim.

Note the three-voice texture of study no. 3, *Folk Song.*

FOLK SONG

United States

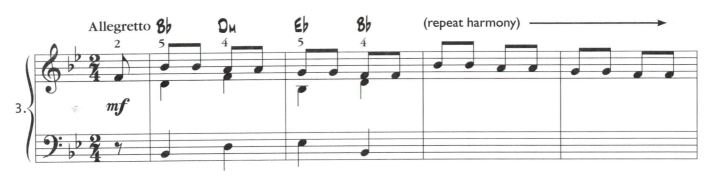

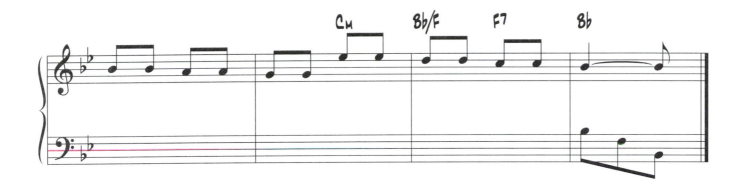

FOLK SONG

Traditional

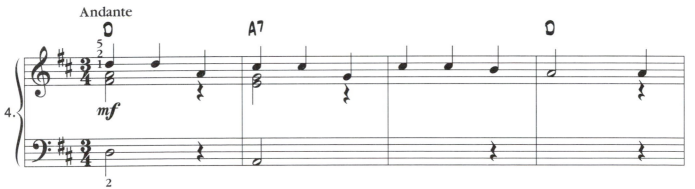

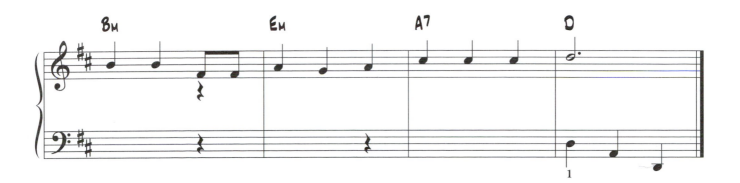

Using Substitute Chords in Accompaniment Patterns

Notice how effective the iii chord becomes when used to harmonize the 7th scale degree in a descending scale line (I–iii–IV–I). Generally, iii moves to a IV chord. Practice the chord pattern several times before attempting the accompaniment to *Finnish Melody*. Note the ii chord used in its first inversion ii⁶. Avoid doubling the 3rd.

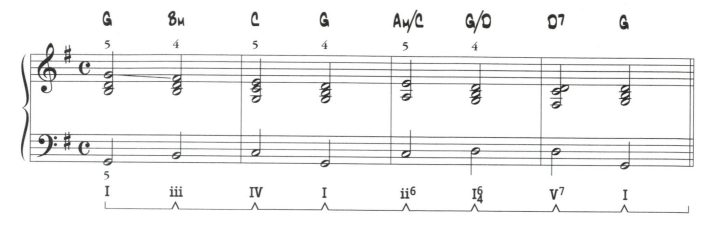

TEACHER: Double the melody one octave higher.

FINNISH MELODY

STUDENT: Analyze and label each chord with a letter name symbol (above) and Roman numeral (below) as shown on page 206. Note all inversions. These chords are used in the accompaniment to *Vive L'Amour*.

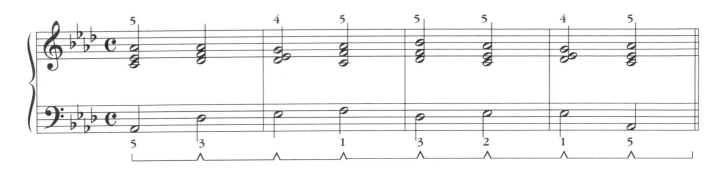

TEACHER: Double the melody one octave higher.

VIVE L'AMOUR

French

Transpose to A major.

A Study Piece Using Substitute Chords

Austrian Carol contains two substitute chords (vi and ii). Study and play this arrangement. Notice the various inversions of chords. Label each chord where the squares appear: G, G/B, D, etc.

AUSTRIAN CAROL
(Study Piece)

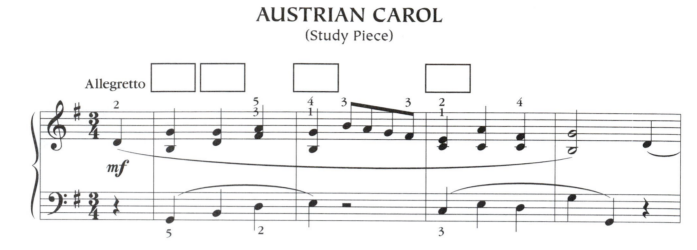

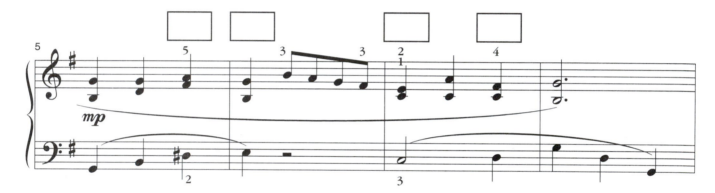

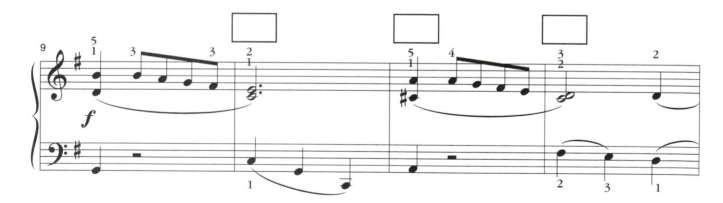

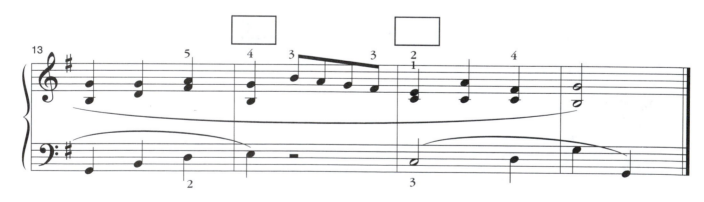

Altered Chords

Examine the circled triad in the first measure of *Deep River*. In root position the triad would be spelled C – E – G♯, similar to a C major triad but with a *raised fifth*. This *augmented* chord creates dissonance and calls for a resolution to a consonant sound. Find and circle three *secondary* chords that occur in consecutive bars. Label each of these substitute chords with letter name symbols and Roman numerals.

DEEP RIVER
(excerpt)

Reverently

Spiritual

Augmented Triads

Complete the exercise below according to the example. Alter the major chord to create an augmented chord by raising the fifth. Augmented chords are symbolized by a + (C+), or aug (C aug).

C   C+   C   G   G+   G   D   D+   D   F   F+   F   A   A+   A

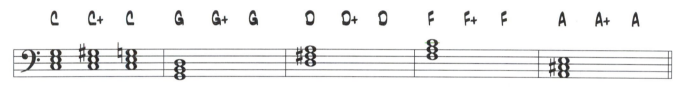

Study the circled triad in the fourth bar of *Melody in F*. This chord, spelled F♯ – A – C, is similar to F♯ minor but with a *lowered fifth*. This *diminished* triad is very active and demands resolution to a more consonant chord. Analyze the other chords in this excerpt. Triads built on the 7th degree of a major scale are diminished (**vii°**).

MELODY IN F
(excerpt)

Rubinstein

Diminished Triads

Complete the exercise below according to the example. Alter the minor chord to create a diminished chord by lowering the fifth. Diminished chords are symbolized by a ° (C°) or dim (C dim).

Cm   C°   Am   A°   Bm   B°   Dm   D°   B♭m   B♭°

NEW SCALES
1. The Pentatonic Scale

Examine the following keyboard diagram that shows two pentatonic scale patterns. The pentatonic scale is a primitive scale consisting of five consecutive tones within the octave. The scale corresponds to the black keys on the keyboard. The pentatonic scale can begin on any black key.

Black Key Patterns (RH)

The pentatonic scale may be played on white keys also. Using the top numbers above, slide the hand right and play D E G A B. Using the lower numbers, slide the hand left and play F G A C D.

White Key Patterns (RH)

2. The Chromatic Scale

A *chromatic* (from chroma – color) scale consists of the twelve pitches within the octave, that is, a scale that uses all of the black and white keys. It is seldom used in its entirety. Examine the following chromatic scale beginning on C.

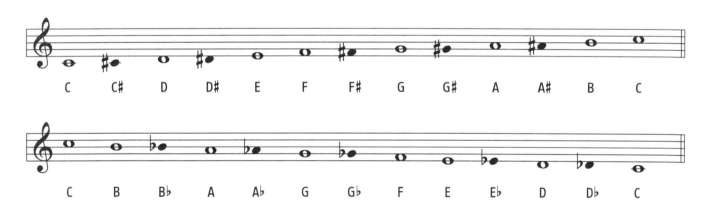

3. The Whole Tone Scale

Another scale that twentieth-century composers, such as Debussy, have used in various ways is the whole tone scale. The *whole tone scale* is a six-note (hexatonic) scale. Study the following diagram that shows the two possibilities for dividing the twelve tones into two patterns. The fingering above the notes is for the RH and the fingering below is for the LH.

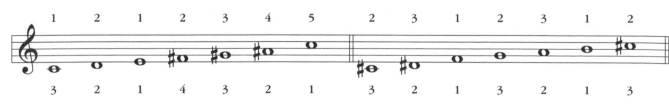

Use of the whole tone scale provides an atmospheric effect when the pedal is employed.

4. The Blues Scale

Any major scale can be turned into a blues scale by playing these tones: 1–♭3–4–♯4 (or ♭5)–5–♭7.

C BLUES SCALE

It is, of course, easier to build the blues scale from the natural minor form of the scale because it already contains a ♭3 and ♭7. ♫ = ♩♪ means that the eighths should be played thus: ♫♩. Divide ♩ values into triplet values, ♩ = ♫♩, with the first two notes of the triplet tied (♫♩).

MOANIN' LOW BLUES

Geoffrey Haydon

Four Harmonization Studies

The following melodies make use of primary chords (I, IV, and V), substitute (secondary) chords (ii, iii, and vi), and altered chords (aug and dim).

SWEDISH FOLK SONG

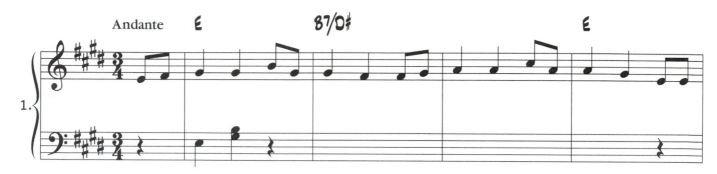

CALYPSO TUNE

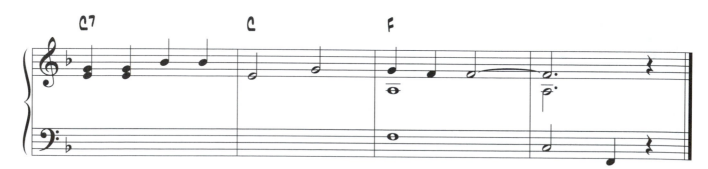

GOIN' HOME

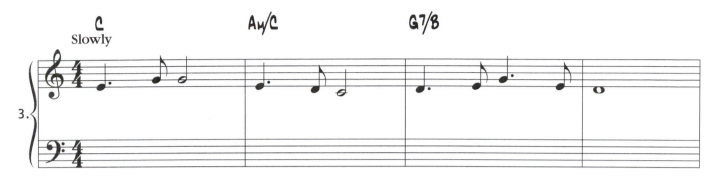

JOLLY OLD ST. NICK

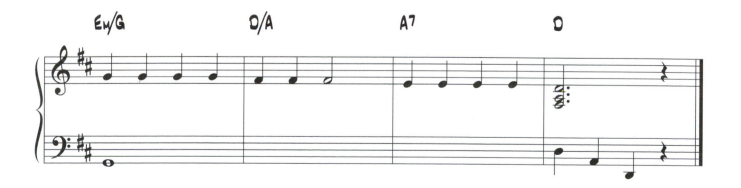

Music for Sight Reading and Transposing

This section contains reading material that emphasizes secondary chords, pentatonic melodies, chromatic passages, and altered chords (augmented and diminished). It also contains review material. Follow the normal reading routine of tapping rhythm, pre-analysis of harmonies, pattern identification, etc. Some of the more challenging exercises might require one-handed reading (RH alone, LH alone, and then HT). Transpose each exercise as suggested. Write the letter name chord symbols in each of the boxes.

GERMAN FOLK SONG

Transpose to G major.

FRENCH FOLK SONG

Transpose to D major.

ITALIAN FOLK SONG

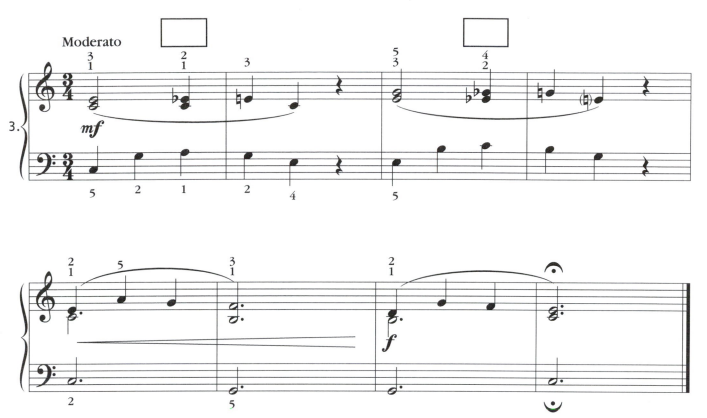

Transpose to B♭ major.

I'M TRAMPING

American

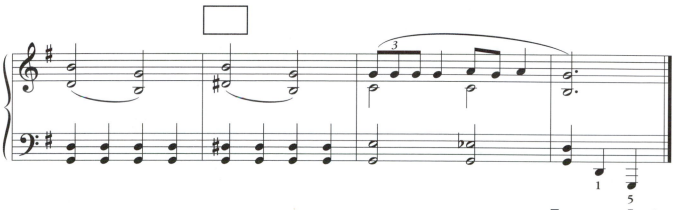

Transpose to F major.

IRISH SEA CHANTEY

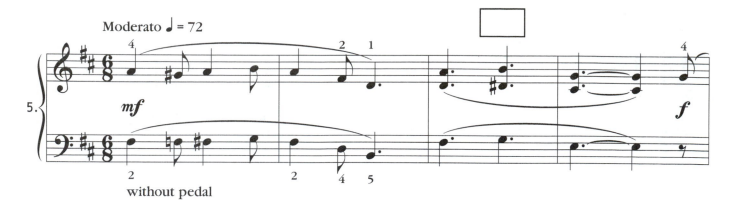

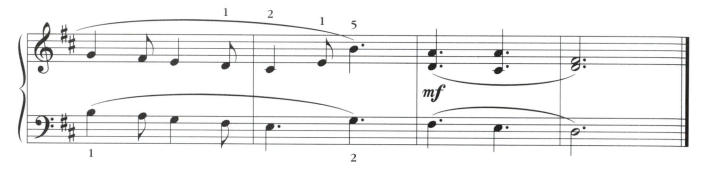

Transpose to C major.

RUSSIAN FOLK SONG

Transpose to E and D♭ major.

In *The Mocking Bird Song,* what scale does the RH play?

THE MOCKING BIRD SONG

Southern U.S.

Transpose to G major.

ITALIAN FOLK SONG

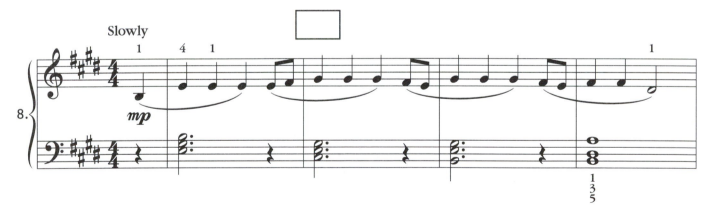

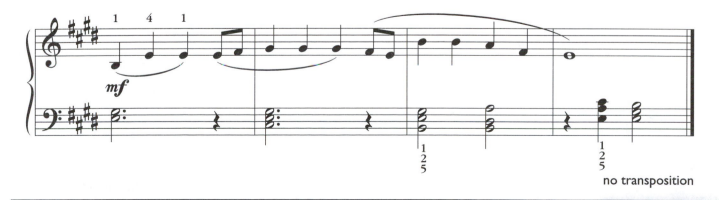

no transposition

BOOK ONE, CHAPTER SIX

SONG TO THE EVENING STAR

Richard Wagner

no transposition

LOTUS BLOSSOMS

Chinese

ped. simile

Transpose to F pentatonic.

Swing Eighth Notes ($\overline{}^{3}\overline{}$) – A Review

You will recall in Chapter 5 the explanation of "straight" 8th notes vs. "swing" 8th notes. In jazz and popular music you will often see = , which means play regular or "straight" 8th notes. You will also see , or , meaning swing the 8th notes. Think (the triplet) taking the space of a note with a slight emphasis on the last note of the triplet. Practice the melodic excerpts below.

ACCOMPANYING
TEACHER: Double the melody one octave higher.

WHEN LOVE IS KIND

English Folk Song
arr. James Lyke

TEACHER: Double the melody two octaves higher.

DRAGGY RAG

music by **Irving Berlin**
arr. **James Lyke**

AMERICAN SONG REPERTOIRE

TILL THE CLOUDS ROLL BY

Jerome Kern
arr. **James Lyke**

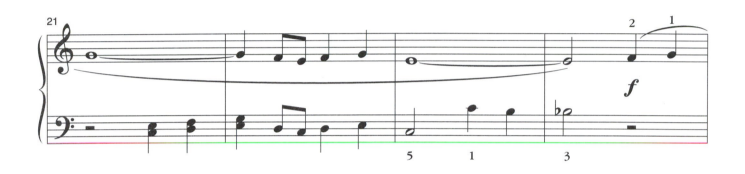

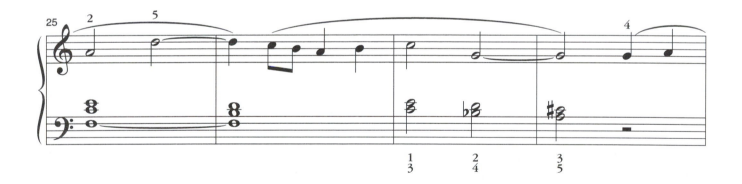

ANY OLD PLACE WITH YOU

music by **Richard Rodgers**
arr. **James Lyke**

STOP, STOP, STOP

music by **Irving Berlin**
arr. **James Lyke**

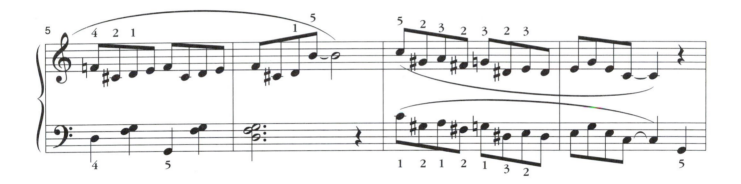

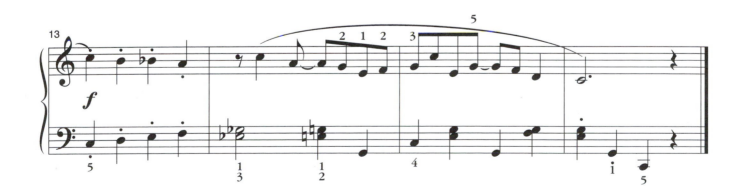

ENSEMBLE REPERTOIRE

FORTY-FIVE MINUTES FROM BROADWAY
Secondo – Teacher

George M. Cohan
arr. James Lyke

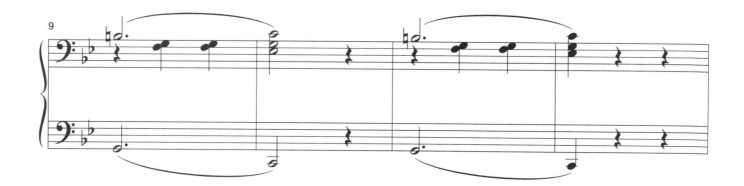

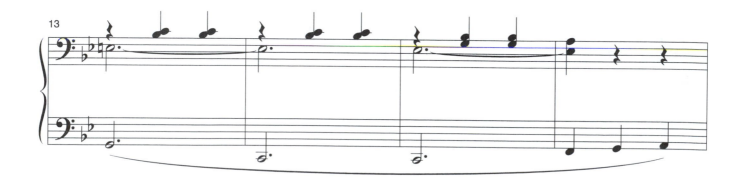

FORTY-FIVE MINUTES FROM BROADWAY

Primo – Student

George M. Cohan
arr. **James Lyke**

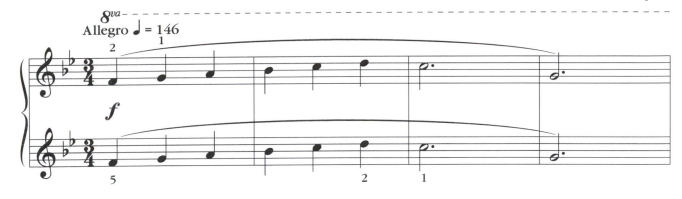

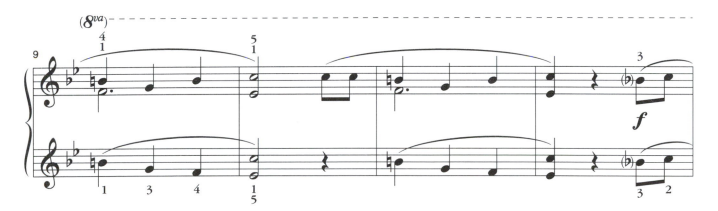

Secondo

a tempo

Primo

TAP DANCE

(Secondo – Teacher)

James Lyke

TAP DANCE

Primo – Student

James Lyke

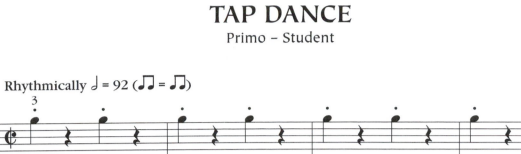

BOOK ONE, CHAPTER SIX

Secondo

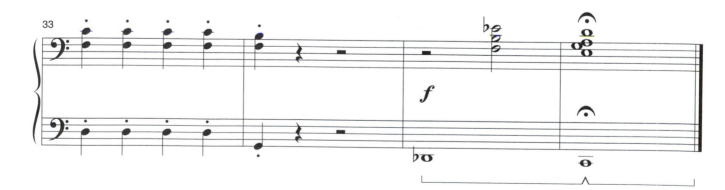

Primo

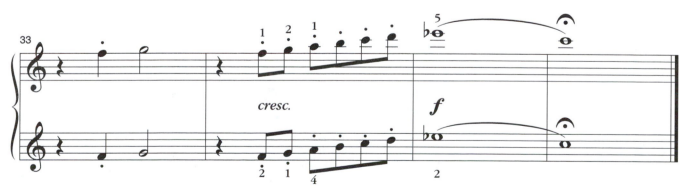

SOLO REPERTOIRE

Practice Plan: In *Minuet*, strive for evenness of sound and touch when performing the triplet figure in measures 1, 3, 9, and 11. Pay special attention to two-note phrases, *staccato* notes, and *legato* phrases.

MINUET

George Phillip Telemann

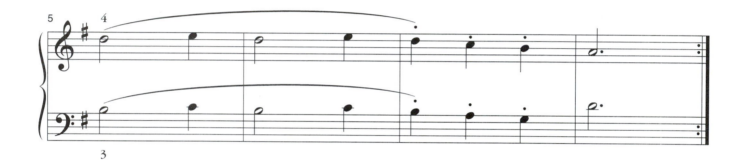

Practice Plan: Practice *German Dance* hands separately beginning with the LH. Pay attention to touch, fingering, and shifts of position. Be satisfied with slow work. Drill difficult spots when hands are put together (HT).

GERMAN DANCE

Franz Joseph Haydn

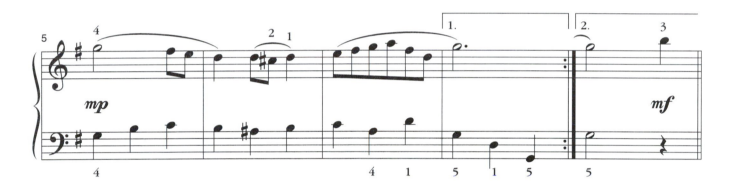

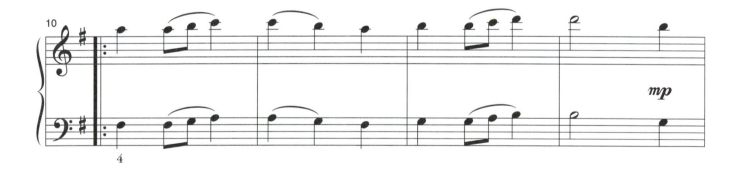

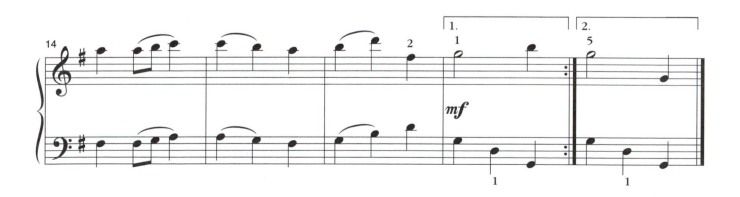

Practice Plan: Before playing *Prelude*, block the RH chord outlines and identify inversions. Down-up wrist movements in the RH should receive careful attention.

PRELUDE

Samuel Maykapar

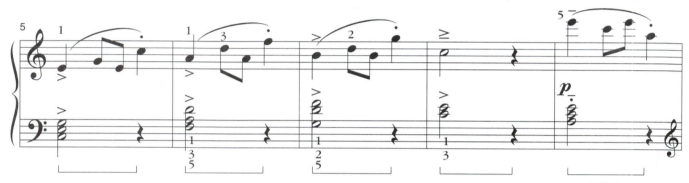

Practice Plan: In *Soldier's March*, pay attention to the dotted 8th followed by a 16th. Play each hand alone with a metronome going from slow to fast very gradually. Then combine the hands, gradually moving from a slow to a quick tempo until you reach *Vivo* (briskly).

SOLDIER'S MARCH

Robert Schumann

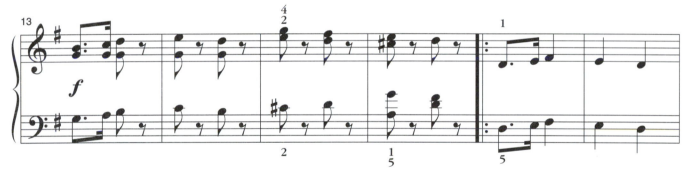

Practice Plan: *Pensive* explores secondary triads in a colorful manner. Pay close attention to the finger-ing, the clef changes, and especially the specific pedaling changes.

PENSIVE

Tony Caramia

Practice Plan: *Sleepy Time* is composed using the pentatonic scale. Master the LH ostinato pattern at first. Take note of the time signature, $\frac{5}{4}$. The group of 5 beats may be thought of as either 2 + 3, 3 + 2, or in groups of 5. Listen for a very *legato* RH.

SLEEPY TIME

Jean Eichelberger Ivey

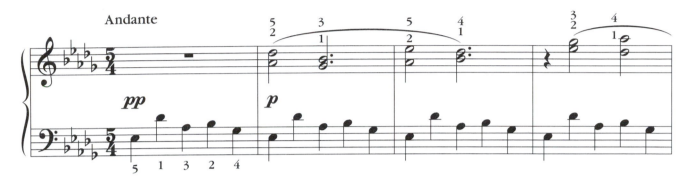

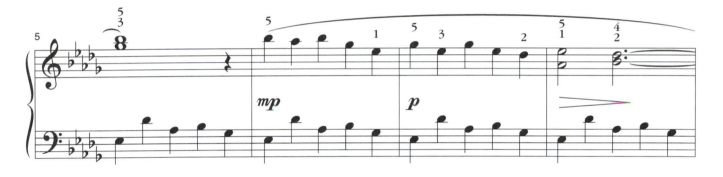

Sleepy Time, from Sleepy Time and Water Wheel, by Eichelberger Ivey.
© 1960 by Lee Roberts Publications, Inc., international copyright secured.
All rights Reserved. Reprinted by permission.

Practice Plan: In *Chromatic Blues*, follow the fingering suggestions carefully. Take note of the hands together scale that occurs four bars from the end.

CHROMATIC BLUES

Tony Caramia

Not fast (can be swung or played with straight 8ths)

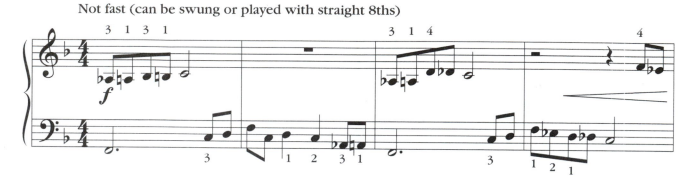

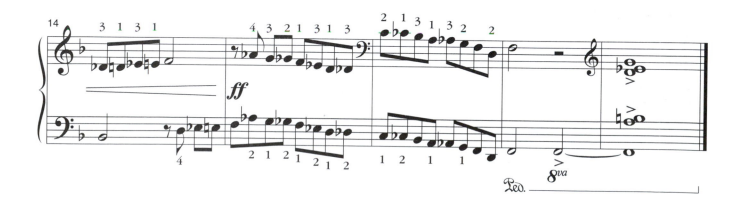

Practice Plan: *Beginning in bar 5 of A Lazy Summer Afternoon, sing out the RH melody over the LH har-mony. In the LH part, be sure to hold down the whole notes for full value. As usual, practice hands alone without pedal. Work towards achieving a good balance between the hands. Finally, add pedal, following the indicated markings.*

A LAZY SUMMER AFTERNOON

James Lyke

MUSICIANSHIP ACTIVITIES

Complete the following exercises that review various topics introduced in Chapter Six.

Secondary Chord Review

Build supertonic (ii) chords in the following keys. Notate root position and both inversions as shown in the example. Label each chord with Roman numerals (beneath) and letter names with appropriate slashes (above).

Follow the instructions above and notate submediant (vi) chords.

Follow the instructions above and notate mediant (iii) chords.

Fill in the RH missing notes for this familiar chord progression. Add letter name symbols above the chords.

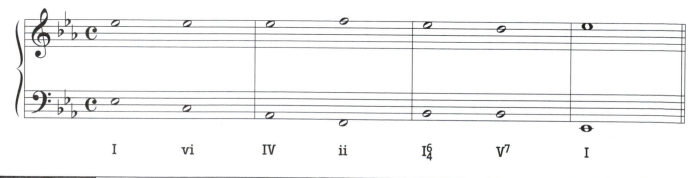

TECHNICAL STUDIES

NEW Major Scales: B♭, E♭, A♭

RH: 4th finger is always on B♭, 3rd finger is always on E♭.

LH: 3-2-1-4-3-2-1 (3).

NEW Major Arpeggios: B♭, E♭, A♭, G♭

Consult Appendix B for a thorough presentation of all scales AND arpeggios.

Slowly practice scales and arpeggios hands together, two octaves.

Improvising

Using the beginnings of the following examples, expand each utilizing four-bar phrases. Maintain rhythmic unity and make use of melodic sequences.

White key pentatonic, LH ostinato

Whole tone, LH ostinato

Blues scale LH bass pattern

Expand to 12 measures using the normal blues chord progression.

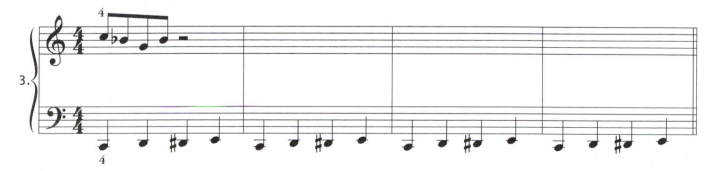

Chromatic Scale Exercise

The complete chromatic scale divides the octave into twelve half steps. Notice that by starting a third apart, and playing in contrary motion, the fingerings become mirrored and are, therefore, the same in each hand.

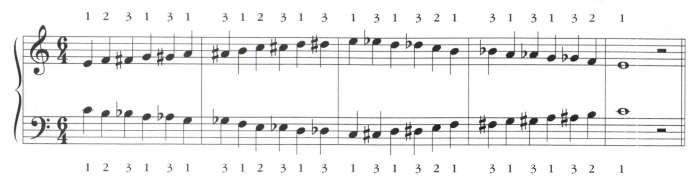

Triad Exercise

Practice the following triad exercise until all adjustments (maj, min, aug, and dim) are mastered. Transpose this exercise to all white major keys.

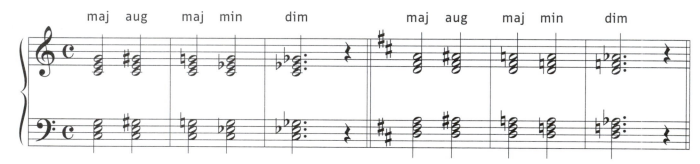

Five-Finger Exercise

Practice this five-finger exercise until all adjustments to the various qualities (major, whole tone, major, minor, etc.) become automatic. Transpose this exercise to all white major keys, i.e., D, E, F, etc.

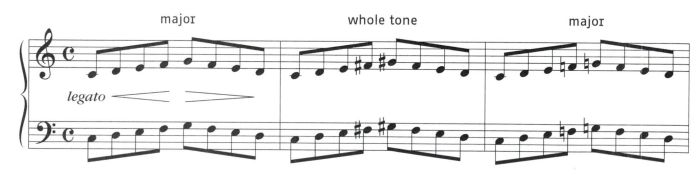

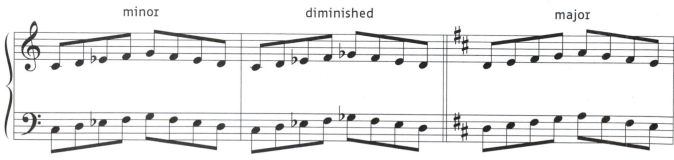

continue

The following *12 Bar Chromatic Blues* combines the 12-bar blues pattern and the chromatic scale. Practice hands separately, then combine the hands (HT) and play as written. Give special attention to the RH chromatic scale fingering.

12 BAR CHROMATIC BLUES

James Lyke

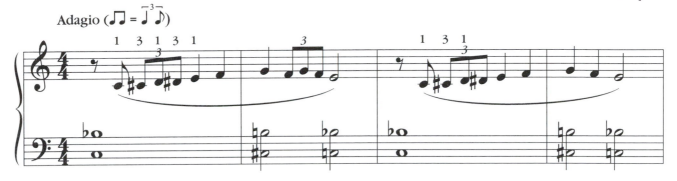

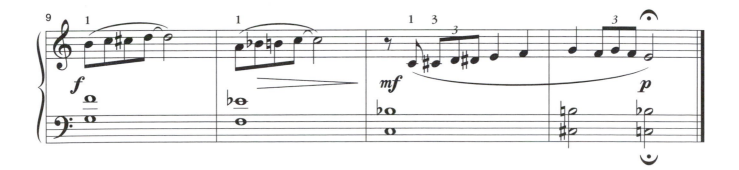

SUGGESTED PLAYING EXAM TOPICS
CHAPTER SIX

1. Play the following chord progressions (found on page 200) in keys suggested by your instructor:
   a) $\text{I–vi–IV–ii–I}_4^6\text{–V}^7\text{–I}$
   b) $\text{I–vi–ii}^7\text{–V}^7\text{–I}$

2. Play one of the harmonization exercises found on pages 204–205 with chords in the RH and single bass tones in the LH.

3. Play all of the following scales:
   a) pentatonic (page 210)
   b) chromatic (page 210)
   c) whole tone (page 210)
   d) blues (page 211)

4. Play one of the accompanying examples found on pages 220 or 221.

5. Play one arrangement from the American Song Repertoire section (pages 222–225).

6. Perform one piece from the Ensemble Repertoire section (pages 226–233).

7. Perform one or two pieces from the Solo Repertoire section found on pages 234–241).

8. Improvise a short piece using any of the three scale patterns found on page 243.

Study the D^7 chords in bars 2 and 6. This chord—not in the key of C—embellishes the next chord V^7 (G), which is in the key. The root of the D^7 chord is a root a fourth below or a fifth above G^7 chord. In this key, the D^7 is termed the *dominant of the dominant* (V^7 of V or V^7 of V^7).

THAT'S WHERE MY MONEY GOES

American

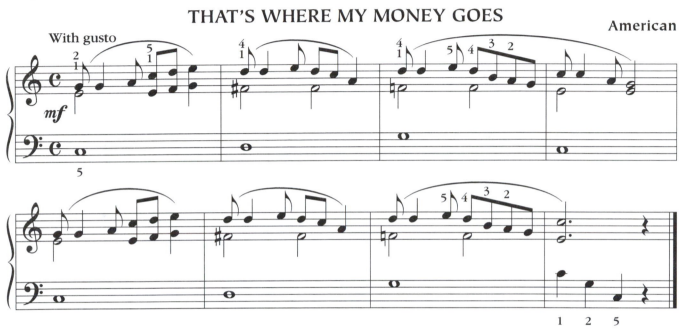

Secondary Dominants

Any triad may be preceded by its own dominant or secondary dominant. These chromatic chords—the most common of which is $V^{(7)}$ of $V^{(7)}$—add color and enrich the harmony. Study the scale degree triads embellished by their respective dominants. Secondary dominants are built a fourth below the root of the triad to which they resolve.

$I \quad V^7 \quad I \qquad ii \quad V^7/ii \quad ii \qquad iii \quad V^7/iii \quad iii \qquad IV \quad V^7/IV \quad IV \qquad V \quad V^7/V \quad V \qquad vi \quad V^7/vi \quad vi$
etc.

Chord Pattern: $I-IV-V^7/V^7-V^7-I$

Practice the familiar $I-IV-V^7$ chords with the added V^7 of V^7. Transpose to F, G, and a few other keys.

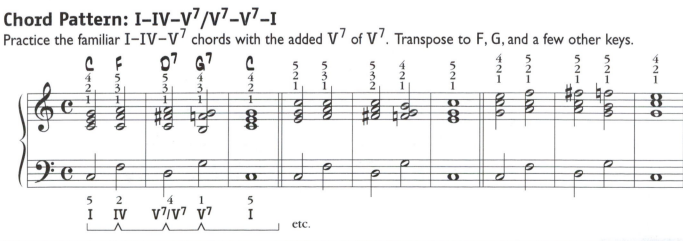

$I \qquad IV \qquad V^7/V^7 \quad V^7 \qquad I$
etc.

Building the Dominant of the Dominant

In any key, there is an easy way to figure out the dominant of the dominant $V^{(7)}$ of $V^{(7)}$. When LH finger 4 plays the second scale degree, mentally build a dominant seventh chord on that tone—major triad with a minor seventh. Then transpose the notes to the RH to conform to the spelling of the chord.

Practice with the $V^{(7)}$ of $V^{(7)}$ and Other Secondary Dominants

Study and play the following arrangements of folk songs containing dominant of the dominant chords and other secondary dominant chords. Analyze each chord with a letter name symbol and Roman numeral.

FLOW GENTLY, SWEET AFTON

Alexander Hume
arr. James Lyke

THE FOGGY, FOGGY DEW

British

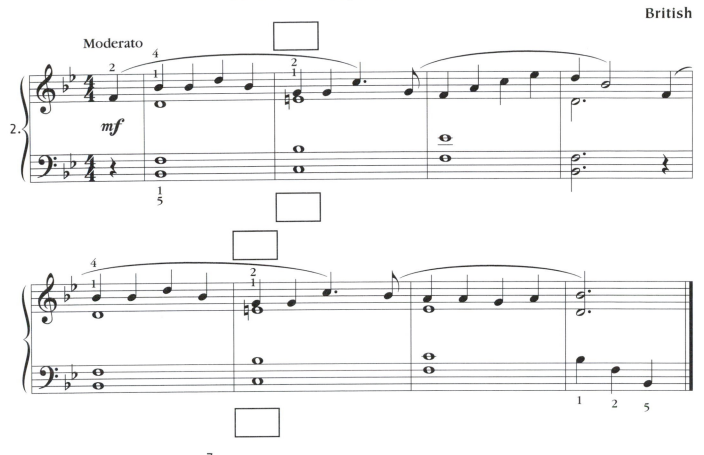

In *Home on the Range,* find a V^7 of IV as well as a minor iv "borrowed" from the parallel minor key. (*Parallel* keys share the same keynote.)

HOME ON THE RANGE
(Chorus)

United States

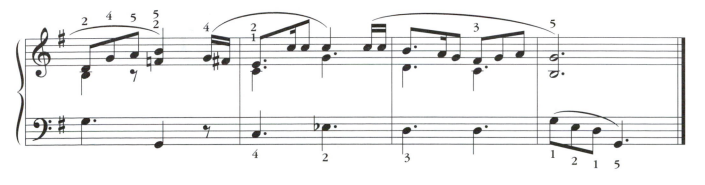

DALMATIAN FOLK SONG

I'M GONNA SING WHEN THE SPIRIT SAYS SING

Spiritual

Spotting the V^(7) of V^(7)

The following excerpts from folk songs contain the V^7 of V^7. Write V^7 of V^7 in the boxes below the chords in examples 2–4. See the example in No. 1. Add your own fingerings wherever necessary.

Brightly

1.

$V^7$of V^7

Moderato

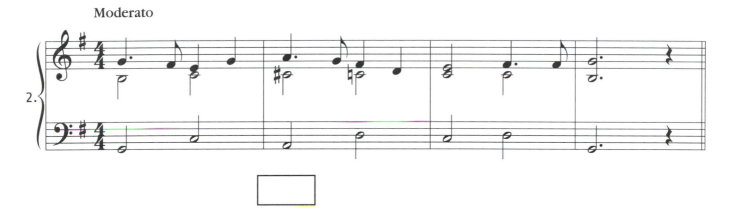

2.

Moderato

3.

Slowly

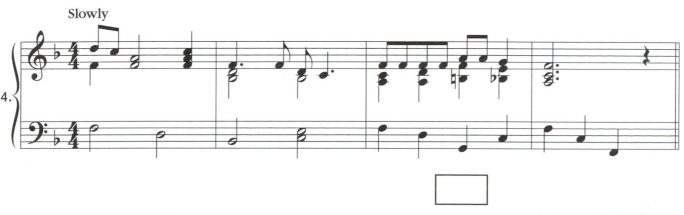

4.

Harmonizing with V^7/V$^{(7)}$ and Other Secondary Dominants

Harmonize the following studies that show the use of V^7 of V$^{(7)}$ and other secondary dominants such as V^7 of IV, V^7 of ii, etc. Continue in the suggested style. Notate your harmonization.

ALL THROUGH THE NIGHT

Wales

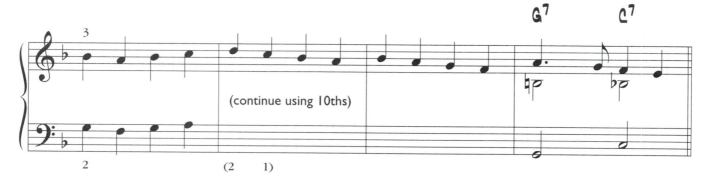

D.C. al fine

HUNGARIAN FOLK SONG

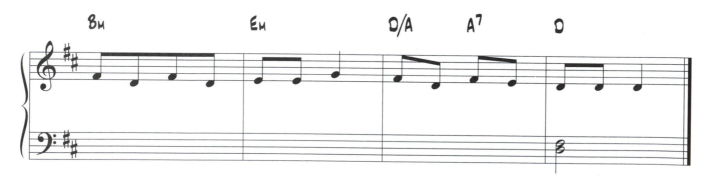

CZECH FOLK SONG

GERMAN FOLK SONG

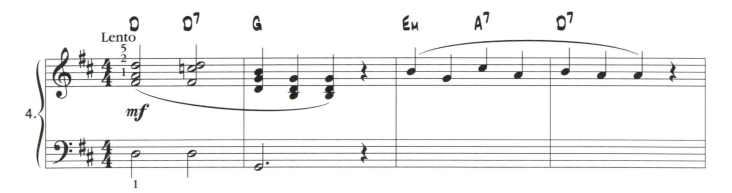

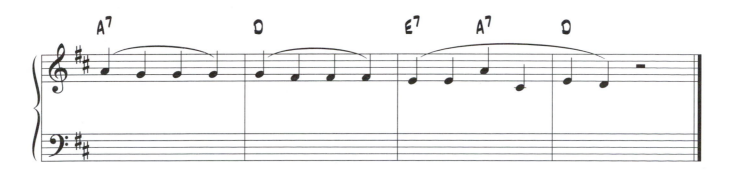

Minor Scales – A Review

Minor scales have three forms: 1) *natural*, 2) *melodic*, and 3) *harmonic*. Study all three built on A.

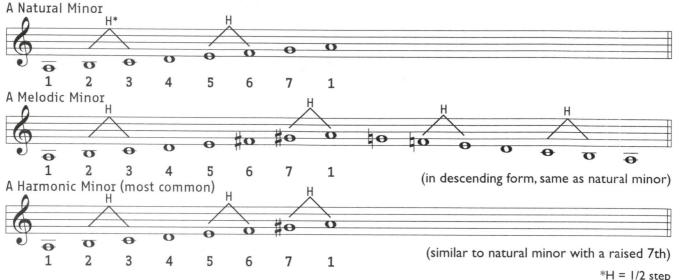

A Natural Minor

A Melodic Minor

(in descending form, same as natural minor)

A Harmonic Minor (most common)

(similar to natural minor with a raised 7th)

*H = 1/2 step

Relative Minor Key Signatures

Minor scales share their key signatures with those of major scales. The minor key signature may be found by counting up three half steps from the minor keynote. C major is the *relative* major key of A minor. A minor is the *relative* minor of C major. To find the relative minor from the major scale keynote, count down three half steps. Study the whole step/half step arrangement of all three forms of the minor scales.

Parallel Keys and Scales

Keys such as A major and A minor share the same keynote. They are considered *parallel* keys. Play the A major scale that follows. Then play the A harmonic minor scale, contrasting it to the major scale. You will notice that in the harmonic minor scale, the 3rd and 6th degrees are lowered one half step. The 7th is the same as in A major.

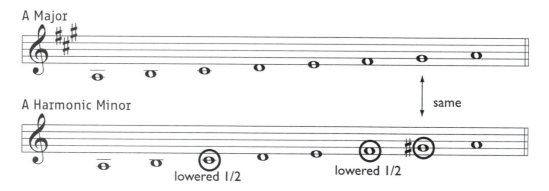

A Major

A Harmonic Minor

same

lowered 1/2   lowered 1/2

i-iv-i$_4^6$-V^7-i Chord Pattern in Minor

Practice this pattern in various minor keys. Analyze each chord with letter name and Roman numeral.

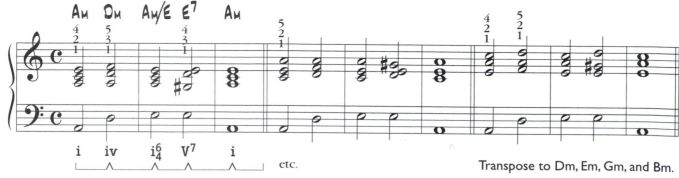

Am   Dm   Am/E   E^7 Am

i   iv   i$_4^6$ V^7 i   etc.

Transpose to Dm, Em, Gm, and Bm.

Chords Built on Scale Tones of the Minor Mode

In harmonic minor, chords built on scale steps i and iv are minor chords; the V chord is major (due to the raised seventh scale degree), as is the VI chord; ii° and vii° are diminished; and III+ is augmented.

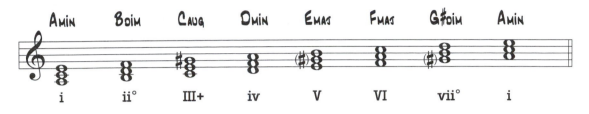

Two Study Pieces in Minor

Determine the minor key of *Two Guitars* (key of one flat, count down three half steps from the major key-note). The raised leading tone, C♯, tells us we are in harmonic minor. The tonic and subdominant chords in a minor key will be minor in quality. Analyze the chords and inversions.

TWO GUITARS

Slovakian

Determine the key of *Russian Folk Song*. Analyze the harmony in each measure.

RUSSIAN FOLK SONG

arr. Beethoven

Study Pieces: Folk Song Arrangements of Melodies in Minor Keys

Study and play the following six folk song arrangements. Analyze each chord and add letter name symbols above the chords.

HUNGARIAN FOLK DANCE

57

PORTUGUESE FOLK SONG

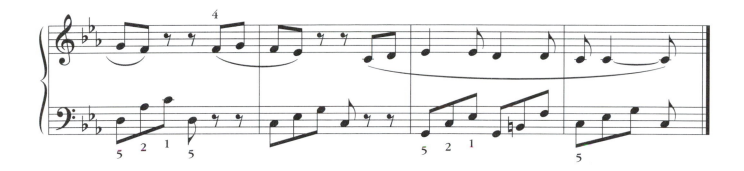

LETTISH FOLK SONG

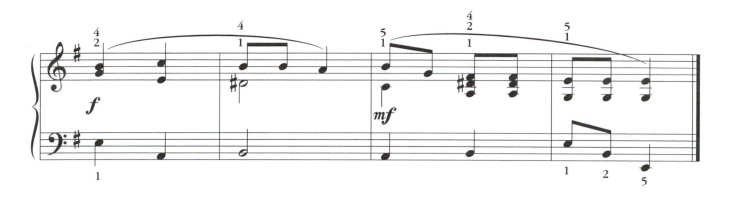

OOK ONE, CHAPTER SEVEN

KALINKA

Russian

MEADOWLANDS

Russian

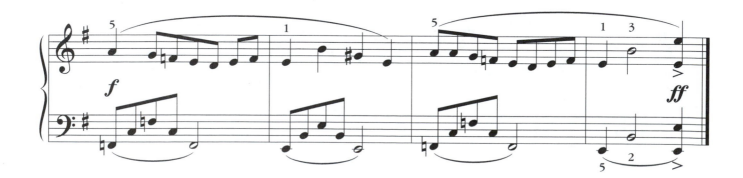

ALL THE PRETTY LITTLE HORSES

American Lullaby

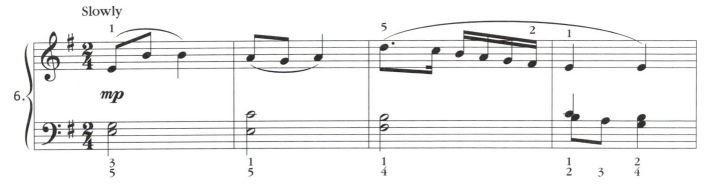

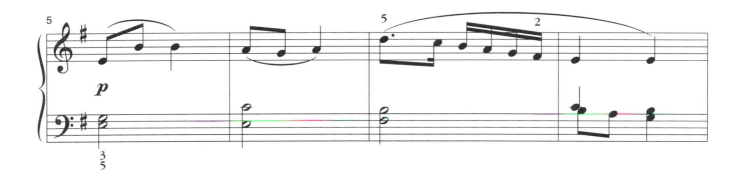

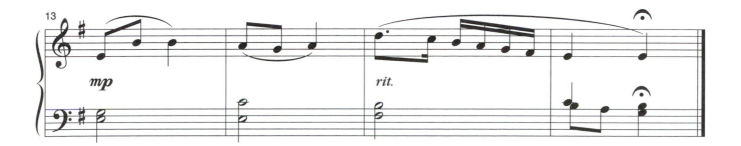

Four Minor Key Melodies to Harmonize

Harmonize the following minor key melodies. Use the suggested style as your guide. Notate and play your arrangements, adding your own fingering where needed.

SPANISH FOLK SONG
(3-voice texture)

Examples 2. and 3. have no chord symbols. Harmonize and notate your arrangement.

ITALIAN FOLK SONG
(3-voice texture)

Here is another harmonization without chords symbols indicated. Use your knowledge to complete *Russian Folk Song* with your own chord choices.

RUSSIAN FOLK SONG

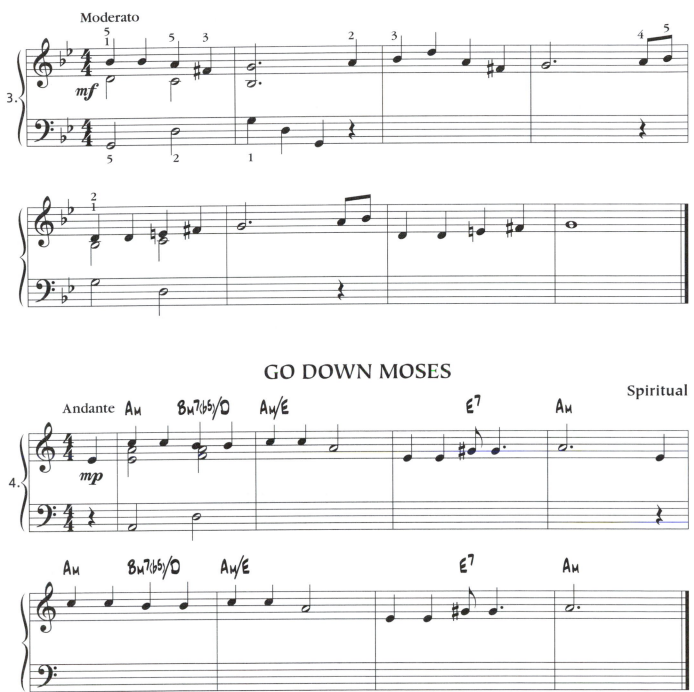

GO DOWN MOSES

Spiritual

In minor keys the seventh chord built on the 2nd scale degree is the half-diminished seventh chord. In jazz harmony these chords are symbolized as either $ii^{\varnothing 7}$ or letter name $m^{7(\flat 5)}$. Notice the use of $Bm^{7(\flat 5)}$ in *Go Down Moses*.

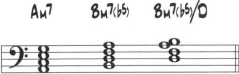

Music for Sight Reading and Transposing

This section contains reading material that emphasizes minor keys and secondary dominants. Follow the reading routine established earlier. Transpose these exercises as suggested.

Minor Harmonies

SPANISH FOLK SONG

Transpose to F minor.

RUSSIAN FOLK SONG

Transpose to G minor.

ITALIAN FOLK SONG

Transpose G minor.

BRITISH FOLK SONG

Transpose to F minor.

MEXICAN FOLK SONG

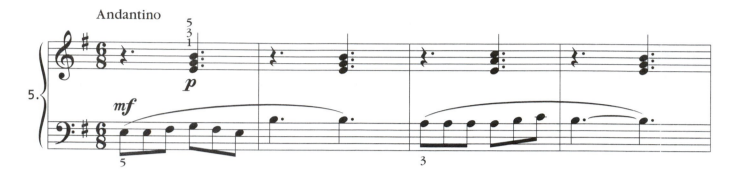

Transpose to D minor.

TROIKA RUSHING

Russian

Transpose to E minor.

In Nos. 7 and 8, locate and circle the secondary dominants. Be able to explain their function.

THE WHITE COCKADE

Scottish

7.

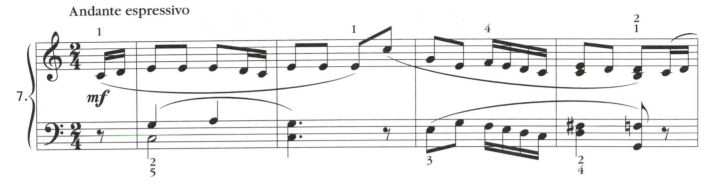

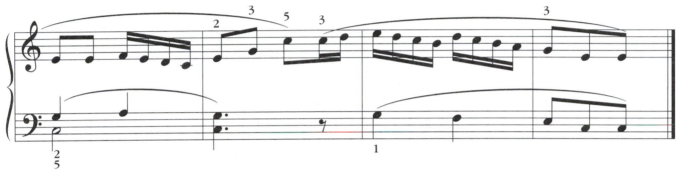

Transpose to D major.

OFT IN THE STILLY NIGHT

British

8.

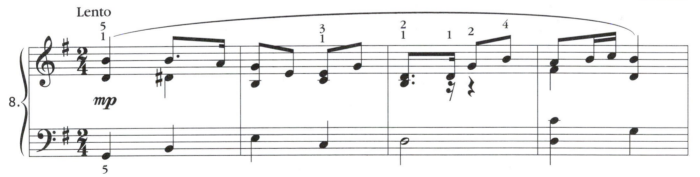

Transpose to F major.

ACCOMPANYING

Practice the I–vi–V⁷/V⁷–V⁷–I progression located in bars 5–9 before learning the rest of the accompaniment. *Cockles and Mussels* includes secondary and dominant of the dominant chords.

TEACHER: Double the melody one octave higher.

COCKLES AND MUSSELS

Irish
arr. **James Lyke**

Transpose to F major.

TEACHER: Double the melody one octave higher.

BEAUTIFUL BROWN EYES

American
arr. **James Lyke**

AMERICAN SONG REPERTOIRE

WHEN THE MIDNIGHT CHOO-CHOO
LEAVES FOR ALABAM'

music by **Irving Berlin**
arr. **James Lyke**

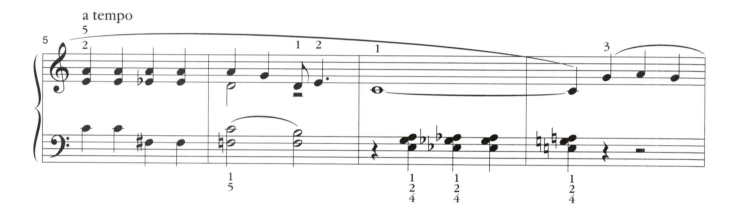

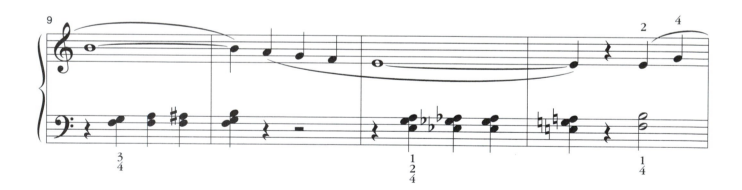

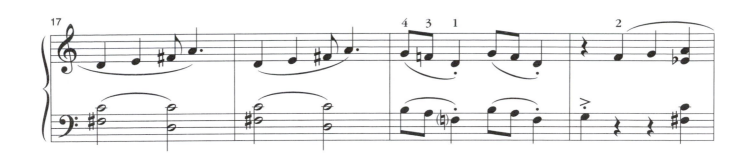

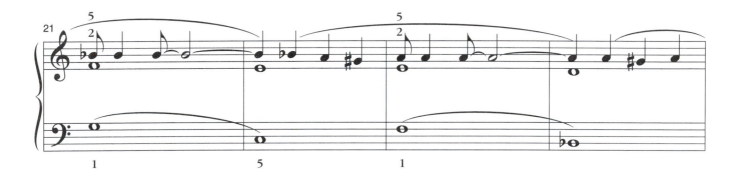

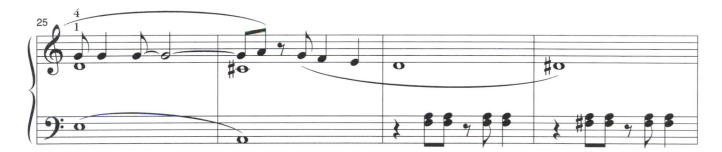

BOOK ONE, CHAPTER SEVEN

270

The Love Nest illustrates the use of many types of seventh chords. Find and name them. Example: in bars 1 and 2—E♭M⁷, Cm⁷, Fm⁷, B♭⁷.

THE LOVE NEST

music by **Louis Hirsch**
arr. **James Lyke**

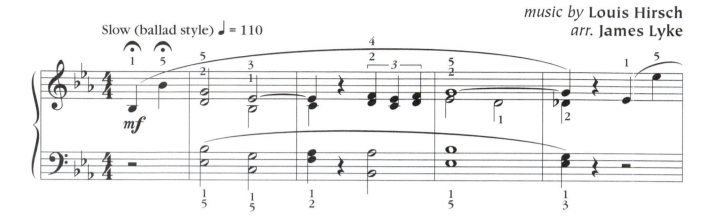

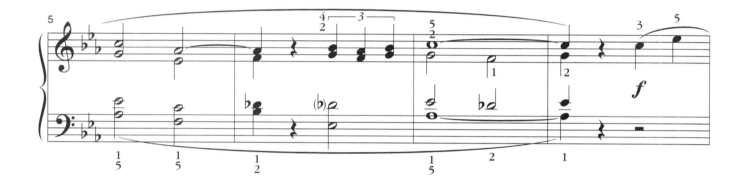

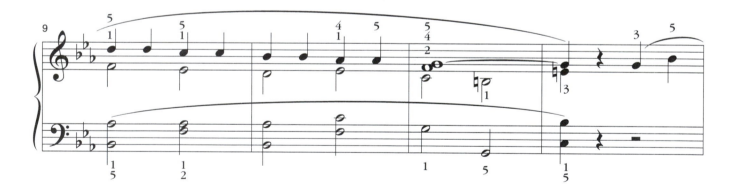

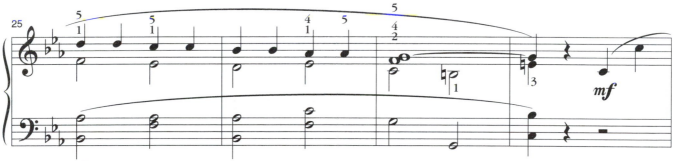

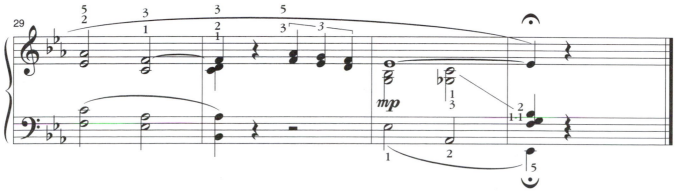

BOOK ONE, CHAPTER SEVEN

ENSEMBLE REPERTOIRE

ALL ABOARD FOR BROADWAY

Secondo – Teacher

music by George M. Cohan
arr. James Lyke

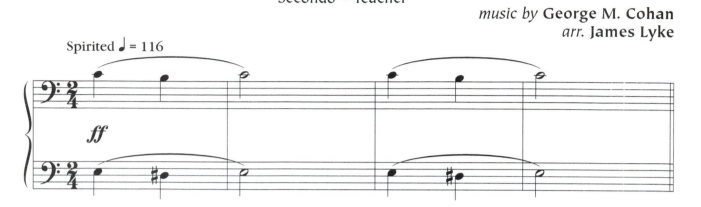

ALL ABOARD FOR BROADWAY

Primo – Student

music by **George M. Cohan**
arr. **James Lyke**

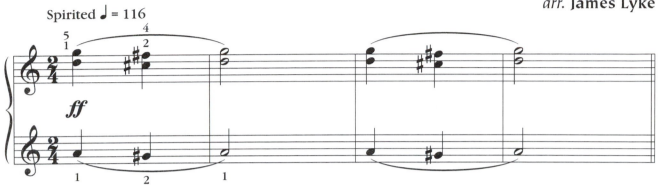

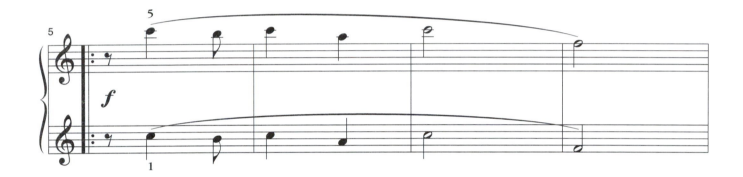

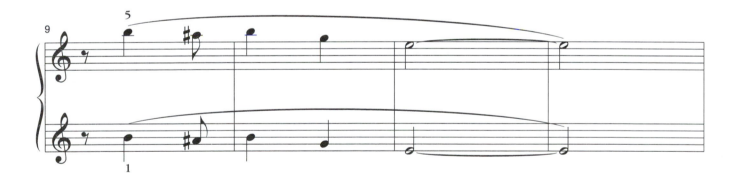

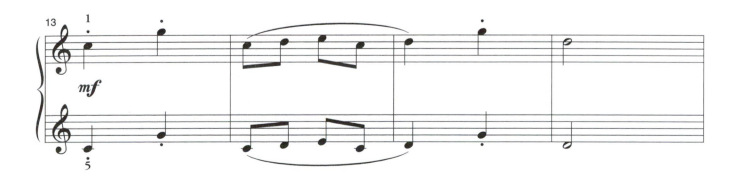

Secondo

Primo

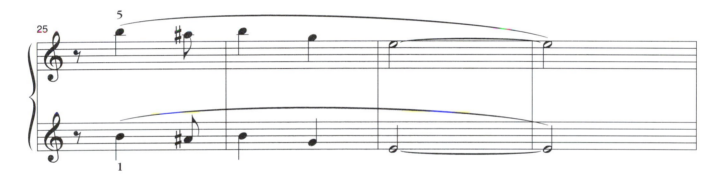

WONDERFUL ONE

Secondo – Teacher or Student

music by **Paul Whiteman** and **Ferde Grofe**
arr. **Geoffrey Haydon** and **James Lyke**

WONDERFUL ONE
Primo – Student or Teacher

music by **Paul Whiteman** *and* **Ferde Grofe**
arr. **Geoffrey Haydon** *and* **James Lyke**

Secondo

ped. simile

Primo

SOLO REPERTOIRE

Practice Plan: Block each outlined RH triad and identify it (Gmaj, Emin, etc.). Then play RH as written thinking about your moves. Block all outlined LH triads and identify them by chord name. When beginning to put the hands together (HT), play all eighth notes *staccato* (finger *staccato*). Finally, play *Prelude from Suite in G* as written.

PRELUDE
(Suite in G)

Henry Purcell

Practice Plan: Fingering is of utmost importance while playing this Telemann composition (see especially measure 8). What form of the minor scale does the F♯ suggest?

ANDANTE IN G MINOR

Georg Philipp Telemann

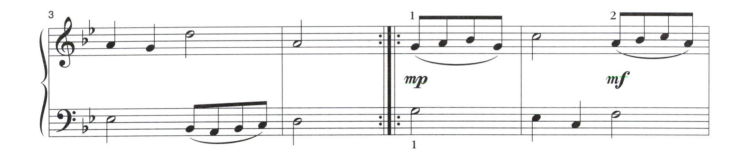

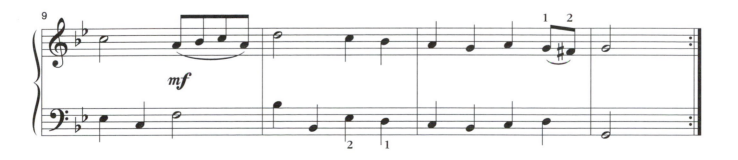

Practice Plan: Play *Minuet in F* without pedal. Drill bars 4 and 16 until the rhythmic figures are under control. At first, exaggerate the RH slurs with gentle lifts of the wrist.

MINUET IN F

Franz Joseph Haydn

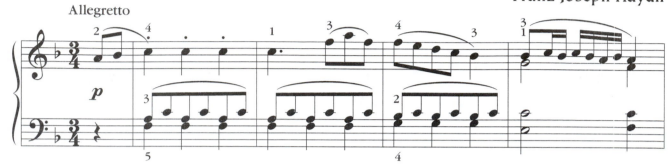

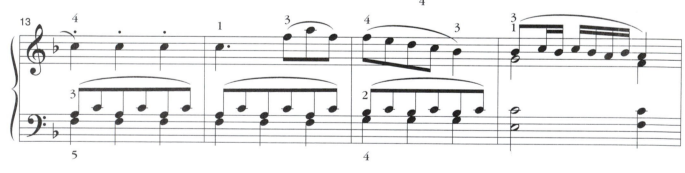

Practice Plan: In *Lost and Found* pedal carefully, listening to the changing harmonies as a guide. Play as smoothly as possible and observe all fingering suggestions.

LOST AND FOUND

Tony Caramia

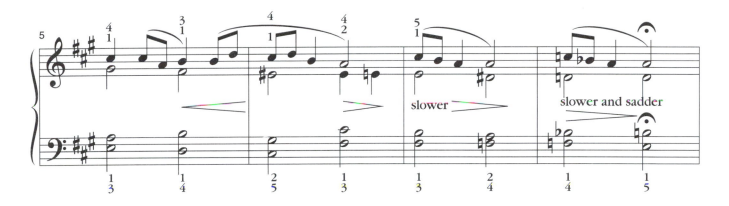

Practice Plan: In the first movement of Beethoven's Sonatina in G Major, first block all of the LH Alberti bass figures and identify each chord. Then play the entire LH part at a comfortable tempo. Play the RH part, slowly at first, being attentive to the various slurs. When putting the hands together (HT), begin slowly and increase the tempo gradually. Play without pedal.

SONATINA IN G MAJOR

(first movement)

Ludwig van Beethoven

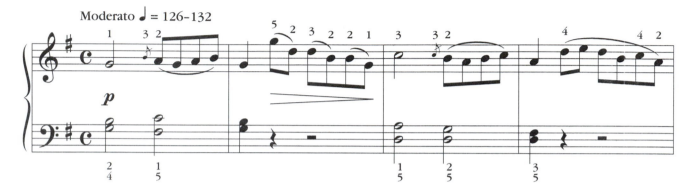

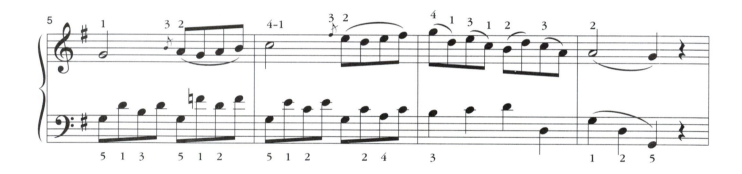

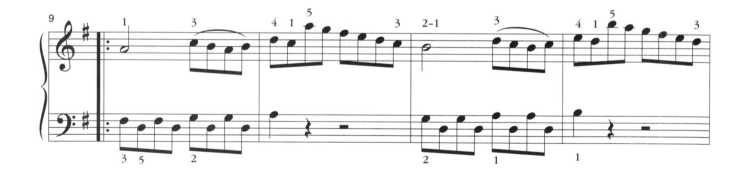

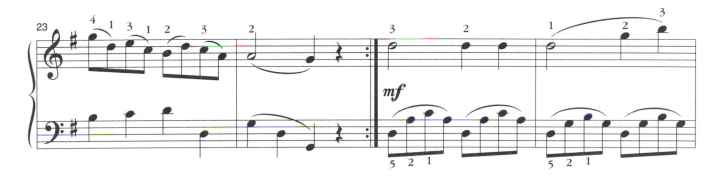

Practice Plan: In *Little Study*, block the chords in each hand. Then play slowly making sure that there are good connections from LH to RH. Analyze the chords in each hand. Play without pedal at first. Then add pedal as indicated.

LITTLE STUDY
(from *Album for the Young*)

Robert Schumann

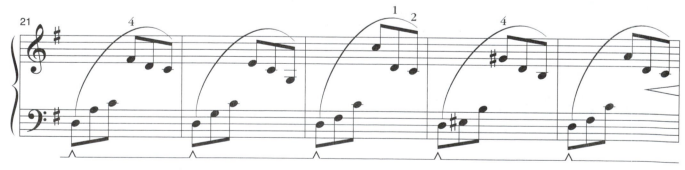

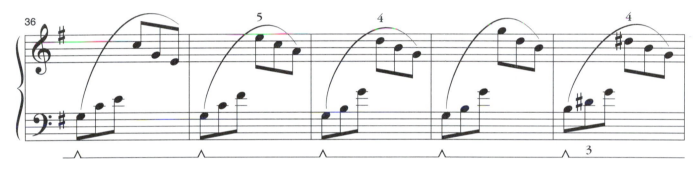

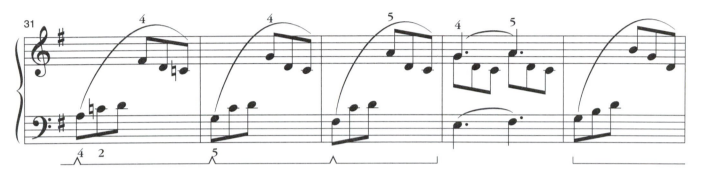

BOOK ONE, CHAPTER SEVEN

Practice Plan: In *Two Will Get You Five*, play the LH alone counting carefully. Then play the RH eighth notes in swing rhythm. Finally, play HT being careful with touch and tied notes.

TWO WILL GET YOU FIVE

James Lyke

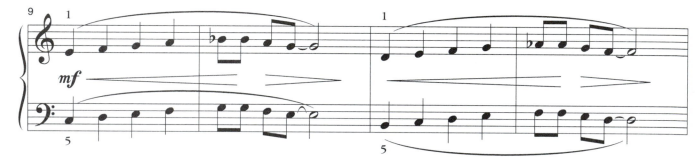

Practice Plan: *Leather Vest* requires careful counting. Subdivide all rhythms at first, paying special attention to the two-measure tied syncopation ♩♩♩♩♩ ♩♩↓♩. in measures 1–2, 3–4, etc. Play with a full tone.

LEATHER VEST

Geoffrey Haydon

BOOK ONE, CHAPTER SEVEN

MUSICIANSHIP ACTIVITIES

Complete the following exercises that review various topics introduced in Chapter Seven.

Chord Progessions in Minor

Fill in the missing tones in the following two progressions. Move to the closest voice to create smooth voice leading.

Chord Progessions with V^7/V

Fill in the missing tones in the following two progressions.

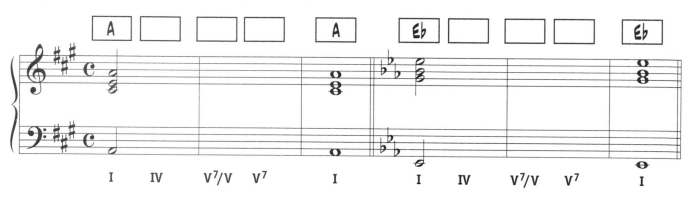

Improvising

While another class member (or the instructor) plays this salsa pattern, improvise a RH melody in E minor. Listen for the harmonic changes.

Andantino - Latin flavor

TECHNICAL STUDIES

Harmonic Minor Scales: c, g, d, a, e

Begin the study of harmonic minor scales. The fingerings are the same as those in the parallel major scales. Consult Appendix B for a thorough presentation of all scales and arpeggios.

Minor Arpeggios: c, g, d, a, e

Begin the study of harmonic minor arpeggios. The fingerings are the same or similar to those in the parallel major arpeggios. Consult Appendix B to check fingerings.

Example: Two Octave Minor Arpeggio, Hands Together (HT) (Play twice slow, twice fast.)

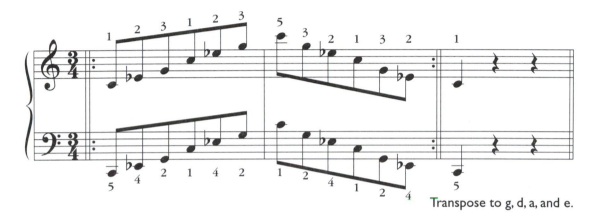

Transpose to g, d, a, and e.

Chromatic Scale Review: Play and learn the RH part of this excerpt from Köhler's *Polka*. This will serve as a review of chromatic scale fingering. The instructor (or another student) can play the LH part so that the focus remains on good fingering in the RH part.

Louis Köhler

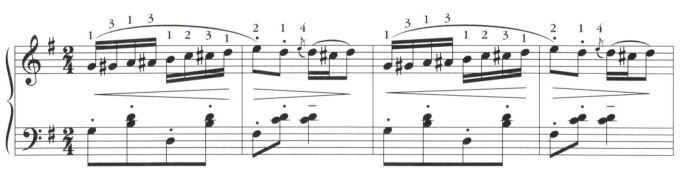

SUGGESTED PLAYING EXAM TOPICS
CHAPTER SEVEN

1. Play one harmonized melody that uses the dominant of the dominant found on pages 248–250.

2. Play the chord progression, i–iv–i_4^6–V^7–i, from memory in these minor keys: cm, dm, em, gm, am, and bm. See page 254 to review the progression.

3. Demonstrate harmonization skill by playing one example from pages 260–261.

4. Play two sight reading melodies from pages 262–265.

5. Accompany the melody to *Cockles and Mussels* (page 266) or *Beautiful Brown Eyes* (page 267).

6. Perform *When the Midnight Choo-Choo Leaves for Alabam'* (pages 268–269) or *The Love Nest* (pages 270–271).

7. Perform the duet (student part) to *All Aboard for Broadway* (pages 272–275) or *Wonderful One* (pages 276–279) from the Ensemble Repertoire section.

8. Perform one or two selections from the Solo Repertoire section found on pages 280–289.

Seventh Chords Built on Various Scale Degrees, Lead Sheet Harmonization, Modes, Harmonization, Reading Studies, Repertoire, Musicianship Activities, and Technical Studies

In Chapter Six, Kern's *Look for the Silver Lining* was used to illustrate secondary chords (ii, iii, and vi). Review these seventh chords in the example below. Complete the letter name analysis in the boxes provided and practice slowly to savor the richness of the various 7ths and their qualities (maj, min, etc.).

LOOK FOR THE SILVER LINING

music by **Jerome Kern**

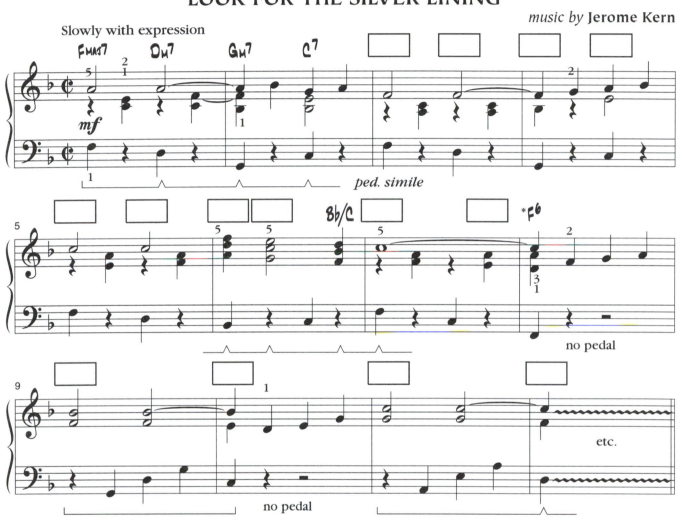

* Sometimes a 6th may be added to a major triad. 6th chords occur often in popular music (see bar 8).

Seventh Chord Qualities

Seventh chords can be built on major scale degrees I, ii, iii, etc. The resulting qualities, such as major and minor 7ths, will be examined in the following pages. The most common types of seventh chords appear below. Build these on various tones. Focus on diminished seventh chords in the last two measures.

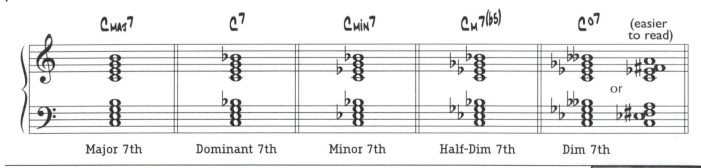

| Major 7th | Dominant 7th | Minor 7th | Half-Dim 7th | Dim 7th |

In the example from Kern's *Look For The Silver Lining*, these seventh chords are used: Dm^7 (vi^7), $Fmaj^7$ (I^7), and $B\flat maj^7$ (IV^7). These chords are in addition to the ii^7 chord that moves to the dominant. Study the various seventh chords built on each scale degree shown below. I^7 and IV^7 are major in quality; ii^7, iii^7, and vi^7 are minor in quality (secondary sevenths); and V^7 is dominant. The $vii^{\o 7}$ is a special chord, half-diminished (diminished triad with a minor seventh.)

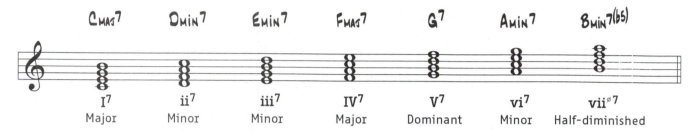

Study the quality of the various seventh chords built on each degree of the major scale above. Block these scale degree seventh chords *in selected major keys* and identify the quality of each chord. Say the Roman numeral, letter name, and quality as you build each chord on scale degrees of each new key. Use both hands and play two octaves apart.

A Special Progression: ii^7–V^7–I^7

In jazz and popular music, the ii^7–V^7–I^7 sequence is known as: "ii–V–I." Look back to the Kern song on page 293. Take note of Gm^7–C^7–F (bar 2 to bar 3), the "ii–V–I" progression. Learn this progression (very gradually) in the six keys shown below. Play each progression twice before moving on to the next. (maj7 = major seventh.)

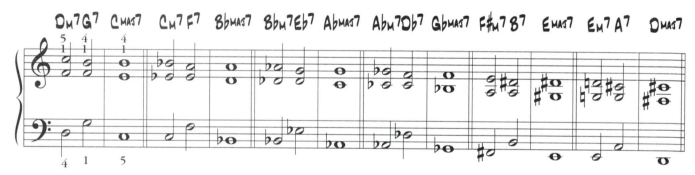

Using vi^7

Another common minor seventh chord is vi^7. Learn this progression in F, C, and G. Later, you will use these harmonies in an accompaniment pattern.

Study Pieces: Folk Song Arrangements Using Various Seventh Chords

Study **and play** the following five arrangements. Analyze the harmony and add letter name symbols in the boxes above the chords.

SOURWOOD MOUNTAIN

United States

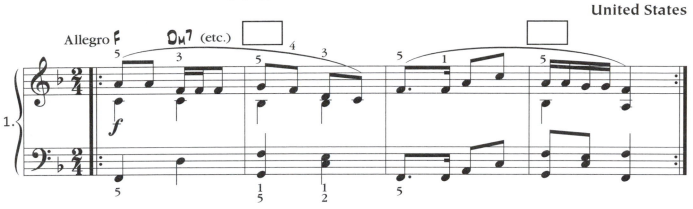

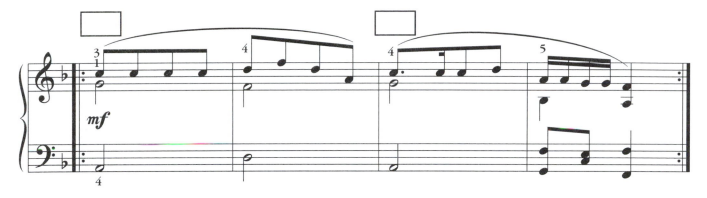

GERMAN FOLK SONG

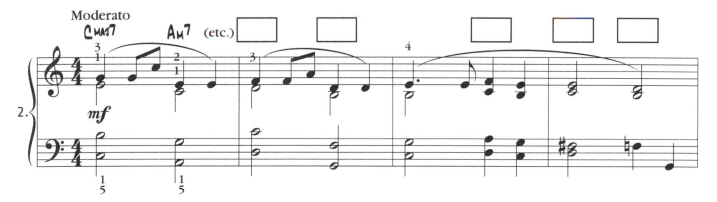

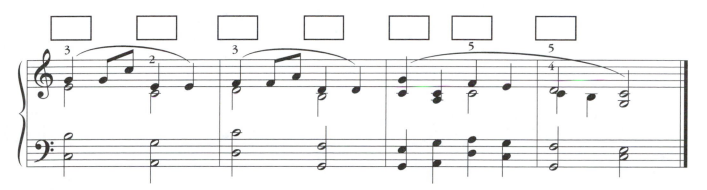

O COME, LITTLE CHILDREN

J.P.A. Schulz
arr. James Lyke

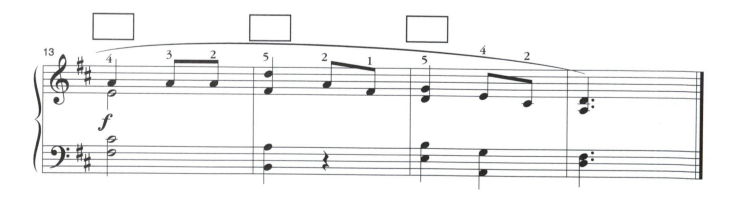

Using the boxes above the measures identify the harmony in Jerome Kern's *Mitzi's Lullaby* and *They Didn't Believe Me*. Use letter name symbols for each 7th chord and identify its quality.

MITZI'S LULLABY

THEY DIDN'T BELIEVE ME

Harmonization Using ii⁷ and Other Secondary Seventh Chords

Harmonize the following melodies that occasionally call for secondary seventh chords. Follow the example at the beginning to attain a good keyboard texture. Notate and finger your arrangements. Keep the harmony limited to mostly three voices.

POLISH LULLABY

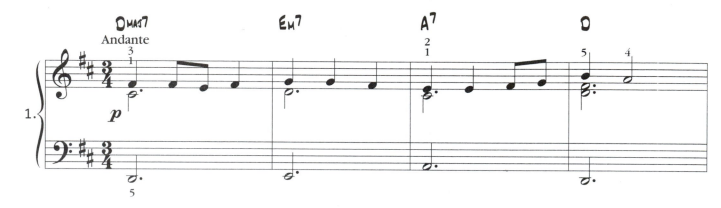

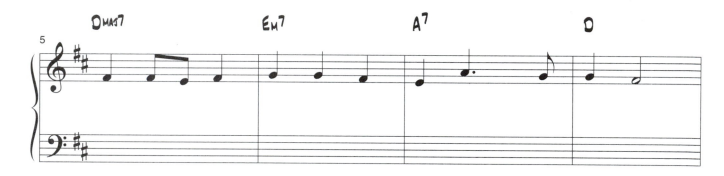

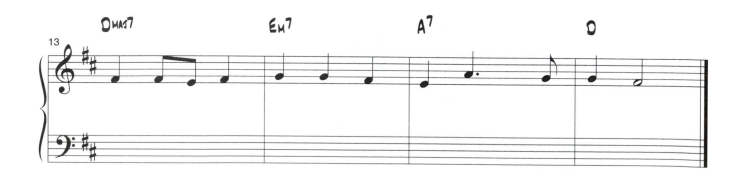

LAS MAÑANITAS

Mexico

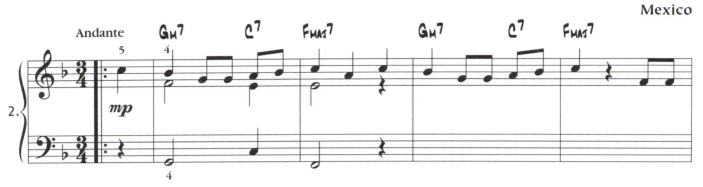

MUSIC ALONE SHALL LIVE

Germany

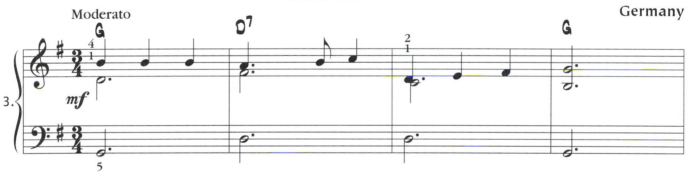

THE LITTLE SHOEMAKER

Janet Gaynor

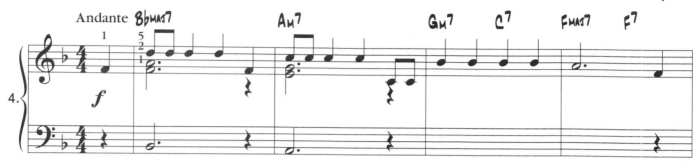

EARLY ONE MORNING

British

Harmonic Review

Place chord symbols above each new chord, then play the arrangement.

AMAZING GRACE

American
arr. James Lyke

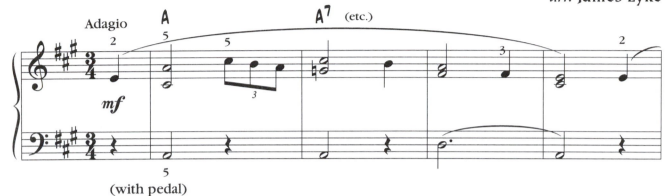

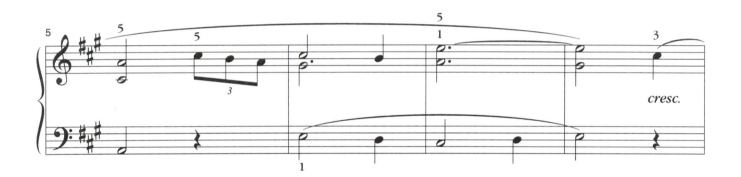

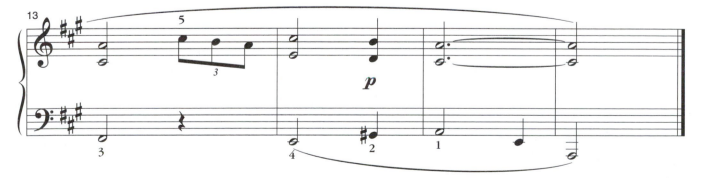

Harmonizing Popular Song Lead Sheets Using Various Types of Seventh Chords

The following two early American popular tunes make use of various types of seventh chords. Study the suggested styles given at the opening of each tune. Some students might find it helpful to notate certain passages (or even the entire arrangement).

Gershwin's tune, *Sunday in London Town*, provides an opportunity to use both the diminished seventh and the half-diminished seventh chords ($m^{7(\flat 5)}$). Mostly, the harmonization requires 3 voices. Occasionally, four voices add richness, especially at the close of phrases.

SUNDAY IN LONDON TOWN

George Gershwin

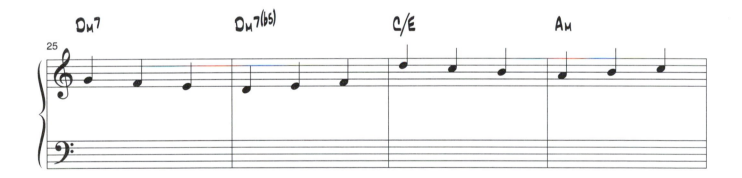

NOTE: n.c. = no chord

FOR ME AND MY GAL

George W. Meyer

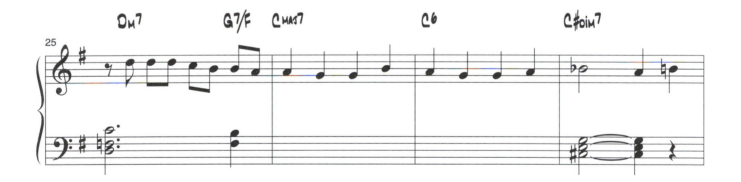

Modes

We have already explored major and minor scales, or *modes*. And we have had experience with other modes such as the pentatonic and whole-tone. The Church modes are centuries old and have been used in folk song melody (particularly in Eastern Europe) and in plainsong (Gregorian chant). The untransposed modes can be played on the white keys of the piano with no accidentals. Two of the modes, Ionian and Aeolian, are constructed with the same half and whole step patterns as the major and natural minor scales. Twentieth century composers have used the church modes to get away from the traditional major and minor sound. Study the white key modes below. Play and listen to them. Analyze how each differs from the familiar major and minor scales.

UNTRANSPOSED MODES

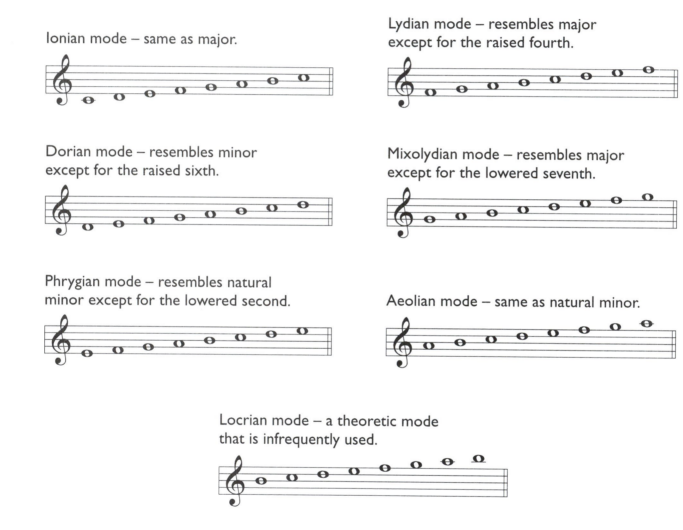

Ionian mode – same as major.

Lydian mode – resembles major except for the raised fourth.

Dorian mode – resembles minor except for the raised sixth.

Mixolydian mode – resembles major except for the lowered seventh.

Phrygian mode – resembles natural minor except for the lowered second.

Aeolian mode – same as natural minor.

Locrian mode – a theoretic mode that is infrequently used.

Transposing the Modes

The modes may be transposed to any key. Always think of the relationship the white key modes have with C major. For example, the Dorian mode on D takes the key signature of C major, which is a major second below D. Therefore, the Dorian mode beginning on E has the same key signature as the major scale located a major second below E—D major—and has two sharps. E Dorian is be spelled: E, F♯, G, A, B, C♯, D, and E. The interval relationship is always maintained. For Phrygian, use the major key signature a major third below the tonic; for Lydian, a fourth below; for Mixolydian, a fifth below (or fourth above); for Aeolian, a minor third above; and for Locrian, a half-step above.

When a piece appears to be modal, and the tonal center has been determined, the mode can be quickly analyzed. For example, if the tonal center appears to be F, and the key signature has five flats, the mode is Phrygian because D♭ is a major third below F.

Four Modal Folk Songs for Study

Study and play the following folk song arrangements that illustrate three different modes. Identify each mode before playing.

CRADLE HYMN
(Aeolian)

Kentucky Folk Song
arr. **James Lyke**

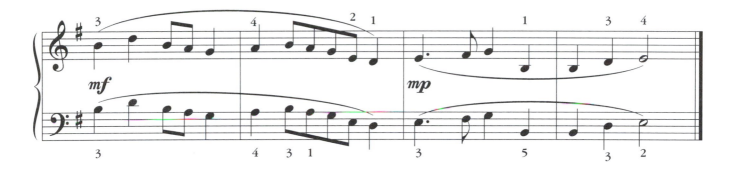

DOWN IN THAT VALLEY
(Phrygian)

Kentucky Folk Song
arr. **James Lyke**

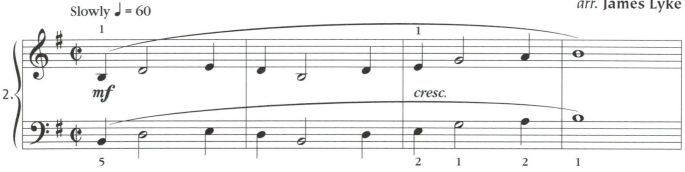

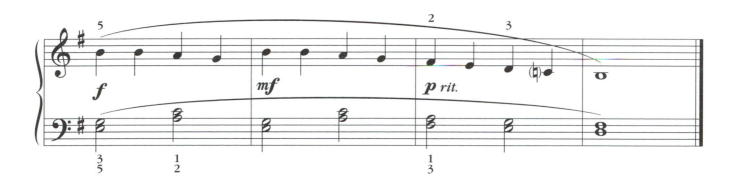

THE DRUNKEN SAILOR
(Dorian)

Chantey
arr. **James Lyke**

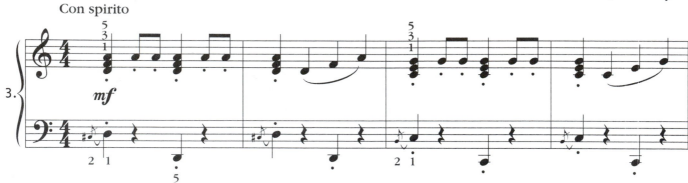

WHEN JOHNNY COMES MARCHING HOME
(Aeolian)

American
arr. **James Lyke**

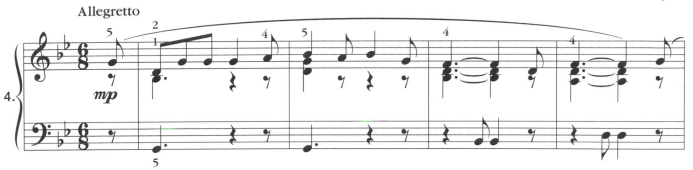

Two Original Modal Pieces for Study and Performance

Study and play *A Smidgeon of Phrygian* and *Mixolydian Mix* to gain additional experience with modal writing. Both are white key (untransposed) compositions.

A SMIDGEON OF PHRYGIAN

James Lyke

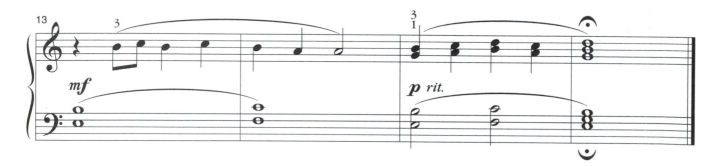

MIXOLYDIAN MIX

James Lyke

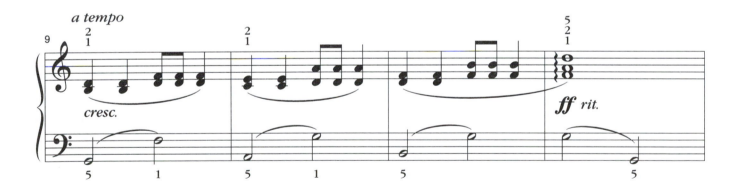

Four Modal Melodies to Harmonize

Harmonize the following melodies according to the suggested style.

SCARBOROUGH FAIR
(Dorian)

British

JOHNNY HAS GONE FOR A SOLDIER
(Aeolian)

Irish

KEYBOARD MUSICIANSHIP

IROQUOIS SONG
(Dorian)

French Canadian

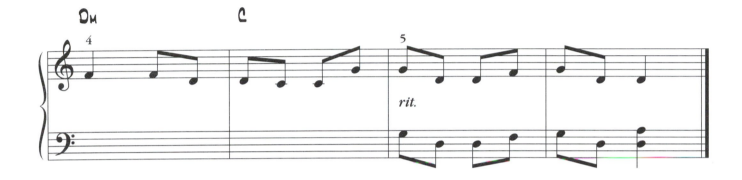

LULLABY
(Aeolian)

Japanese

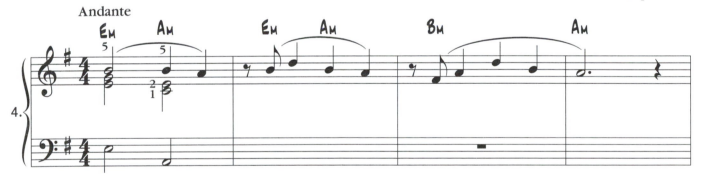

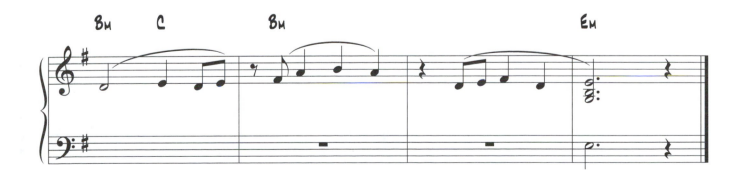

Music for Sight Reading and Transposing

The pieces in this section contain diatonic seventh chords, secondary chords and secondary dominants, and minor and modal music. Analyze all seventh chords (Dm^7, FM^7 etc.) before sight reading.

Diatonic Sevenths

DANISH FOLK SONG

Transpose to G major.

LEAVE HER JOHNNY

Transpose to F major.

CALYPSO SONG

Caribbean Islands

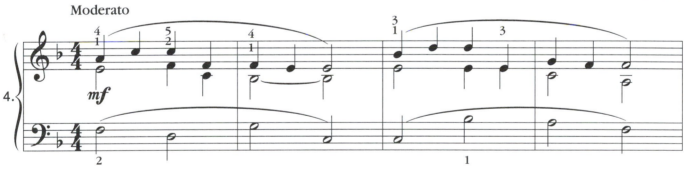

Transpose to F major.

BOBBY SHAFTO

British

Transpose to G major.

MEXICAN FOLK SONG

Transpose to G major.

HEY, BETTY MARTIN

United States

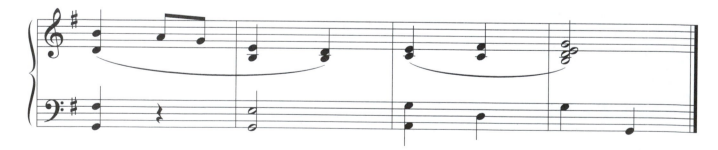

Transpose to F major.

Minor and Modal (nos. 7–11)

KATIUSHA

Russian

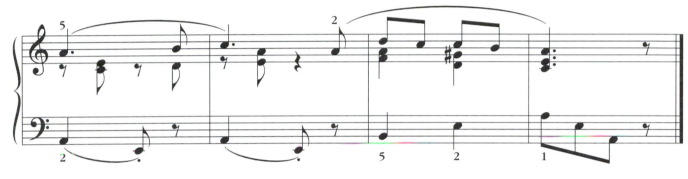

Transpose to G minor.

IN THE VALLEY

Russian

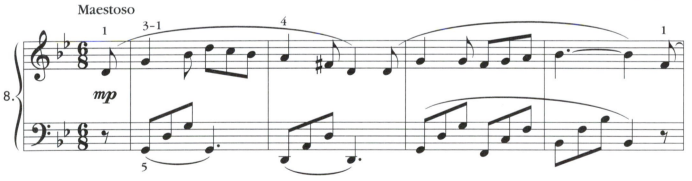

Transpose to A minor.

BOOK ONE, CHAPTER EIGHT

318

THE TAILOR AND THE MOUSE

British

9.

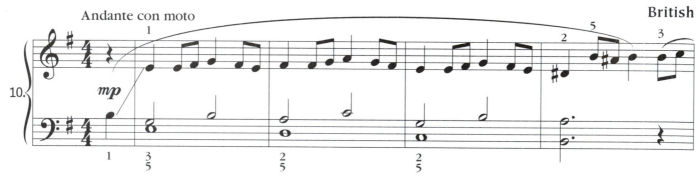

Transpose to B aeolian.

THE OAK AND THE ASH

British

10.

Find secondary (substitute) chords and secondary dominants. Write the chord symbol above each chord.

FOLK TUNE

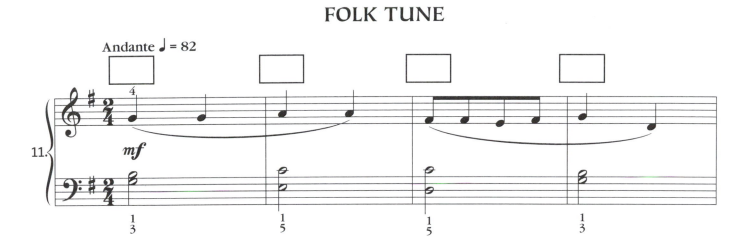

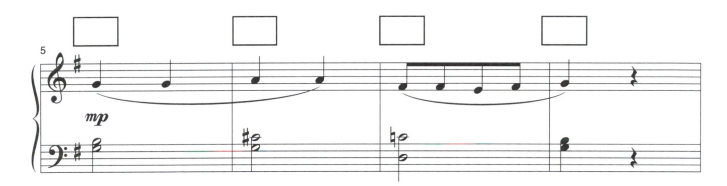

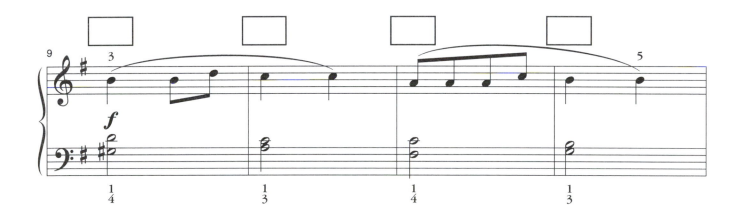

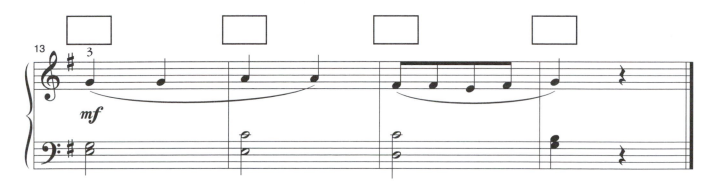

Transpose to F and A major.

BOOK ONE, CHAPTER EIGHT

ACCOMPANYING

Before learning the accompaniment to *Peg O' My Heart*, block each chord in half notes (LH and RH together). Analyze each chord and place letter name symbols above the accompaniment part. Then play as written.

TEACHER: Double the melody two octaves higher.

PEG O' MY HEART

music by **Fred Fisher**
arr. **James Lyke**

(a typical ii⁷–V⁷–I⁷ pattern)

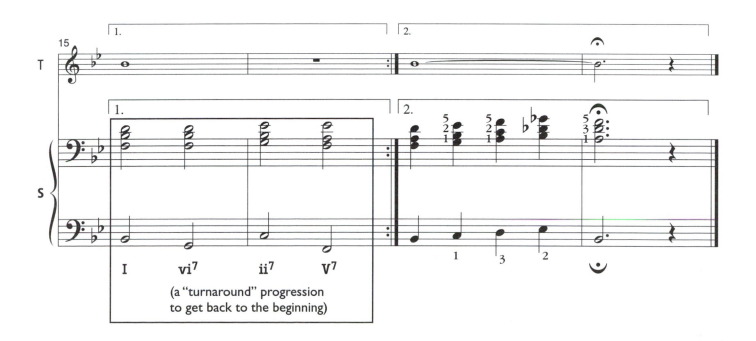

I   vi⁷   ii⁷   V⁷

(a "turnaround" progression
to get back to the beginning)

My Buddy uses diminished seventh chords very effectively. Find an example of an augmented dominant.
Label all harmonies in the usual way.

TEACHER: Double the melody one octave higher.

MY BUDDY

music by **Walter Donaldson**
arr. **James Lyke**

BOOK ONE, CHAPTER EIGHT

AMERICAN SONG REPERTOIRE

TAKE ME OUT TO THE BALL GAME

music *by* **Albert von Tilzer**
arr. **James Lyke**

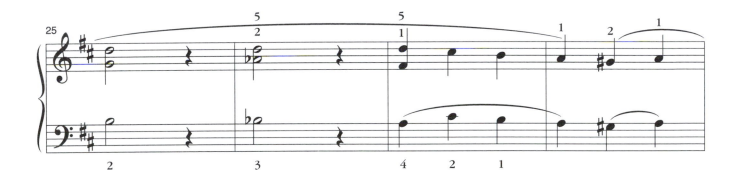

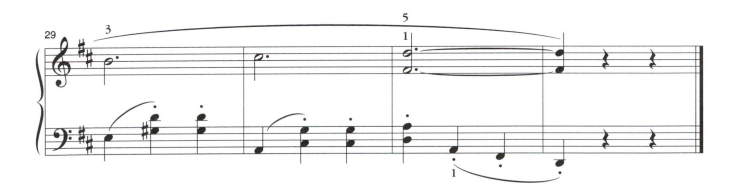

BOOK ONE, CHAPTER EIGHT

THEY DIDN'T BELIEVE ME

music by **Jerome Kern**
arr. **James Lyke**

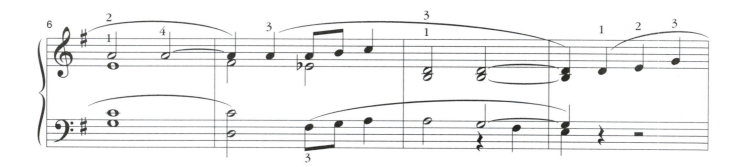

ENSEMBLE REPERTOIRE

The secondo part of *Look for the Silver Lining* provides an opportunity to work with various types of seventh chords. Analyze the chords and work through the fingering. The tempo should allow fluency with the chord changes. The secondo part is highly recommended for the student.

LOOK FOR THE SILVER LINING
Secondo – Student or Teacher

music by **Jerome Kern**
arr. **James Lyke**

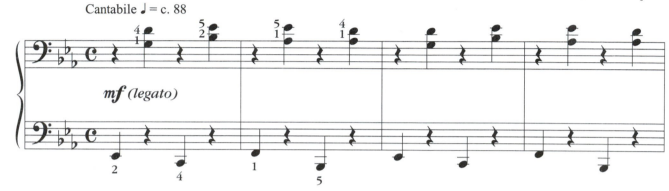

LOOK FOR THE SILVER LINING

Primo – Teacher or Student

music by **Jerome Kern**
arr. **James Lyke**

BOOK ONE, CHAPTER EIGHT

Secondo

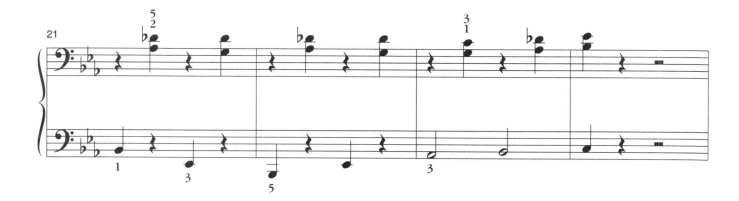

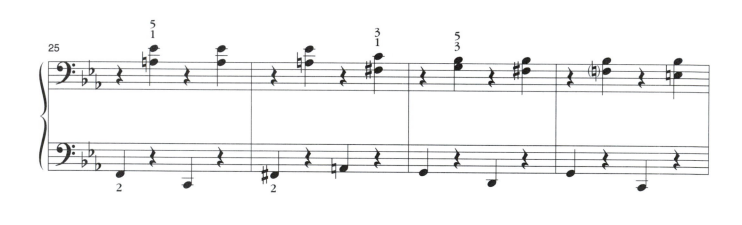

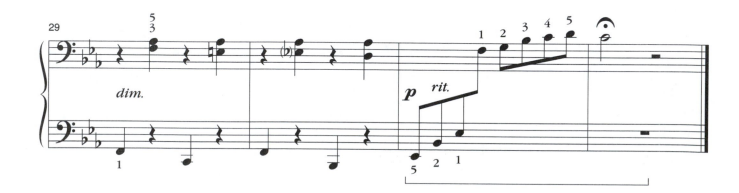

Primo

SHE'S MY BABY

Secondo – Teacher

George Gershwin
arr. **James Lyke**

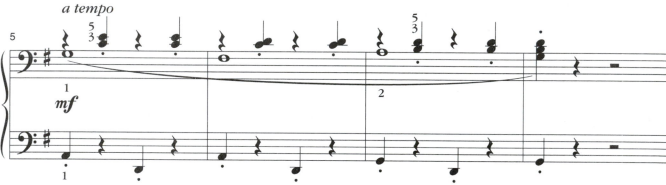

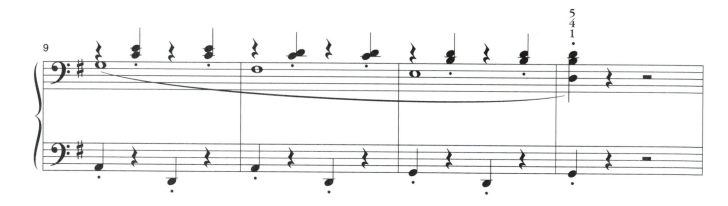

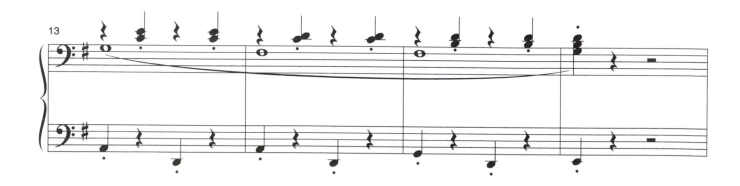

SHE'S MY BABY
Primo – Student

George Gershwin
arr. **James Lyke**

Moderato ♩ = 48

(secondo)

rit.

a tempo

8va throughout

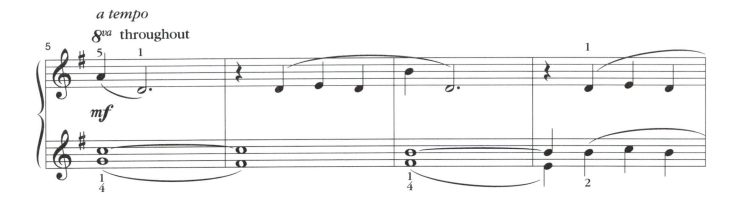

mf

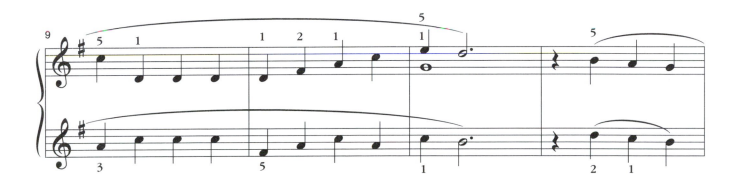

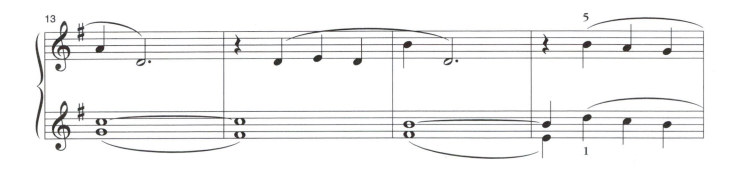

BOOK ONE, CHAPTER EIGHT

Secondo

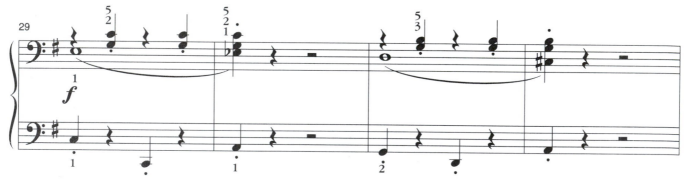

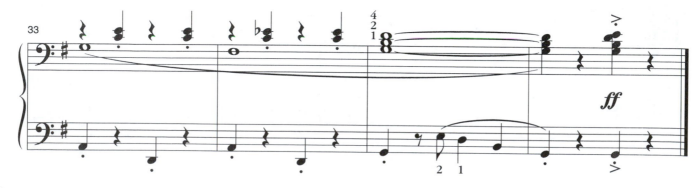

Primo

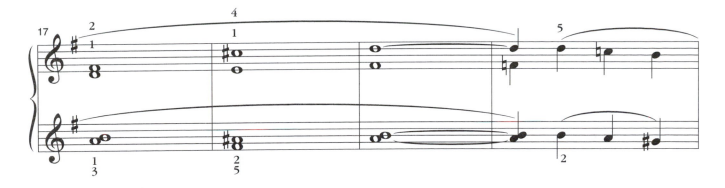

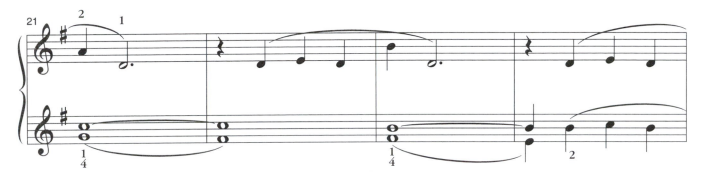

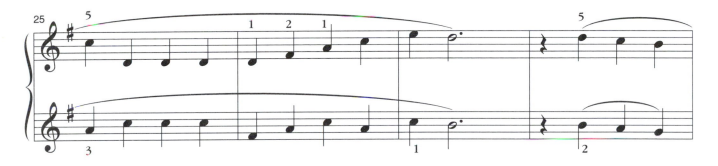

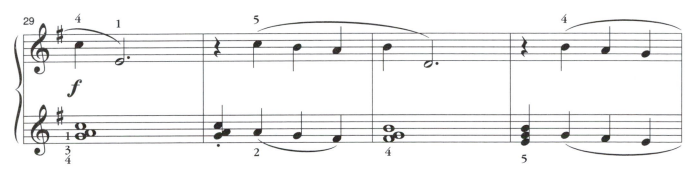

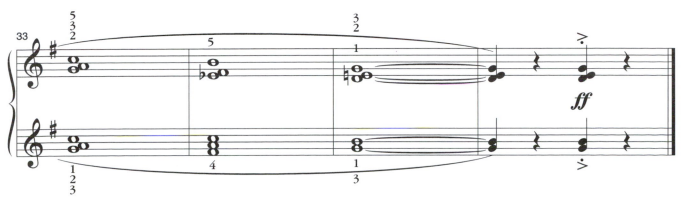

SOLO REPERTOIRE

Practice Plan: Slightly detach the quarter notes in Bach's *Minuet*. Be attentive to the phrase markings in each hand. Give rests full value.

MINUET

J.S. Bach

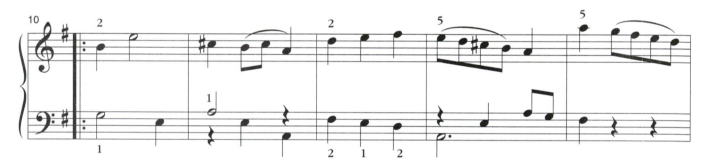

Practice Plan: In *Allegro in B Flat*, practice hands separately with the given fingerings. Perform proper 2-note slurs, keeping finger tips firm and utilizing a down – up wrist motion. Put the hands together (HT), playing slowly at first, gradually increasing the tempo to Allegro.

ALLEGRO IN B FLAT

W.A. Mozart

Practice Plan: In *Waltz*, it will take much LH practice to be comfortable with the leaps between bass note and chords. The RH ornaments (trills) need lightness and rapidity. Pay attention to fingering. Work from a slow tempo to the indicated tempo.

WALTZ
(abbreviated)

Frédéric Chopin

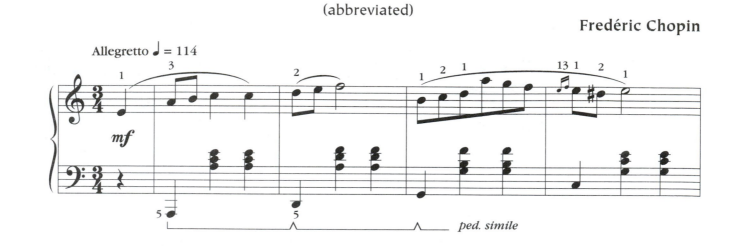

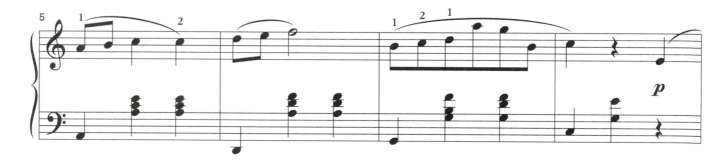

Practice Plan: *Pattern in Color* uses various types of seventh chords. Analyze each chord, placing letter name symbols above each chord. Leave out neighboring tones when reading the chords for analysis. Practice hands alone several times before combining RH and LH.

PATTERN IN COLOR

Alec Wilder

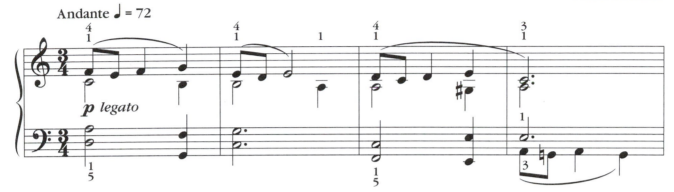

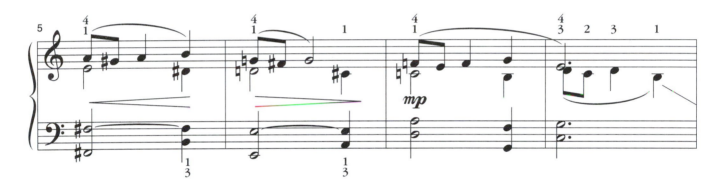

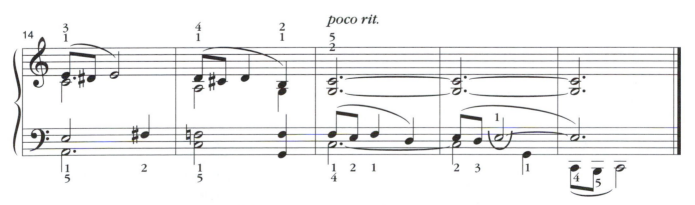

Practice Plan: In *Along the Seine*, first block the LH intervals. Isolate measures 1-4, 17-20, and 34-36 to practice the quick shifts. Strive to bring the melody (RH or LH) to the foreground. Careful pedaling is required.

ALONG THE SEINE

James Lyke

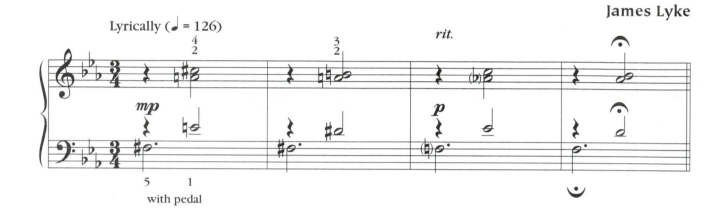

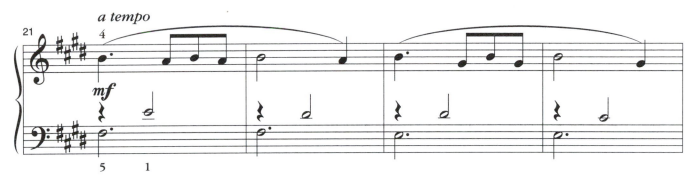

BOOK ONE, CHAPTER EIGHT

Practice Plan: An invention is a contrapuntal study piece. *Invention for Piano* contains aspects of bi-tonality—right hand in C major against left hand in D minor. In the section with harmonic intervals, the right hand mirrors the left hand. Technical features emphasized are five-note scale figures in both hands and two-note slow trills in both hands. As usual, play hands separately before putting the hands together (HT).

INVENTION FOR PIANO

Emma Lou Diemer

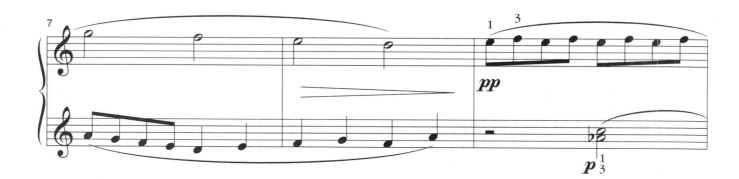

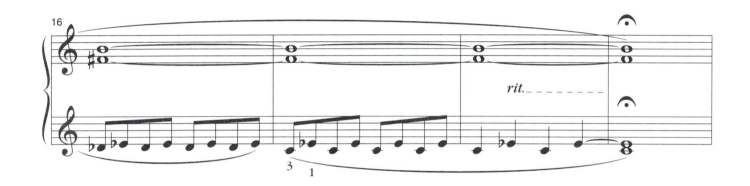

Practice Plan: In *Ragtime* good coordination is required to perform the rhythms correctly. Practice tapping certain measures hands together on the fallboard. Isolate measure 3 and measures 29-32 in order to practice the chromatic fingering. Be careful that the 4ths in bars 13-18 sound together.

RAGTIME

James Lyke

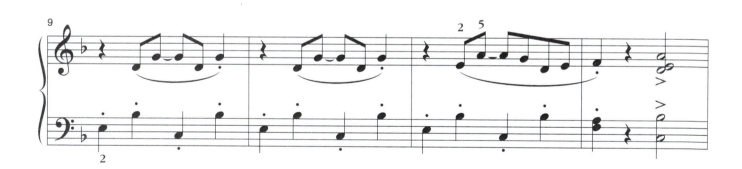

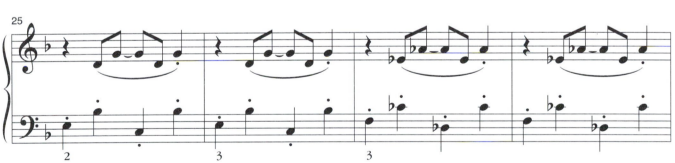

BOOK ONE, CHAPTER EIGHT

Practice Plan: Be sure to follow all fingering in *So Cool!* Play with a smooth and relaxed touch.

SO COOL!

Tony Caramia

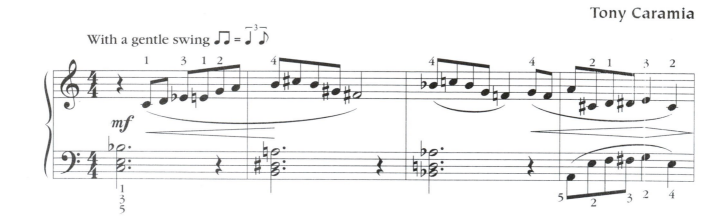

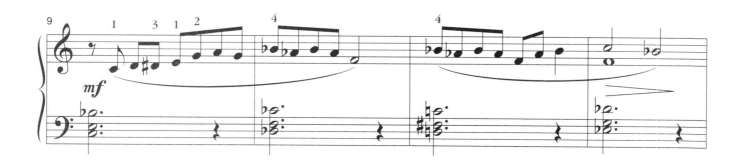

Practice Plan: *Swing Street* has some sophisticated harmonies that require careful scrutiny. You will find some instances of dominant sevenths sliding to a major seventh from a half step above. Analyze this composition and add chord symbols. Practice in the usual way (LH alone, RH alone, HT very slowly with a steady beat) before working up to the indicated tempo.

SWING STREET

Geoffrey Haydon

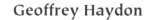

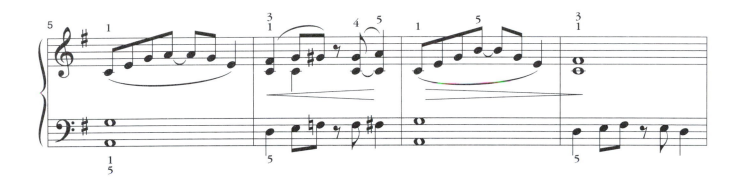

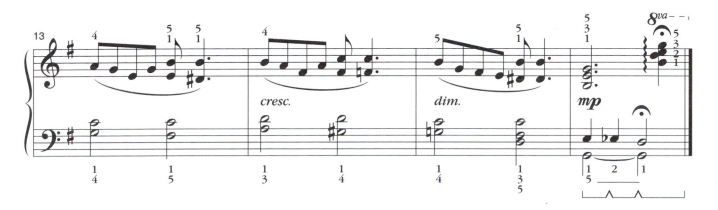

MUSICIANSHIP ACTIVITIES

Complete the following exercises that review topics introduced in Chapter 8.

Build close position seventh chords in both treble and bass clefs on the tones given below. Double-check the chord quality before notating each chord.

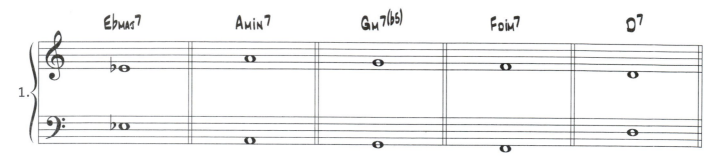

Analyze and label the following chords with letter name symbols.

Notate the following three modes from the given starting note.

G Lydian mode

E Dorian mode

F Mixolydian mode

Modal Improvisation

Using the LH ostinato tango figure, improvise RH melodies in the Phrygian mode on white keys. Repeat several times until a satisfactory cadence is reached.

Complete the following 4-voice progression and add the missing seventh to each chord. Label the chords with letter name symbols in the boxes. Play the progression.

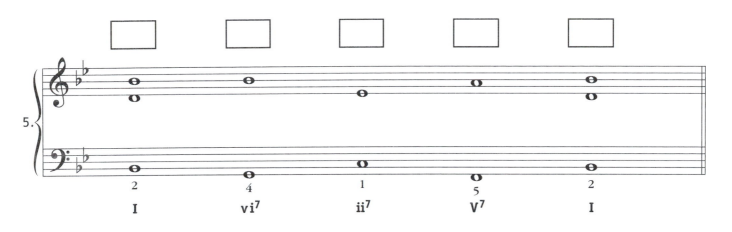

Complete the following 4-voice progression and add the missing third to each chord. Label the chords with letter name symbols in the boxes. Play the progression.

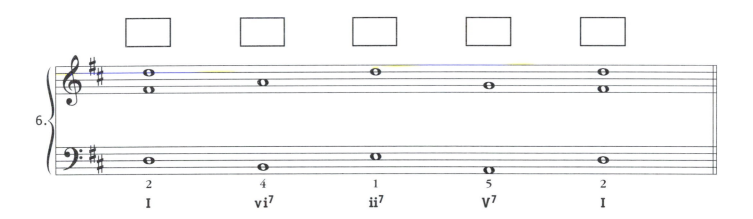

TECHNICAL STUDIES
Harmonic Minor Scales: f and b
Continue the study of harmonic minor scales. The fingerings of the F and B harmonic minor scales are the same as those of the parallel major scales. Consult Appendix B for a thorough presentation of all scales and arpeggios.

Minor Arpeggios: f and b
Continue the study of minor arpeggios. The fingerings of the F and B minor arpeggios are the same or similar to those of the parallel major arpeggios. Consult Appendix B to check fingerings.

SUGGESTED PLAYING EXAM TOPICS
CHAPTER EIGHT

1. Play the I–vi^7–ii^7–V^7–I chord progression in the keys of F, G, D, and B♭. See the bottom of page 294 for review.

2. Play a harmonization example from the lead sheets for *Sunday in London Town* (pages 302-303) or *For Me and My Gal* (pages 304-305).

3. Build and play modes built on white keys. Be able to transpose each mode to another key (page 306). Perform one arrangement of a modal folk song found on pages 307-309.

4. Play one or two sight reading studies found on pages 314-319. Transpose your selection to the suggested key.

5. Play the accompaniment to *Peg O' My Heart* (pages 320–321) or *My Buddy* (pages 322–323).

6. Perform one piece from the American Song Repertoire section found on pages 324-327.

7. Perform one ensemble piece found on pages 328-335.

8. Perform one or two solos from the Solo Repertoire section found on pages 336-347.

Musical Terms

Accelerando (accel.)	gradually increasing the speed or tempo.
Accidental	sharp, flat, natural, double sharp, double flat used separately from those in key signatures.
Adagio	slow, but quicker than Largo and Lento.
Agitato	agitated; restless.
Allegretto	lively; slower than Allegro.
Allegro	quick; lively; rapid.
Andante	moderately slow, but flowing easily (walking tempo).
Andantino	a little faster than Andante.
Animato (Animando)	lively; animated.
Arpeggio	playing the notes of a chord consecutively (harp style).
Assez vif (vite)	rather quickly.
A tempo	in time. A return to the original tempo after a ritard or accelerando.
Blues	slow style of music employing jazz rhythms.
Cadence	a close in melody or harmony. The end of a phrase.
Calma	calm, quiet.
Calypso	folk song from the Caribbean region with syncopated rhythms.
Cantabile	in singing style.
Cesura (//)	a complete separation.
Chorale	old form of psalm or hymn tune of the early German Protestant Church.
Coda	a passage added to the end of a composition.
Con	with.
Con anima	with animation; life.
Con brio	with fire; spirit.
Con fuoco	with fire.
Con moto	with motion.
Con Spirito (spiritoso)	with spirit.
Crescendo (cresc.)	gradually becoming louder.
Da Capo (D.C.)	from the beginning.
Dal Segno (D.S.)	repeat from the sign.
Decrescendo (decresc.)	gradually becoming softer.
Diminuendo (dim.)	gradually softer.
Dolce	sweetly; softly.
Ecossaise	a lively Scottish dance.
Espressione	expression, deep feeling.
Espressivo	expressive.

Fermata	a pause or hold.
Fine	the end.
Forte (f)	loud.
Fortissimo (ff)	very loud.
German Dance	a dance related to the Minuet in $\frac{3}{4}$ time.
Giocoso	happy; playful; mirthful.
Glissando	rapid sliding movement upward or downward across white or black keys using one or more fingers.
Grave	slow; solemn.
Grazioso	gracefully; elegantly.
Handset	placement of hands over a "set" pattern of notes.
Inversion	regrouping of the notes in an interval or chord. For example, a triad (3-note chord) can have two inversions in addition to its root position.
Largo	slow; stately.
Legato	smooth; connected; bound together. The reverse of staccato.
Leggeramente	lightly.
Leggiero	light; rapid; delicate.
Lento (Lent, Fr.)	slow, between Largo and Adagio.
Loco	play as written.
Maestoso	majestic; dignified.
Marcato	marked; emphasized.
March	music intended for marching (as in a parade).
Marcia	march.
Meno	less.
Menuet (Minuet)	a slow, stately dance in $\frac{3}{4}$ time.
Metronome	device to determine tempo (speed) in music; measured in beats per minute, ex. ♩ = 72.
Mezzo	half.
Mezzo Forte (mf)	half or moderately loud.
Mezzo Piano (mp)	half or moderately soft.
Minuet	dignified dance in triple meter.
Moderato	moderate.
Molto	very much; exceedingly.
Mosso	motion; movement.
Nocturne	night piece, sentimental or poetic character.
Ostinato	recurring figure, usually in the bass.
Pastoral (Pastorale)	portraying a rustic or rural scene.
Pensieroso	thoughtfully; pensively.

Musical Terms (cont.)

Pesante	heavy.	Sempre	always; continually.
Piano (*p*)	soft.	Sforzando (*sfz* or *sf*)	forced; a strong accent.
Pianissimo (*pp*)	very soft.	Simile	the same.
Piu	more.	Sonatina	a short sonata with two to three
Poco	a little, rather.		(sometimes four) movements.
Poco a poco	little by little; by degrees.		The first movement generally has
Portato	disconnected; neither staccato nor legato.		two themes (exposition) followed by a development section and a
Presto	fast.		recapitulation section.
Primo	the first (upper part) of a piano duet.	Sostenuto	sustained; unhurried.
		Spirito	animation, spirit.
Quadrille	a dance in five sections derived from an old French folk dance.	Staccato	detached; separated.
		Subito	suddenly.
Rag	syncopated piano piece, forerunner of jazz.	Syncopation	accent on a weak beat commonly used in ragtime, jazz, and popular music.
Rallentando (rall.)	gradually becoming slower.		
Religioso	in a religious manner.	Tranquillo	tranquil; calm.
Ritardando (rit.)	retarding; getting slower and slower.	Transposition	playing of music from one key to another.
Rubato	robbed; stolen. The rhythmic flow is interrupted by dwelling slightly on some melodic notes and slightly hurrying others.	Troppo	too much.
		Upbeat	pickup note(s).
		Vivace	animated; lively.
Scherzo	light, humorous piece of music.	Vivo	lively; briskly.
Secondo	the second (lower part) of a piano duet.	Waltz	popular dance (slow to moderately fast) in triple meter ($\frac{3}{4}$).

Musical Signs

sharp	♯	accent and sustain	
flat	♭	break or breath mark	,
natural	♮	rolled or "strummed" chord	
double sharp	×	tenuto mark – sustain	
double flat	♭♭	triplet	
fermata	⌢ or ⌣	accent	
repeat sign	‖: :‖	endings	1. 2.
tie		pedal	Ped. ※
slur		acciaccatura	
staccato		ottava	*8va*
portato (see Glossary)		swing	

Part 1: Major Scales and Arpeggios

Major Scales – Two Octaves

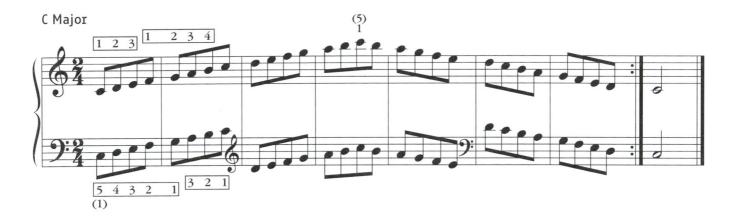

When putting hands together, notice that the thumbs fall on the tonic, and the third fingers play together on the third and sixth scale degrees. This will hold true for the scales of C, G, D, A, and E.

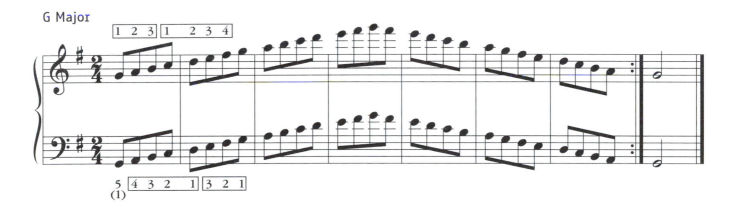

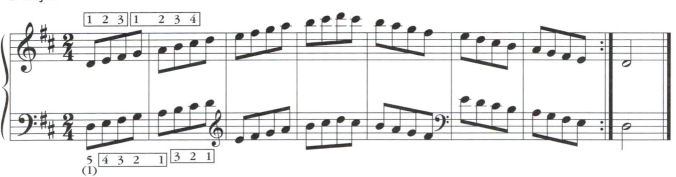

354

A Major

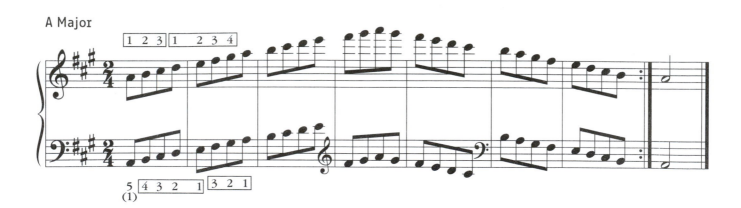

E Major

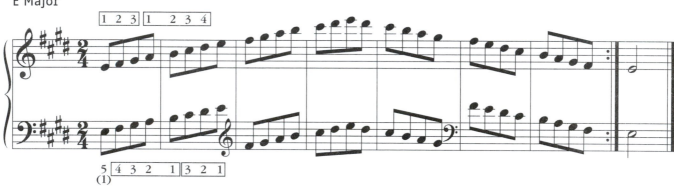

B Major

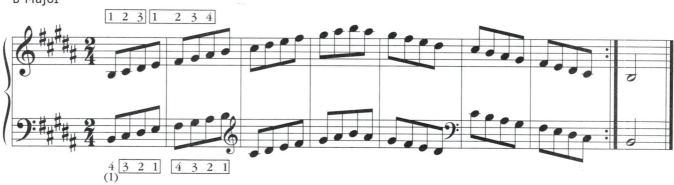

F Sharp Major

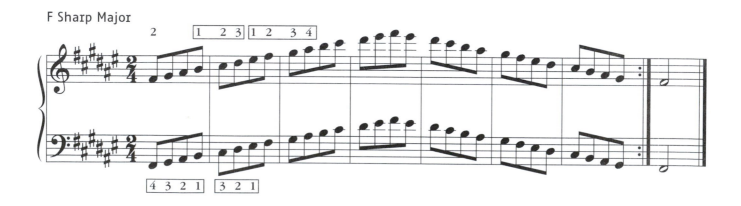

Tetrachord Minor Scales:

Study the scales below, and sing solfege as you play
Stem down = LH, Stem up = RH

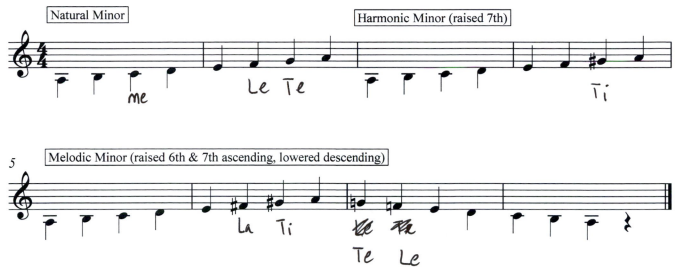

For the final exam, be able to create (in tetrachord form)
all 3 forms of minor scale on any tonic while you sing do-based solfege.

Wyatt Graff

C Sharp Major

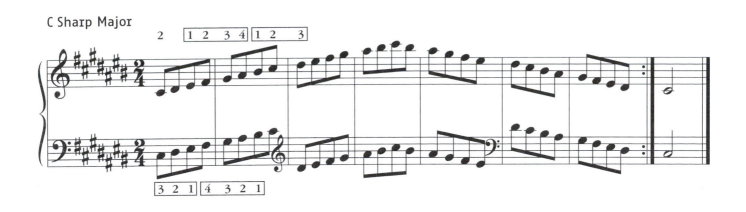

Flat Scale Fingerings

Study the following flat major scale fingering principles. (1) The fourth finger of the right hand always plays B flat. Knowing this makes it possible to figure out any right hand flat scale fingering. In any major flat key, simply place the right hand fourth finger on B flat and let the other fingers fall on adjacent scale tones in the key. Determine the groups of three and four. (2) The fingering pattern in the left hand for the keys of B flat, E flat, A flat, and D flat is 3 2 1 | 4 3 2 1. This fingering may also be used for the F scale, but the traditional LH fingering is the same as C major (5) 4 3 2 1 | 3 2 1. When using the 3 2 1 | 4 3 2 1 pattern, the fourth finger of the left hand is always placed on the new flat in the new key. The order of the scales below begins with F major and proceeds through the circle of fourths, i.e., F, B flat, E flat, and so on. Learn these scales gradually and be guided by your teacher as to various ways to practice the scales.

F Major

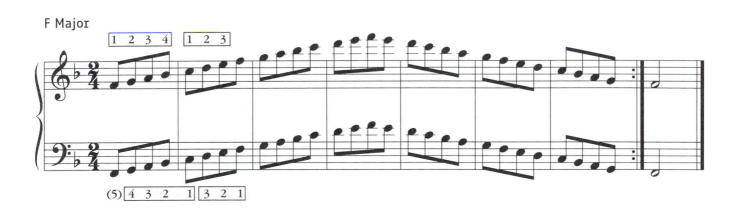

B Flat Major

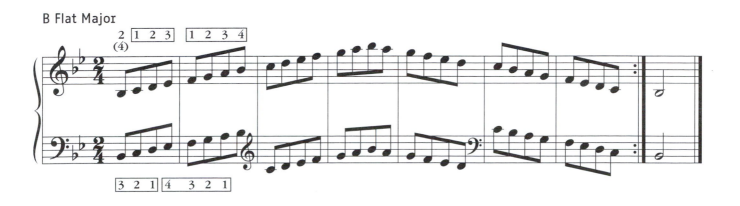

E Flat Major

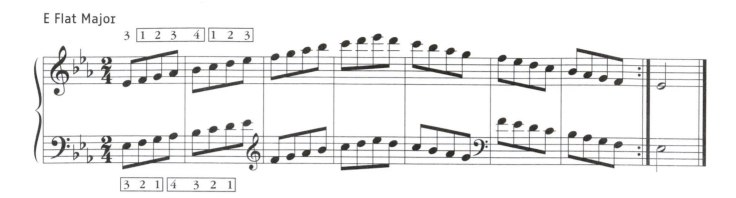

A Flat Major

D Flat Major (enharmonic with C Sharp Major)

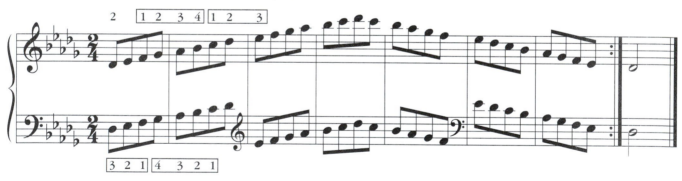

G Flat Major (enharmonic with F Sharp Major)

C Flat Major (enharmonic with B Major)

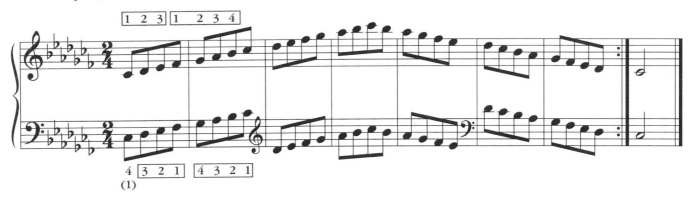

Major Arpeggios – Two Octaves

Add arpeggio practice immediately following scale practice. Learn the fingerings carefully. Slide the thumb under quickly.

C Major   G Major

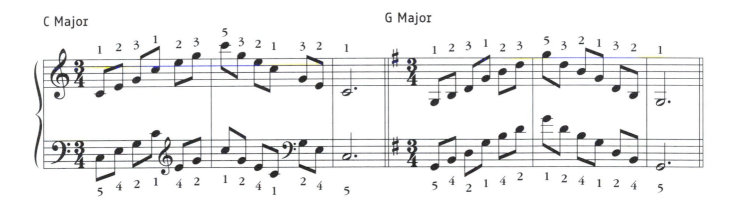

D Major   A Major

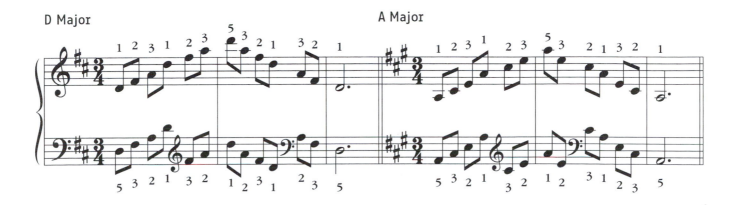

358

E Major

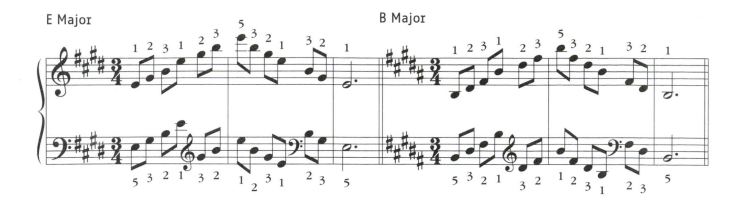

B Major

F Sharp Major
(G Flat Major)

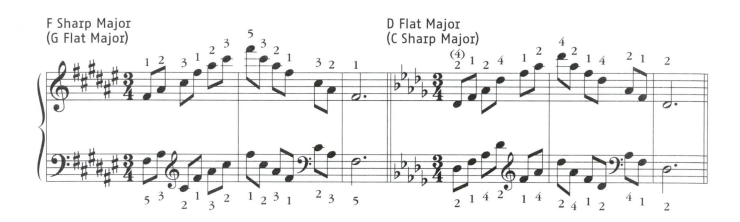

D Flat Major
(C Sharp Major)

A Flat Major

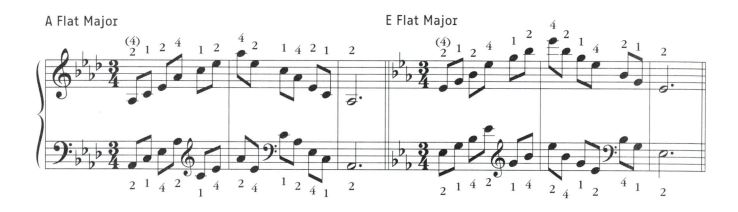

E Flat Major

B Flat Major

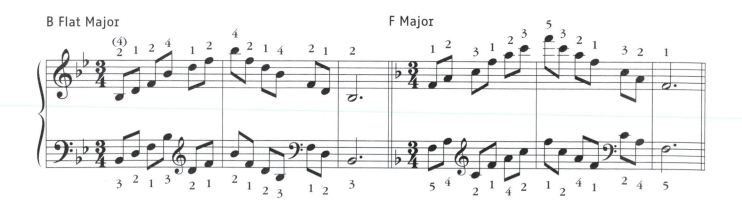

F Major

Part 2: White Key Minor Scales and Arpeggios

C Harmonic Minor Scale

C Minor Arpeggio

D Harmonic Minor Scale

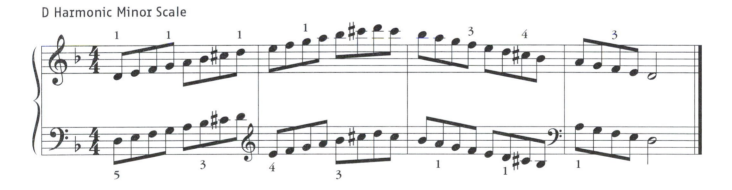

D Minor Arpeggio

E Harmonic Minor Scale

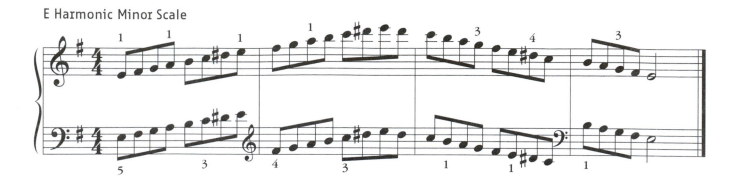

E Minor Arpeggio

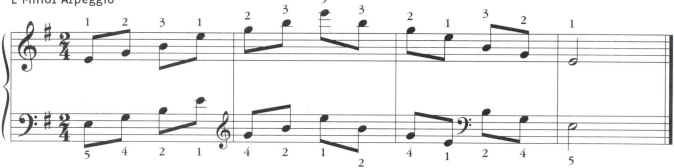

F Harmonic Minor Scale

F Minor Arpeggio

G Harmonic Minor Scale

G Minor Arpeggio

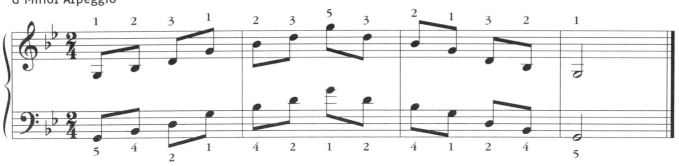

A Harmonic Minor Scale

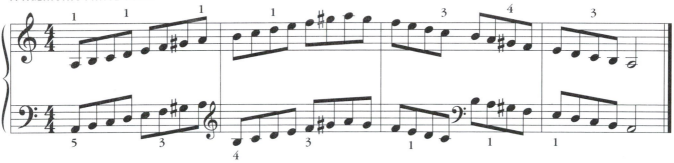

A Minor Arpeggio

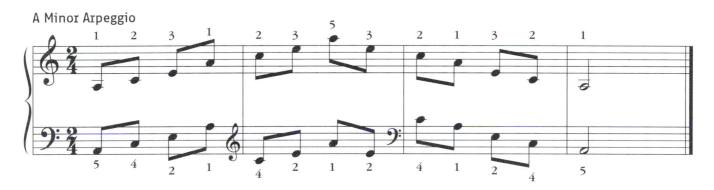

B Harmonic Minor Scale

B Minor Arpeggio

BOOK ONE, APPENDICES

LEAD SHEETS

JOLLY OLD SAINT NICHOLAS

Traditional

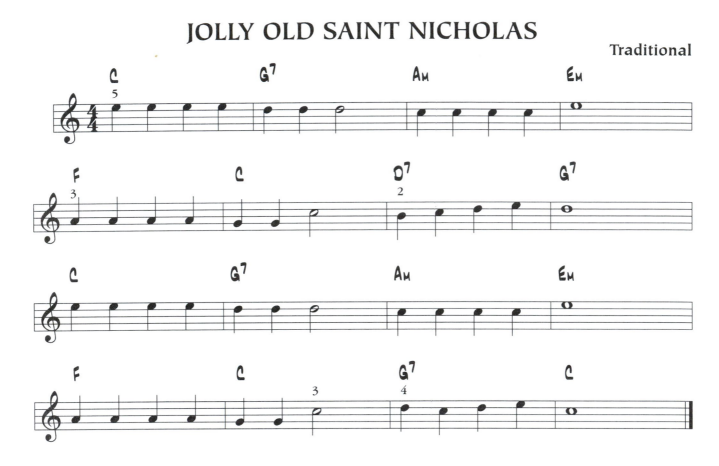

JOSEPH DEAREST, JOSEPH MINE

German

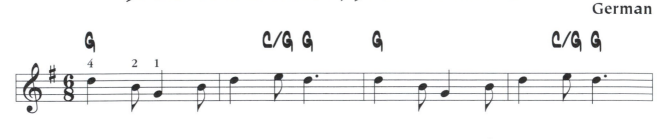

HANUKKAH SONG

Israeli

O CHRISTMAS TREE

German

HANUKKAH HYMN

Israeli

MID OX AND DONKEY

French

LULLABY MY LITTLE SON

Norwegian

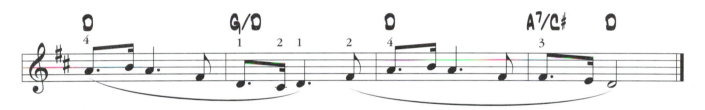

BESIDE THY CRADLE

German

SOLO ARRANGEMENTS

I SAW THREE SHIPS

English
arr. James Lyke

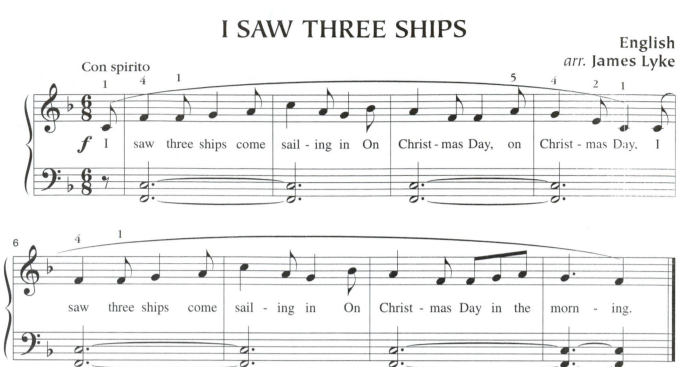

PAT-A-PAN

French
arr. James Lyke

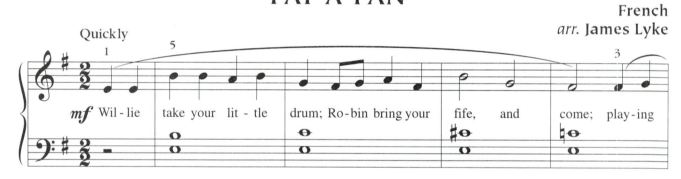

MY DREIDEL

Hebrew
arr. **James Lyke**

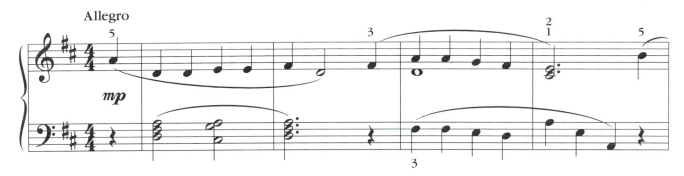

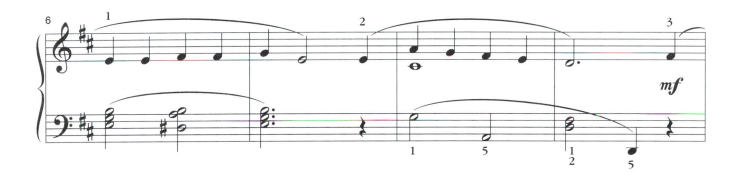

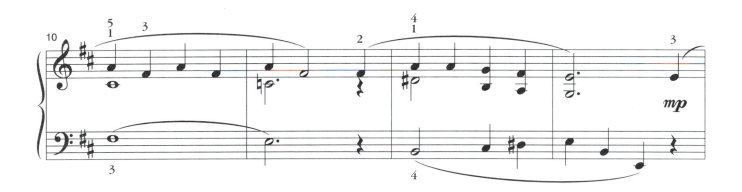

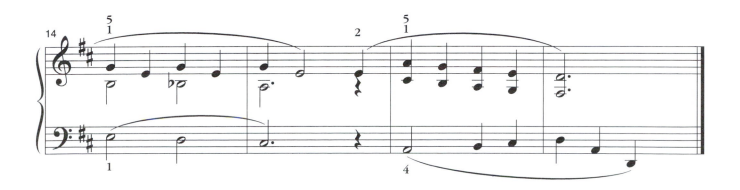

GOOD KING WENCESLAS

English
arr. James Lyke

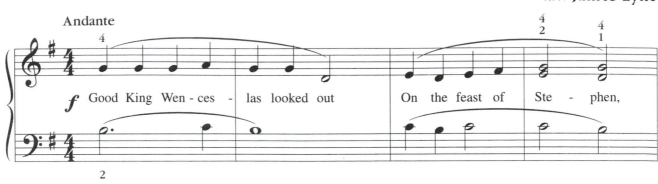

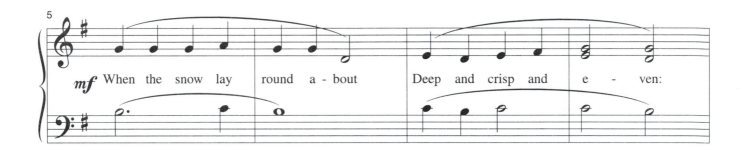

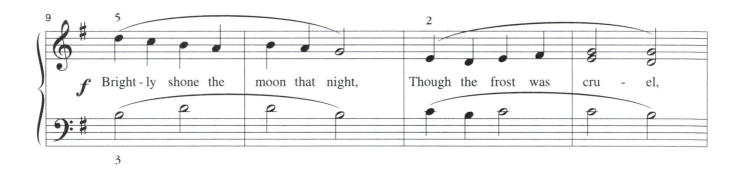

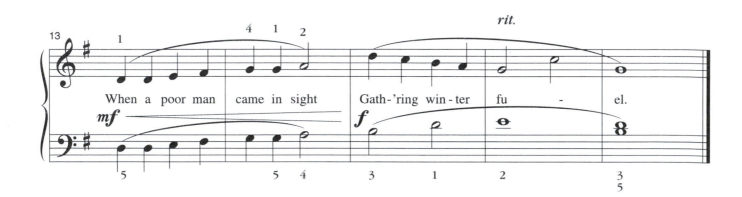

DING! DONG! MERRILY ON HIGH

French
arr. Christos Tsitsaros

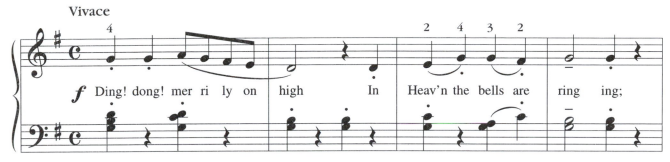

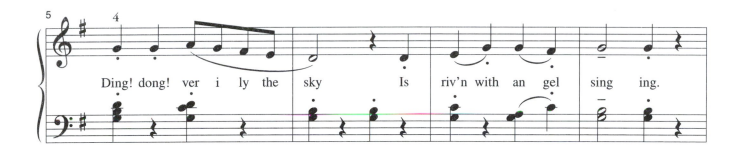

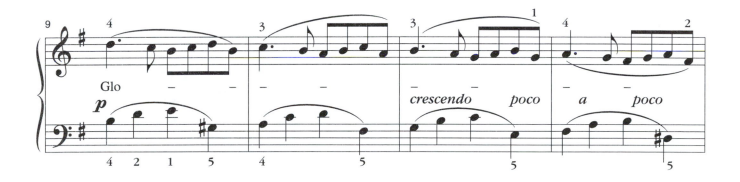

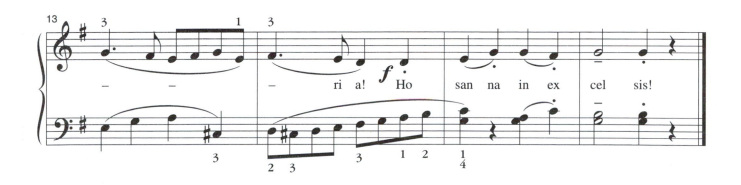

I WONDER AS I WANDER

Appalachian Carol
arr. James Lyke

Slowly ♩ = 78

with pedal

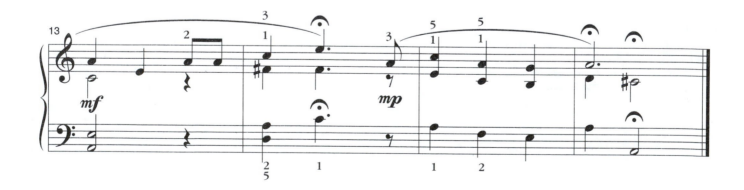

SILENT NIGHT

Franz Gruber
arr. **Tony Caramia**

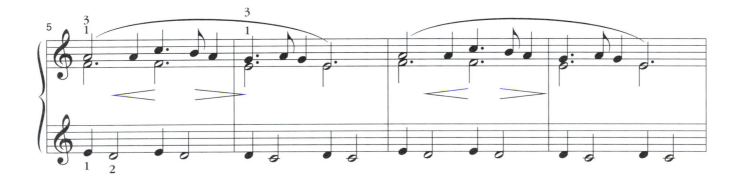

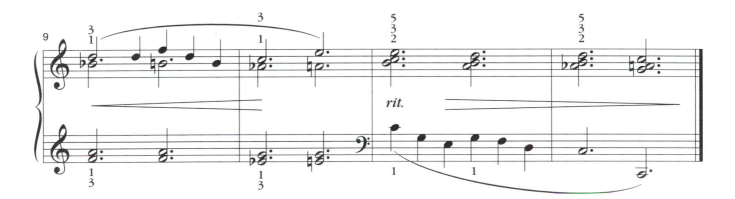

DUET ARRANGEMENTS

SEE THE DEAR LITTLE JESUS

Secondo – Teacher (or Student)

Polish Carol
arr. **James Lyke**

Andantino

with pedal

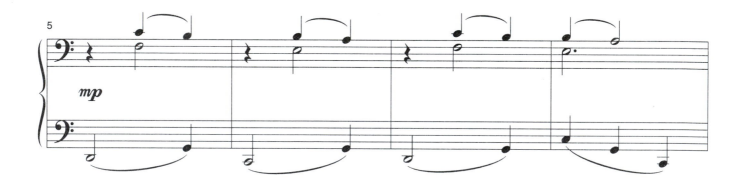

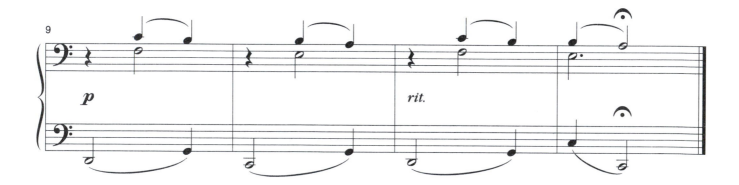

SEE THE DEAR LITTLE JESUS

Primo – Student (or Teacher)

Polish Carol
arr. **James Lyke**

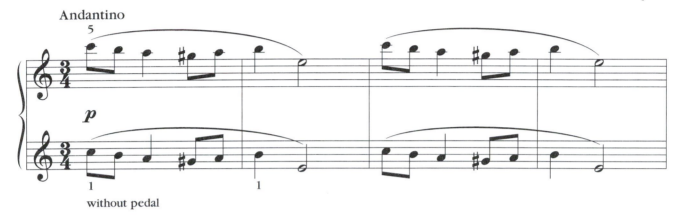

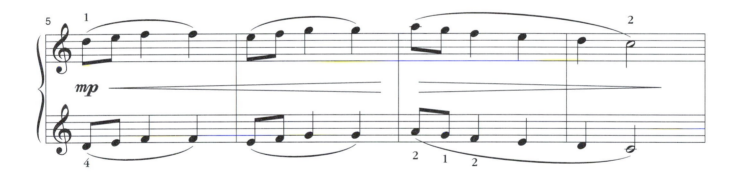

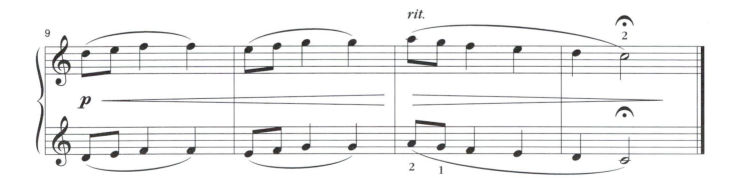

PARADE OF THE WOODEN SOLDIERS

Secondo – Teacher (or Student)

music by **Leon Jessell**
arr. **James Lyke**

stacc. simile

PARADE OF THE WOODEN SOLDIERS

Primo – Student

music by **Leon Jessell**
arr. **James Lyke**

Secondo

Primo

appendix E

American Song Repertoire (ASR), Accompaniments to Folk and American Popular Songs (ACC), Study Pieces (SP), and Arrangements of Holiday Songs (HS)